Southern Literary Studies

FRED HOBSON, SERIES EDITOR

THOMAS RUYS SMITH

River of Dreams

Imagining the Mississippi before Mark Twain

LOUISIANA STATE UNIVERSITY PRESS

BATON ROUGE

Published by Louisiana State University Press
Copyright © 2007 by Louisiana State University Press
All rights reserved
Manufactured in the United States of America
First printing

DESIGNER: Michelle A. Neustrom
TYPEFACE: Adobe Garamond Pro
PRINTER AND BINDER: Edwards Brothers, Inc.

LIBRARY OF CONGRESS CATALOGING-IN-PUBLICATION DATA

Smith, Thomas Ruys, 1979–
River of dreams : imagining the Mississippi before Mark Twain / Thomas Ruys Smith.
p. cm. — (Southern literary studies)
Includes bibliographical references and index.
ISBN-13: 978-0-8071-3233-3 (alk. paper)
1. Mississippi River—In literature. 2. American literature—19th century—History and
criticism. 3. American literature—1783–1850—History and criticism. 4. United States—
Civilization—1783–1865. 5. United States—Civilization—19th century. I. Title.
PS217.M58S65 2007
810.9'372—dc22
2006032210

For Arianna

The Mississippi! [. . .] A river of mighty, unbroken solitudes, rolling amid undreamed wonders of vegetable and animal existence. But, as in an hour, this river of dreams and wild romance has emerged to a reality scarcely less visionary and splendid. What other river of the world bears on its bosom to the ocean the wealth and enterprise of such another country?—a country whose products embrace all between the tropics and the poles! Those turbid waters, hurrying, foaming, tearing along, an apt resemblance of that headlong tide of business which is poured along its wave by a race more vehement and energetic than any the old world ever saw. Ah! would that they did not also bear along a more fearful freight.

HARRIET BEECHER STOWE, 1851

Contents

Acknowledgments

So said Mark Twain: "I don't care much for gratitude of the noisy, boisterous kind. Why, when some men discharge an obligation, you can hear the report for miles around." Hoping to be neither noisy nor boisterous, I am nonetheless very pleased to have this opportunity to offer some brief words of thanks. It's been a number of years since this book's conception, and though I cannot name everyone who has been of help in that period, I hope they are all aware of my gratitude for any kindnesses done me.

I'll begin at the beginning. This book can trace its genealogy a long way back, to work done as an undergraduate at St. John's College, Cambridge. As such, I would particularly like to thank Richard Beadle, John Kerrigan, Con Coroneos, and Paul Giles for providing me with invaluable instruction and inspiration at such a vital time. I could not have received a better start.

What they helped to begin, Eric Homberger helped bring to fruition. To Eric, my doctoral supervisor at the University of East Anglia, I owe a significant debt. I could not have hoped for more support or better advice. His criticisms have always been infallible, and he is a remarkable academic role model. Many others in the School of American Studies at UEA also read chapters of this book and offered sterling advice—to name only a few: Richard Crockatt, Allan Lloyd-Smith, Christoper Bigsby, and Sarah Churchwell. I thank them and everyone else in the department. I am now proud to call them my colleagues.

I would also like to offer my gratitude to all those in the Department of English at University College London, particularly Henry Woudhuysen and Mark Ford. I spent a very enjoyable and productive term there in 2006, and I thank them all for their hospitality.

Other miscellaneous thanks, no less significant: to James H. Justus, for reading the manuscript and offering some essential comments; to Alfred Bendixen, for much interest and assistance; to Bridget Bennett, for her valuable advice and support; to Marie Jeanne Rossignol and Marc Chénetier at the Université Paris VII–Denis Diderot, organizers of the 2003 *Stemming the Mississippi Conference* and subsequent editors of a special edition of the *Revue Française D'Études Américaines* in which a modified portion of chapter 3 appeared; to Neil Brody Miller, for his correspondence and for allowing me to quote from an unpublished conference paper; and to Simon Dovar and Nils Davey, the super-talented men who designed the map for this book. And to the librarians: at the Rare Books and Music Reading Room in the British Library; at the Howard-Tilton Memorial Library at Tulane University; at the Historic New Orleans Collection; and at the Widener and Houghton Libraries at Harvard. They all provided priceless assistance.

Special thanks, of course, go to my editor, John Easterly, Lee Sioles, Cynthia Williams, and all those at Louisiana State University Press. John has provided unfailing assistance and advice. Thanks also to Fred Hobson for some invaluable comments on the entire manuscript. This is a better book for the efforts of all at LSUP. The same is certainly true for Susan Brady, my copy editor, who deserves special notice and has my sincere gratitude.

Which almost brings me up to date. And so last, but certainly not least, some inadequate words of personal recognition. Profound thanks and love to my family, the Haberis family, and my friends: I am grateful to you all. I know that my grandfather, Frank Ruys, would very much liked to have seen this book—so I mention his name here in tribute. To my parents, Kathleen and Peter, goes my heartfelt appreciation for their constant encouragement; I am sure that they can both recognize their separate influence in these pages. And to Arianna, my wife, goes my unceasing gratitude for her patient and loving companionship throughout every moment of this journey—truly, my island in the stream.

RIVER OF DREAMS

The Antebellum Pan-Mississippi World

The American Nile
"Ultima Thule"

We came in sight of what had long been the subject of our conversations, our inquiries, and curiosity, the far-famed Mississippi. It is a view, which has left on my mind a most deep and durable impression, marking a period, from which commenced a new era in my existence [. . .] The country on this side had still some unbroken associations with our native land. This magnificent river, almost dividing the continent, completely severed this chain [. . .] The Mississippi [. . .] at that time was to the great proportion of the American people, as it was to us, the "ultima Thule"—a limit almost to the range of thought.
TIMOTHY FLINT, 1826

This noble and celebrated stream, this Nile of North America, commands the wonder of the old world, while it attracts the admiration of the new.
ZADOK CRAMER, 1814

Two speeches—two prophecies, in fact—bookend the decades in which the Mississippi rose to cultural prominence; they narrate, in miniature, the journey taken by the river in antebellum American life and thought. In New Orleans late in 1803, Napoleon's colonial prefect Pierre Clement de Laussat prepared to reclaim possession of Louisiana for France. Of course, news of the Louisiana Purchase had been announced on July 4, and Laussat knew that he was accepting possession only to formally hand it to America in a matter of days. Addressing an assembly of Louisianans, Laussat struck an optimistic note about that prospect. "You will be incorporated," he assured them, "with a nation already numerous and powerful, renowned besides for its industry, its patriotism, and the degree of civilization and knowledge it possesses." More importantly, perhaps, revenue was practically guaranteed. "Your country will become an immense warehouse or place of deposit, affording you countless profits," he promised, reaching for a rhetorical trope that would be echoed throughout the antebellum years: "The Nile of America, the Mississippi, which flows, not through parched deserts of sand, but through the most extensive and the most fertile plains of the new world, will soon see its bosom darkened with a thousand ships belonging to all the nations of the earth, and mooring at the quays of another Alexandria."[1]

From a vision of harmony, to one of schism. Speaking before the Senate in 1858, Senator J. H. Hammond of South Carolina felt it was time "to bring the

North and South face to face, and see what resources each of us might have in the contingency of separate organizations." "Through the heart of our country," he asserted, meaning the South, "runs the great Mississippi, the father of waters, into whose bosom are poured thirty-six thousand miles of tributary streams [. . .] Can you hem in such a territory as that?" The valley of the Mississippi, Hammond continued, was "now the real and soon to be acknowledged seat of the empire of the world":

> The sway of that valley will be as great as ever the Nile knew in the earlier ages of mankind. We own the most of it. The most valuable part of it belongs to us now; and although those who have settled above us are now opposed to us, another generation will tell a different tale. They are ours by all the laws of nature; slave labor will go to every foot of this great valley where it will be found profitable to use it, and some of those who may not use it are soon to be united with us by such ties as will make as one and inseparable.

The Mississippi River, that American Nile—an analogy at once aspirational and accusatory, speaking of empire, profit, slavery, and liberation—ran powerfully through the antebellum imagination, uniting and dividing, creating and destroying as it flowed. So much had changed for the river of dreams in sixty years, and so little.[2]

Rivers have ever been sacred symbols of civilization—Euphrates, Nile, Jordan, Tiber, Rhine, Thames—as they have of time, of life, of consciousness, of death. Human culture has always flourished on the banks of a defining river that flows throughout a nation's conception of itself, mixing history and mythology in its waters, providing an image of idealized nationhood while narrating the story of society in the raw. "The river," Wyman Herendeen has written, "in geography and as an image, takes on the characteristics of the culture of which it is a part [. . .] What it most resembles is protean nature itself: mutable yet constant, gaining meaning by virtue of human ability to make something of it. Thus its specific significance will vary from age to age." In the decades before Mark Twain enthralled the world with his definitive representations of the antebellum Mississippi, the river had already played such an essential role in American culture and consciousness. Throughout the period, the river was a powerful symbol of both American's conception of itself, and the world's conception of America. How, then, was the Mississippi imagined and reimagined in the antebellum years?[3]

The river appeared in a host of representations—from printed page to moving canvas, from high culture to low—that developed and transformed as America changed. From empire building in the Louisiana Purchase to the trauma of the Civil War, the Mississippi's dominant symbolic meanings tracked the powerful forces operating within the nation through which it flowed. The giant river was a commercial thoroughfare that drew millions to its waters, united disparate elements, and brought together a uniquely diverse range of characters. It was simultaneously connective tissue, borderline, and crossing point; a channel of slavery and a path to freedom; a lonely wilderness for explorers and the setting for a fashionable tour; a pastoral paradise and an industrial powerhouse; a place of salvation, and a notorious underworld. It was America's river, physically and culturally at the heart of the nation; but it was also, to apply Timothy Flint's phrase, "ultima Thule": distant, strange, mysterious, magical. The story of the imagined Mississippi River is the story of antebellum America. The neglected ways in which the Mississippi needed and demanded to be imagined before Mark Twain therefore form the subject of this book.

As Twain understood, "the Mississippi is well worth reading about." His countless readers have long agreed—but the fertile antebellum river frontier where he grew up, and from which he drew the essential ingredients for his definitive portraits of America, remains largely untilled. Having been blessed with an embarrassment of riches while researching and writing this book, I find it difficult to fathom that neglect. It is hard to think of a significant antebellum American who did not, at some point, feel compelled to think and write about the Mississippi. In the pages that follow, presidents, politicians, authors, poets, painters, and international celebrities of every variety describe the way that they experienced and imagined the river in the antebellum years. As John Sears has highlighted, "It was inevitable, when [Americans] set out to establish a national culture [. . .] that they would turn to the landscape of America as the basis of that culture." The river had a vital role to play in that process, and this is the first time that its antebellum story has been told in all its rich multiplicity.[4]

While asserting that no previous account has focused its attention solely on the Mississippi's role as a prominent feature in antebellum culture, it is also important to note that this book builds on the work of others. The river has generated a voluminous amount of published material. Numerous anthologies of Mississippi writings have been produced, and, used with caution and awareness, they can be useful as a guide to important antebellum material. Notable examples are B. A. Botkin's *Treasury of Mississippi Folklore* (1955), Wright Morris's *The Mississippi River Reader* (1962), and John Francis McDermott's *Before Mark Twain: A Sampler of Old, Old Times on the Mississippi* (1968). Collections of river stories—like Ray Samuel et al.'s *Tales of the Mississippi* (1955), Walter Havighurst's *Voices on the River* (1964), and Michael Gillespie's *Come Hell or High Water* (2001)—are equally prevalent, but since they are predominantly anecdotal they are only of limited use. McDermott's anthology is the most useful, dedicating itself to antebellum material and selecting its passages judiciously. Indeed, McDermott is owed a debt by all students of the cultural history of the river since as a researcher, author, and editor of books on the First West and the Mississippi River he made an extraordinary amount of antebellum material—often lost or long forgotten—readily available. His *Lost Panoramas of the Mississippi* (1958), for example, remains the most thorough investigation of that subject, and still the only book-length treatment.

Other writers have produced important works focused on very specific aspects of the river's antebellum life. The history of river travel and transportation has been well served. Leland D. Baldwin's *The Keelboat Age on Western Waters* (1941) is beginning to show its age but is still an informative treatment of the early years of man's movement along the Mississippi. Michael Allen's *Western Rivermen, 1763–1861* (1990) has supplanted it, and his investigation of the antebellum nonsteam boatman is also a fascinating piece of social history. Louis Hunter's *Steamboats on the Western Rivers: An Economic and Technological History* (1949) is the seminal work on western riverboats, and is far more wide-ranging in its material than its title would suggest. It remains an indispensable reference work that is unlikely to be improved upon. The social development of the river, and its increasing urbanization and industrialization in the antebellum years, can best be traced in John Reps's *Cities of the Mississippi* (1994), which also provides a mine of visual images of the river and river towns.

In terms of cultural history, there is a greater paucity of seminal works. Alongside McDermott's publications, Walter Blair and Franklin Meine's *Half-Horse, Half-Alligator, The Growth of the Mike Fink Legend* (1956) is a vital study of one of the Mississippi's antebellum cultural icons. James Lal Penick's *The Great Western Land Pirate: John A. Murrell in Legend and History* (1981) is an indispensable work that provides a vital corrective to the plethora of myths and legends that have grown up around the river's favorite wayward son. Other than Penick's work, the underworld of the Mississippi has been notably ill served. Robert M. Coates's *The Outlaw Years: The History of the Land Pirates of the Natchez Trace* (1930) set the trend for perpetuating myths as fact and anecdotes as contemporary evidence. Ann Vincent Fabian's *Card Sharps, Dream Books and Bucket Shops, Gambling in Nineteenth-Century America* (1990) and Jackson Lears's *Something for Nothing, Luck in America* (2003), while useful, treat the Mississippi as a small

4

part of a larger discourse. Here, however, all of these strands are united. This book is a new panorama of the antebellum river that allows the Mississippi to stand front and center in its own story—not in miniature, and not as mere backdrop.

The structure of this book is chronological, though it is a gentle chronology that allows for a freedom of association across five chapters that span the antebellum decades. This approach was suggested very much by the material itself, since there was a discernible development of the dominant cultural representation of the Mississippi over time. Progressively, the river represented a dream of empire; a fertile frontier; an uneasy fashionable tour; a moving panorama; and an underworld, leading to war and eventual cultural resurrection. Charting these changing roles, it is impossible to ignore the accelerated form of cultural and societal growth peculiar to the New World at this time—a span of decades, a human life, incorporating the social and cultural growth of centuries.

Chapter 1 examines the Mississippi's turbulent transformation into an American river following the Revolution, a process dramatically marked by international power wrangling and individual subterfuge. As a distant promised land, the Mississippi tantalized the nation—especially those moving west—with visions of future prosperity and divine design. An extraordinary number of Revolutionary figures (Thomas Paine, Joel Barlow, Gilbert Imlay, Citizen Genet, George Rogers Clark, General Wilkinson) were drawn into a nexus of covert imperial plots and conspiracies that focused on the river. The defining relationship of the period was, however, between the river, Thomas Jefferson, and the American people. Jefferson was a Mississippi Moses who never saw the river, but whose shifting imperial vision proved critical during its symbolic and practical Americanization—its simultaneous annexation into Jefferson's so-called Empire of Liberty, and its inauguration as the jugular of slavery. Chapter 2 takes up the story of the river as a magnetic frontier now within the remit of a growing young nation. The river's cultural role was intimately connected to the rise of Andrew Jackson. Jackson's victory against the British at New Orleans in 1815 ensured that the icon first and perhaps most powerfully associated with the Mississippi in the antebellum years was the backwoods rowdy: Mike Fink, Davy Crockett, T. B. Thorpe's Jim Doggett, and scores of lesser-known, though no less potent, frontier "alligator-horses." Like Jackson himself, these new and definitive Americans toiled on, along, and against the Mississippi in the presteamboat years, worked on its waters in the years of the ascendance of steam, and, most importantly, proliferated in the Jacksonian press, disseminating the spirit of their times.

At the same time that Jacksonian river heroes rose to cultural prominence, innumerable travelers reached the river in the Golden Age of the steamboat, including the greatest number—and most influential—of European commentators. Chapter 3 is concerned predominantly with their accounts, and their reactions to the world of the alligator-horses. Narratives by the likes of Frances Trollope, Dickens, Thackeray, Frederick Marryat and Harriet Martineau had the greatest impact both internationally and in America itself. It was their accounts of the Mississippi, slavery, and the social world of the steamboat cabin that were most alive to the river's symbolic qualities as an artery of the Jacksonian nation. Accordingly, their judgments of both river and America were not always favorable. But when sympathetic commentators, like Harriet Martineau, found a communion with the Mississippi, its symbolic resonances became very different.

The post-Jackson Mississippi was increasingly understood visually—evidence of the changing nature of the river frontier—and chapter 4 is concerned with the pictorial attempts to understand an industrialized river. John James Audubon spent years on the river, but was more interested in its feathered inhabitants; George Caleb Bingham was concerned with its human population, and was the first to cast the alligator-horses, retreating into the past, in iconic visual poses. But as the Mississippi became increasingly industrialized, in keeping with its social and economic development, the most popular solution to the problem of visually representing the river was found in a blend of industry and art. The moving panoramas of the Mississippi chimed perfectly, in content and tone, with the movement, expansionism and westward trajectory of America. As well as a visual counterpoint to manifest destiny, these "useful illusions" pointed the way forward to something far more modern: simulation. As the antebellum years drew to a close, and as sectional differences eroded the cultural value of previous river icons, the dark undercurrents of the Mississippi became stronger. They are the subjects of chapter 5. It had always been a river of shadows, smoke, and mirrors, but as war approached, the Mississippi's ambiguous reputation for mystery increasingly took center stage. Slavery, often in strange and unexpected ways, was deeply connected to the popular representations of crime along the river. The illicit aspects of river life often featured prominently in travel accounts and popular fiction—particularly mystery novels and yellow-backs. But this was a trend that would find its ultimate expression in Melville's 1857 novel, *The Confidence-Man*—a fittingly bleak endpoint to antebellum imaginings of the river for a country poised for war.

When war came, it was immediately understood that the Mississippi was vitally important militarily; as the most vivid symbol of slavery and the South, its possession was also a symbolic imperative. Along its waters—waters that joined and divided—two different Americas had developed, represented by two men who knew the river well: Abraham Lincoln and Jefferson Davis. Postwar, the river's meaning in national life was uncertain—until one of the river's antebellum sons resurrected, reimagined, and revitalized its symbolic potential. Mark Twain's representations of the Mississippi proved definitive; but only one so steeped in the antebellum river, culturally as well as physically, could have produced the iconic Mississippi that still flows powerfully through a wide and fertile floodplain in American literature.

Perhaps, in some regards, Twain is ironically to blame for the relative neglect of the Mississippi. On the one hand, it is arguable that without him this book would not exist, not least because his interpretations of the river have ensured that the antebellum Mississippi is an environment that persists in the collective sense of America and its physical and imaginative identity. And yet without Twain, perhaps this area of study would have been mined much earlier: Twain's readings of the antebellum river have been taken as authoritative, eclipsing truly contemporary interpretations—the readings of the mythical Mississippi in flux that are the subject of this book. Twain spent his childhood by the river, was a part—as a printer's devil—of the print culture that grew up around the river, and, as a young man, lived the flush, peripatetic life of a steamboat pilot, on and along the river. Aspects and echoes of almost all of the material in this book are locatable in Twain's work. This was his world, and he knew it intimately. Speaking of the classical world, Herendeen has described the way that societies have traditionally acculturated their rivers: "As society masters the environment, writers acquire greater control over the literary images in that world, as we see in the rivers of the creation myths and in Homer and Virgil, for example. The poet's skills as 'maker' become more formalized, the river tamer." As such, this book can also be read as an introduction and complement to the life and work of Mark Twain, Mississippi river tamer.[5]

Some final establishing comments about approach and methodology are necessary. In exploring the different meanings of the trope of the Mississippi in antebellum America, the greatest effort has been made to use exclusively antebellum material. This has not always been possible, and reference to memoirs and reminiscences published after the Civil War have sometimes been necessary to fill important gaps. As a rule, this has not been necessary, and when given a choice between ante- and postbellum material, contemporary sources have always been prioritized. Furthermore, though this book draws on a wide variety of sources, textual and visual, it is centrally concerned with the dominant cultural roles played by the Mississippi in the antebellum years. By and large, though by no means exclusively, priority has been given to material that was readily available within the antebellum American public domain—the more prominent and popular the better.

This approach is necessary when telling the story of the prevailing ways in which America (and the wider world) imagined the Mississippi; but it has a reciprocal effect on the narrative. As they did in antebellum culture, white male voices dominate. It is vital to assert, and to appreciate, that the story of the dominant cultural meanings of the antebellum Mississippi is not the whole story of the river in the decades before the Civil War. Indeed, the moments in this book when disenfranchised voices, removed from obvious sources of power and influence, indelibly make their mark on the imagined Mississippi are in many ways the most revealing. Today, one need only turn to Thomas Buchanan's *Black Life on the Mississippi: Slaves, Free Blacks, and the Western Steamboat World* (2004) to appreciate, for example, the way in which, away from the general gaze, black river workers created "a pan-Mississippi community that nourished collective challenges to authority, as well as opportunities for personal gain [. . .] places where hidden communication networks sustained the slave community." This and other such vital, untold histories need to be brought to light. But a caveat: since this book does not attempt to provide a comprehensive history of the antebellum Mississippi, it engages with such stories only at the moments when they intersected with the dominant cultural conceptions of the river.[6]

"IT IS OUR NILE, OUR MYTHIC STREAM"

This intersection was absolutely apparent within the prevailing association of the Mississippi as American Nile, particularly in terms of its relationship to slavery. As the dominant tropes of the river in the antebellum years, apparent within each of the chapters that follow but not always explicitly expressed, they require some further introductory comment. As cultural themes, they stand behind all other antebellum representations of the river. The vogue for all things Egyptian developed in the late eighteenth century. It was spurred on by the discovery, by Napoleon's troops, of the Rosetta Stone in 1799, and reached a peak in the early decades of the nineteenth century after its deciphering. In London in 1818, a satirical article in the *Morning Chronicle* described the trend: "My eldest boy rides on a sphynx instead of a rocking-horse, and my youngest has a pap-boat in the shape of a crocodile. My husband has built a water-closet in the form of a pyramid."[7]

But what did the Nile signify for antebellum readers? On the one hand, perhaps the dominant interpretation, it was as the Rev. Aveling described it in 1855: "In ascending the NILE, literally or mentally, we advance towards the primeval source of civilization and government; light upon the first schools of science and art, and discover one of the chief birth-places of the religions of man." But on the other, it was the biblical river of slavery: "A river," Philip Gosse wrote in 1850, "mighty and renowned, indeed, but one whose name would be chiefly associated in the mind of Israel with memories and traditions of bitter captivity, the "iron furnace" of Egyptian bondage." At the time when, in John Irwin's words, "the analogy between the Nile and the Mississippi/Missouri was a commonplace," both readings of the Nile were vital for the river's cultural life.[8]

For the earliest European settlers along the Mississippi, the analogy was immediately apprehended: they found pyramids. Mounds along the river were evidence of a great and powerful civilization that once existed on the Mississippi. "It is claimed for the Egyptians," wrote George Gale in 1867, "that they became the fathers of geometry from the necessity of dividing out to the tillers of the soil the overflowed bottoms of the Nile; but the Mound-Builders have exhibited the most exact geometrical skill in many of their embankments and inclosures." For example, the great fortified mound of the Choctaws, "Nanih Waya," in what is now Winston County, Mississippi, "was an oblong mound forty to fifty feet high, and covering at the base about an acre [. . .] protected by a circular earthen rampart, ten feet in height and thirty to forty feet in width, with several entrance gaps, and enclosing an area of about one square mile." James Adair, the first white man to describe such mounds, was driven to one conclusion: "From the most exact observations I could make in the long time I traded among the Indian Americans, I was forced to believe them lineally descended from the Israelites, either while they were a maritime power, or soon after the general captivity; the latter however is the most probable."[9]

The settlers on the Mississippi soon developed their own Egyptian associations, expressing their desires for the future through the names they hopefully awarded their towns: Cairo, Memphis, Thebes, Karnak, Alexandria. English traveler Mrs. Houstoun, having "passed [. . .] Troy, and other places, with grandiloquent and ancient names," felt only the "*shade* of ridicule" which came from the contrast with their "modern nothingness." But Americans found nothing ridiculous about their aspirations. Sometime in the early nineteenth century, the southern tip of Illinois at the confluence of the Mississippi and Ohio rivers became known as "Egypt," in legend because it provided corn in a time of hunger. "And hence the title Egypt applied thereto," wrote the *Cairo Delta* in 1849: "It was certainly very properly applied for the region does possess all the advantage of fertility and climate which marked ancient Egypt at a time when the sons of the Patriarch Jacob were compelled to go hither to buy corn, because the famine was sore in all the land of Canaan." When Andrew Jackson, John Overton, and James Winchester founded a town on the Chickasaw Bluffs, Winchester looked to Egypt for its name: "the general advantages of Memphis are owing to its being founded on the Mississippi, one of the largest and most important rivers on the globe, and the high road for all the commerce of the vast and fertile valley through which it flows. This noble river [. . .] may with propriety be denominated the AMERICAN NILE."[10]

Alongside dreams of progress and civilization for this "Egypt of the West," as Lincoln described the Mississippi Valley in his second State of the Union address in 1862, stood the issue of slavery. In Hammond's vision of the American Nile in 1858, slavery was a vital component of the proud future of the Mississippi Valley. Predominantly, however, the association was felt as Lincoln and others intended it, as both a condemnation and a hope for liberation: "this is indeed true slavery," wrote Augustin Cochin of the biblical river of bondage, "and the Nile has looked on the sufferings of which the Mississippi to-day is the witness." Whatever else it might have been in the antebellum years, the Mississippi was unavoidably the river of slavery. Harriet Beecher Stowe's description of the river, carrying "a fearful freight, the tears of the oppressed, the sighs of the helpless, the bitter prayers of poor, ignorant hearts to an unknown God," or the iconic image of Uncle Tom rescuing Eva from the Mississippi, would have been enough to ensure that this association was profoundly and widely felt. But the black men and women, both slave and free, who actually experienced the Mississippi also left their own records of their lives on the artery of slavery—and reacted to the river in complex, conflicted ways that were profoundly open to its symbolic meanings.[11]

Slaves certainly felt the association between the Mississippi and the Nile. Fugitive slave Andrew Jackson, heading toward the Ohio and freedom, remembered: "I had heard about the Israelites when they fled from the slavery of Egypt. I thought I was like them." In this equation, of course, the Ohio featured as Jordan to the Mississippi's Nile, the chance of freedom juxtaposed with the certainty of slavery. As Josiah Henson described (even though he worked on the Mississippi and was not immune to the charm of life on its waters), the river was felt most powerfully in this grim capacity:

> I know not what most men see in voyaging down the Mississippi. If gay and hopeful, probably much of beauty and interest. If eager merchants, probably a golden river, freighted with the wealth of nations. I saw nothing but portents of woe and despair. Wretched slave-pens; a smell of

stagnant waters; half-putrid carcasses of horses or oxen floating along, covered with turkey buzzards and swarms of green flies [. . .] My faith in God utterly gave way. I could no longer pray or trust. He had abandoned ·me and cast me off forever. I looked not to him for help. I saw only the foul miasmas, the emaciated frames of my negro companions; and in them saw the sure, swift, loving intervention of the one unfailing friend of the wretched,—death!

Writing early in the twentieth century, Charles Alexander concluded unequivocally: "Going down the Mississippi River to the slave was much like going to hell and perhaps more dreaded because more real."[12]

So it was, and so the river appeared most frequently in antislavery works. And yet, that was not the whole story. Though unavoidably the river of slavery, the black men and women who lived and worked along the Mississippi in the antebellum years frequently wrote of finding something more resonant in its waters. Of course, though not often symbolically figured in that role, the river could offer the path to physical freedom. John Joseph, fleeing slavery, remembered: "I travelled on till I came to the Mississippi river, and when I saw the river I was afraid [. . .] In despair I was almost ready to cast myself into the river, and thus put an end to my existence, when I caught sight of a boat tied to a tree, which I gladly loosened and in it let myself float down the river, trusting in him who is able to preserve them that put their trust in him, as well on the mighty deep as on the land."[13]

Remarkably, however, for both slave and free black men and women, the Mississippi could also act as the catalyst for mental transformation, offering the chance of a more profound liberation. The Mississippi River "attracted me like a magnet," remembered John P. Parker, "for as soon as I was free to move in my own selected direction I made straight for the river." "Life on the Mississippi River," wrote William Wells Brown, who labored, while a slave, as a steamboat waiter, "is an exciting one." It was, however, an anonymous fugitive slave who produced a vision of the river most compellingly in opposition to Josiah Henson's river of death. Fleeing slavery, and wary of "being arrested and taken back," the nameless man "hid away in a secluded spot on the banks of the Mississippi River." While there, the natural world effected an extraordinary moment of self-discovery: "I waited for the coming of another night. All was silence around me, save the sweet chant of the feathered songsters in the forest, or the musical ripple of the eddying waters at my feet [. . .] I then turned to the rising moon as it peered above, ascending the deep blue ether, high in the heavens, casting its mellow rays over the surrounding landscape, and gilding the smooth surface of the noble river with its silvery line [. . .] It was then and there that I studied nature in its lonely grandeur, and saw in it the goodness of God [. . .] I resolved that I would be a bondman no longer." The idea of the Mississippi as American Nile must inevitably have played into such influential moments of identification with the river—not the Nile of slavery, but the Nile as cradle of civilization. Contemplating the "beautiful and classic obelisk of Luxor, removed from Thebes, where it had stood four thousand years, and transplanted to the Place de la Concorde, at Paris," William Wells Brown read of the "noble daring of Sesostris, the African general, who drew kings at his chariot wheels." His reaction was profound: "I felt proud of my antecedents, proud of the glorious past, which no amount of hate and prejudice could wipe from history's page." In every chapter that follows, whatever the dominant cultural incarnation of the river, these stories are also present—sometimes implicitly, often prominently.[14]

If it is no longer much thought of as America's Nile, the Mississippi's power abides. It is still capable, on a whim, of shrugging off man's checks and controls to wander as it wishes. The river—or just those four assonant syllables—is still capable of eliciting extraordinary emotions and powerful collective memories. Because of the mercurial nature and almost unintelligible scope of the physical river, the imaginary Mississippi has not just been its attendant or shadow: it has been necessary, vital, and, perhaps, the more true—especially in the remarkable years before the Civil War. The Mississippi River, in its role as the antebellum river of dreams, is the focus of this book.

Empire

Jefferson and "the Mississippi We Must Have"

We beg you to trace the Mississippi from the ocean—survey the innumerable rivers
which water your western territory, and pay their tribute to its greatness—examine their
luxuriant soil which those rivers traverse: then we ask, can the God of wisdom and nature have created that vast country in vain? [. . .] Can the presumptuous madness of man
imagine a policy inconsistent with the immense designs of the deity? Americans cannot.
Address to Congress from the sixth Kentucky convention, 1788

It is the last of Gods creation and the Seventh day came before it was quite finnish'd.
ELIZABETH HOUSE TRIST, 1784

Ensconced in Washington at the beginning of 1803, the destiny of the Mississippi in flux and its waters closed to American trade, Thomas Jefferson gathered
his latest thoughts about the river whose destiny had occupied him for decades.
He sat down to write to M. Dupont de Nemours in the hope that his influential old acquaintance would be able use "all the good offices in his power" to
intervene in the events that were unfolding. Jefferson saw the ominous question
mark surrounding the destiny of Louisiana and the Mississippi River as "a crisis
the most important the United States have ever met since their independence."
It would decide, he felt, the young nation's "character and career." Spain had
secretly retroceded Louisiana to France in 1800. Jefferson, pessimistic (at least to
Dupont) about this international wrangling, asserted that "the occlusion of the
Mississippi is a state of things in which we cannot exist." Diplomatic solutions
were being sought: James Monroe had been sent to join Robert Livingston in
Paris, ostensibly to purchase New Orleans for the United States. But Jefferson
was prepared to consider other options. The use of the Mississippi was "so indispensable" that America would not "hesitate one moment to hazard our existence
for its maintenance." If diplomacy failed, Jefferson obliquely warned, "we see the
destinies we have to run, and prepare at once for them." What appeared to be
"an almost invisible point on the horizon" was in fact "the embryo of a tornado
which will burst on the countries on both sides of the Atlantic." For the right to
navigate the Mississippi and deposit goods at New Orleans, Jefferson appeared
willing to take the United States to war with Napoleon.[1]

As Jefferson well knew, this was only in keeping with the turbulent imperial history of the Mississippi River. It had been plagued, since its European discovery in 1541, by colonial strife, countless failed adventures, and scores of unrealized dreams. Prominent on the global stage and a powerful symbol in international politics, the river passed through many hands before its final Americanization. First Spanish, then French, then Spanish again; half-British, then half-American, and, finally, half-French once more: as the flags changed so did the dreams and meanings attached to the river. Hernando de Soto's discovery of the Mississippi was a telling lesson: he did not comprehend what he had found and was buried in its waters soon after. The Spaniard's grave went unvisited by white men for almost a century and a half, until France, moving down from Canada, picked up the imperial baton. The legendary Rene-Robert Cavalier, Sieur de La Salle traveled down the river by canoe in 1682 and officially claimed Louisiana for "Louis le Grand," "from the mouth of *the great river* [. . .] and as far as its mouth at the sea." He, too, died on its banks, but not before his pioneering efforts had aligned Louisiana with and around the Mississippi. The river took pride of place as the central artery of France's sprawling colony.[2]

By the late eighteenth century, La Salle's imperial vision had been largely reduced to a series of sad villages and plantations strung out along the river—St. Phillipe, Corne de Cerf, Bellefontaine—inhabited sometimes by only a few families precariously keeping the dream of a Mississippi empire alive. Most are now long forgotten. One of their countrymen was distressed at what he found along the river in 1795: "Nothing is to be seen but houses in ruins and abandoned." Despite the demise of many French settlements, New Orleans prospered. In 1763, the Spanish became the titular owners of Louisiana when, at the end of the French and Indian Wars, France ceded the territory to her ally to avoid further British gains. Despite initial conflict with the French settlers, there was growth as well as decay. By 1783, the Spanish held garrisons at Natchez (precariously) and St. Louis. Next to New Orleans, St Louis was the biggest settlement on the river, though by 1810 it still contained only 1,400 residents. Cahokia, Illinois, began life as a French mission in 1699. Like other river towns—Kaskaskia, Prairie du Rocher, Cape Girardeau, Ste. Genevieve, Plaquemine, and St Charles—it was a small but significant settlement by the end of the eighteenth century. New Madrid (L'Anse à la Graisse) dated from 1789 and was supported by a diminutive force; the Chickasaw Bluffs (later Memphis) had been settled by a few families; a fort was begun at Walnut Hills (later Vicksburg) in 1790; the fort at Baton Rouge had fallen into disrepair.[3]

The dream of Mississippi colonization was early taken up by Anglo-Americans who, despite official restrictions, filtered westward. The lure of the river was stronger than governments—and, in Frederick Turner's words, "when the English colonists crossed the Alleghanies they escaped from the control of mother colonies as well as of the mother country." As early as 1699, Edward Randolph, the surveyor general of His Majesty's Customs for North America, reported the consternation caused by the construction of Fort Maurepas on Biloxi Bay: "I find the Inhabitants [of Charleston] greatly alarmed upon the news that the French continue their resolution to make a settling at Messasipi River." The British traded with lower-Mississippi tribes like the Chickasaws and Choctaws throughout the eighteenth century. Indeed, Thomas Welch had crossed the Mississippi and established a trading post by 1698. The British briefly found a firm foothold on the river when they gained towns like Natchez and Kaskaskia in the peace of 1763. During the Revolutionary War, however, the Spanish retook Natchez along with Florida; the Americans took Kaskaskia and the Northwest. Therefore, after peace in 1783, Britain was also forced to orientate its riverine ambitions north-south, down from Canada and up from New Orleans.[4]

In the twenty years from American Independence to the Louisiana Purchase, the Mississippi emerged into a new and heightened state of imperial uncertainty. At the heart of the river's many imaginings, the central figure in this period of debate, machinations, and empire building was Thomas Jefferson. He never traveled to the West to see the river that so often occupied his thoughts, but his understanding of and fascination with the Mississippi was crucial in securing the river politically and culturally for America. What the river meant to Jefferson was very closely allied to what the river meant and came to mean in the larger mythology of the United States. This is all the more true since Jefferson's relationship with the river was not static—it developed over time and sometimes appeared inconsistent. The position that Jefferson took in 1803 was twenty years and an ideological shift away from his conception of the western situation at the end of the Revolution; America followed. As politician, president, and geopolitical strategist, he slowly came to understand, with great clarity, the importance of the Mississippi for the young America—and, vitally, its centrality in his conception of America as the expanding "Empire of liberty" (a phrase that Jefferson first used in 1780, in a letter to George Rogers Clark specifically urging him to protect America's western river frontier). Jefferson was the presiding spirit behind the complex maneuvers which prefaced the Louisiana Purchase, and he dealt— often willingly, sometimes less so—with a motley cast of adventurers, foreign schemers, explorers, and political rivals. In the end, Jefferson's vision was definitive. Yet while the complex imperial meanings of the Mississippi underwent profound transformations in the national consciousness, further shifts soon followed. Exploration and steam symbolically ushered in the Americanization of the river, and firmly pointed toward the future.[5]

"A NEW DISCOVERY OF AMERICA"

After the Revolutionary War, the Mississippi River was a potent symbol of the West for Americans—both irresistible lure and emphatic borderline. "The Mississippi Valley," as Alexis de Tocqueville famously described it, echoing the rhetoric of the early river frontier, "is, all in all, the most magnificent dwelling that God has ever prepared for the habitation of man [. . .] the still-empty cradle of a great nation [. . .] almost a new discovery of America." From threatening wilderness, to chimerical dream, to the hub of American commerce and empire, the Mississippi stimulated a heady mixture of desires. It was the Revolution that unleashed them, and veterans were the most significant figures in its immediate future. According to the Treaty of Paris of 1783, the subjects of Great Britain and the United States were guaranteed free and unmolested navigation of the Mississippi. The pioneering settlers—both Loyalist and Revolutionary veterans—who blazed trails into Kentucky, Tennessee, and the Ohio territory, accordingly sighted their lines of desire along the Western Rivers, down the Mississippi to New Orleans. Disastrously, in 1784, Spain closed New Orleans and the Lower Mississippi to American trade (as it remained until 1795)—a response to the flood of migrants who represented a threat to the fragile Spanish empire. This created an economic blockade. In Temple Bodley's words, although the West's "virgin soil yielded superabundant products, the cost of transporting them over the mountains was greater than they would sell for there." In the early American West, anger and resentment—directed at both Spain and the East—grew. "This vast and restless population," wrote the Spanish governor in 1794, "menacingly ask for the free navigation of the Mississippi. If they achieve their object, their ambitions would not be confined to this side of the Mississippi." He was correct: perilous colonial designs, schemes for self-aggrandizement, and imperial fantasies bred exponentially.[6]

Numerous vested interests and the importance of the Atlantic trade for the East meant that western grievances were not unfounded. Many in the East were unconcerned about, even opposed to, American access to the Mississippi—so much so that in 1785, John Jay, appointed by Congress to negotiate a treaty with Spain, was prepared to sacrifice the navigation of the river for twenty-five years in return for lucrative trade routes. Though that plan collapsed, it was not without support. Jefferson, in *Notes on the State of Virginia* (written in 1781 in response to the questions of François de Barbé-Marbois, another important figure in the river's destiny), described the Mississippi as "one of the principal channels of future commerce for the country westward of the Alleghany." Nonetheless, as Julian Boyd has described, at precisely this moment he had "for some months been concentrating attention primarily on developing the Potomac route to tap northwestern trade and bring it to Virginia ports." As Thomas Abernethy concluded, "Jefferson, and doubtless a majority of eastern Virginians, agreed with Washington in his indifference to the navigation of the Mississippi."[7]

For Washington, the answer to the Mississippi problem lay not in the opening of the river but in improved overland transportation. The president wrote to Governor Benjamin Harrison on October 10, 1784, outlining his conception of the problem, spurred by observations made on a tour of the West: "the western states [. . .] stand as it were upon a pivot [. . .] They have looked down the Mississippi, until the Spaniards, very impolitically I think for themselves, threw difficulties in their way; and they looked that way for no other reason than they could glide gently down the stream, without considering, perhaps, the difficulties of the voyage back again, and the time necessary to perform it in, and because they have no other means of coming to us but by long land transportations and unimproved roads." Washington underestimated the western pull of the river, and focused instead on the betterment of Virginia. Improve the roads, he believed, "and then see what an influx of articles will be poured upon us [. . .] and how amply we will be compensated."[8]

James Madison—often in tune with the needs and desires of the people of the Western Rivers—disagreed. On August 20, 1784, he wrote to Jefferson, evidently hoping to persuade his friend that the navigation of the Mississippi was a matter of importance above and beyond local interests. The letter—redrafted, reworked—was one of the crucial visions of the Mississippi en route to its Americanization. In terms that were designed to appeal, Madison addressed the subject of Mississippi navigation via the rising price of tobacco and the increase in demand for land on the Ohio: "What think you of a guinea an acre being already the price for choice tracts with sure titles?" The only impediment to continued increases in both would be the "impolitic and perverse attempt in Spain to shut the mouth of the Mississippi against the inhabitants above." Of course, such an action would only be temporary since, "[Spain] can no more finally stop the current of trade down the river than she can that of the river itself."

Madison began his argument in favor of continued American access to the river with an appeal to "justice and the general rights of mankind," which everyday acquired "weight from the progress of philosophy and civilisation." Spain would have to be careful, since that time would not be "distant [. . .] when, in spite of all precautions the safety of her possessions in this quarter of the globe must depend more on our peaceableness than her own power." Madison turned to the examples of European rivers—"the Rhine, the Maese and the Scheld as well as the Elbe and Oder"—and asserted that Spain could "not surely so disregard the usage of nations" for the case "of the Missisipi is probably the strongest in the world." The settlement of the West, he concluded, "will much depend on the free use of the Missisipi." Thus, the expansion of Americans into the "vacant land of the United States lying on the waters of the Missisipi" would be accompanied by a concomitant increase in "all the productions of the American soil required by Europe." Crucially, this would mean that "the establishment of internal manufactures" would "be long delayed": "Reverse the case by supposing the Missisipi denied to us and the consequence is that many of our supernumerary hands who in the former case would be husbandmen on the waters of the Missisipi will on the latter supposition be manufacturers on those of the Atlantic." Whether or not it was a result of Madison's vision of the Mississippi as the key to imperial expansion, or as the artery that promised to feed, extend, and guarantee the longevity of a pastoral America, Jefferson's attitude to the river underwent a shift. His removal to France, and a concomitant awareness of that nation's continuing aspirations for the river, must also have proved decisive. And more personal stimulus was provided by a voice which, though small, was prophetic.[9]

In 1774, Elizabeth House had married a British officer, Nicholas Trist, stationed in America. Before the Revolution he left the army to invest in the western lands through which he had often traveled. Trist, like many Loyalists, settled in Natchez, still a British holding at the time. While Nicholas made his way in the West, Elizabeth remained in Philadelphia at her mother's boardinghouse. Mary House's pension attracted a prominent caliber of visitor, and Thomas Jefferson was one of them. Elizabeth and Jefferson became friends, and when Martha Jefferson died in 1782, Jefferson turned to Elizabeth for help with his children. Throughout this period of their acquaintance, the West must have dominated conversation. Elizabeth continually looked to the day when she could join her husband on the Mississippi. The international situation prevented Elizabeth from making her western journey until 1783—a moment when Jefferson himself was first looking to sponsor western exploration. So it was that when she set out for the West, Trist determined to keep a journal so that Jefferson's "Philosophical mind" could "gather information."[10]

Trist's record of her flatboat odyssey to Natchez is the first female travel account of its kind, the direct predecessor of the narratives that would dominate Mississippi discourse in the coming decades. It succinctly established lasting travelers' tropes. Having reached the Mississippi by June 13, 1784, Elizabeth "arose in expectation of seeing the Grand Riviere"; expectation soon turned to despair. Mosquitoes, sawyers, a lack of provisions, and the river's "awfull and Melancholy" appearance soon led Trist to conclude, "I don't like this river." With a dislocated perception that Dickens, for one, would have recognized, Trist attempted to explain why:

> I have various Ideas about this river:—[I] sometimes conceit—I am got
> to the fag end of the world; or rather that it is the last of Gods creation
> and the Seventh day came before it was quite finnish'd. At other times, I
> fancy there has been some great revolution in nature, and this great body
> of water has forced a passage w[h]ere it was not intended and tore up all
> before it.

Counterbalancing that was the powerfully heterogeneous sense of the frontier that Trist evoked. Imperial powers feuded over the imperial destiny of the river, imagining rigid lines of demarcation. In practice, things were much more fluid; the official Spanish closure of the river could not stop its inevitable flow of commerce and interaction. American, British, Spanish, and French colonists intermingled through the currents of trade and sympathy engendered by shared hardship. Seeing some "poor french men who had their boat sunk," Trist "gave them the good news of their boat being near at hand." Hearing that a Spanish fort was "in want of flour," Trist's boatmen went to trade. Meeting a starving family from Natchez, Trist's party "gave them some flour [. . .] tea and sugar." Nearer Natchez, a "Mullato Woman [. . .] was exceeding kind to us [. . .] everything she had was at our service." Her last diary entry, on July 1, 1784, optimistically imagined the completion of her journey and her imminent meeting with Nicholas: "Perhaps a boat may just be setting of, and he will be glad to see me." But Nicholas had died in February. The young widow had to dispose of her husband's western holdings. In 1785, Trist still wrote to Jefferson in Paris that she looked forward to giving him "an account of my peregrination." Her journal must therefore stand alongside the other sources working on Jefferson at this time.[11]

In 1786, Jefferson revealed his newly formulated concerns for the future to Archibald Stewart, and they were on a continental scale: "Our confederacy," he wrote from Paris, "must be viewed as the nest from which all America, North and South is to be peopled." The river was to be vital to America's imperial expansion. His conclusion was profoundly simple: "the navigation of the Mississippi we must have." This sentiment was amplified a year later to Madison. Jefferson felt very "uneasy" about "the possibility that the navigation of the Mississippi may be abandoned to Spain." While insisting that he "never had any interest westward of the Alleghany," and never would, Jefferson understood that "the act which abandons the navigation of the Mississippi is an act of separation between the eastern and western country." He feared that if those inhabitants of the Mississippi Valley "declare themselves a separate people, we are incapable of a single effort to retain them." For Charles Miller, therefore, the "establishment of American rights to the Mississippi [. . .] became one of [Jefferson's] most important causes."[12]

Even then, Jefferson could be strikingly inconsistent. In 1790, two years after his apparent concern about the possible dissolution of the westward-spreading union, he wrote (disingenuously?) to William Carmichael, the American minister to Spain, that it was "not our interest to cross the Mississippi for ages, and will never be our interest to remain united with those who do."[13] Whatever westward visions were forming in Jefferson's mind, were aspirations for the trans-Mississippi still a leap too far? Given that Jefferson had already, by 1790, attempted to sponsor exploration across the Mississippi, this remains a contradiction. Within the same month, he produced his first extended piece of work on the Mississippi, writing as secretary of state. A set of instructions to Carmichael, they were extended and published two years later. In terms reminiscent of Madison's earlier correspondence, Jefferson set out the case for American rights to the Mississippi:

> If we appeal to [. . .] the law of nature and nations [. . .] as we feel it written on the heart of man, what sentiment is written in deeper characters than that the ocean is free to all men, and their rivers to all their inhabitants? Is there a man, savage or civilized, unbiased by habit, who does not feel and attest this truth?

Rather more pithily, Jefferson evoked Roman law: "*flumina publica sunt,*" or "rivers belong to the public" (Jefferson's translation). Morally and legally, Jefferson argued, the United States had a right to the use of the Mississippi.[14]

Vital to the political development of the American Mississippi, Jefferson played an equally essential role in its cultural development—or at least, the promulgation of certain important visions of the river. "While I was in Europe," Jefferson wrote to William Dunbar in 1804, having read his "ingenuous paper on the subject of the Mississippi," "I had purchased everything I could lay my hands on which related to any part of America, and particularly had a full collection of the English, French and Spanish authors, on the subject of Louisiana." A letter to James Madison in May 1788, provides a small but telling example of Jefferson's collection of geographical works, and the interest of the Mississippi for the founding fathers: "You remember the report, drawn by Governor Randolph, on the navigation of the Mississippi [. . .] I lent it to Dr. Franklin, and he mislaid it, so that it could never be found."[15]

It was this collection—the fruit of "unremitting researches" and certainly unrivaled of its kind—that proved crucial. Jefferson was the repository of western geographical lore. E. Millicent Sowerby's catalogue of Jefferson's library— as purchased by Congress in 1815 to replace those lost when the Capitol was burnt—reveals an astonishingly full bibliography of the seminal pre-1803 works on the Mississippi. These volumes were often the work of the extraordinary individuals who had played a central role in the river's history, their names echoing the imperial changes to which the river had been subject: Father Jacques Marquette; Joutel and Tonti (both members of La Salle's expedition); Father Louis Hennepin; Pierre Charlevoix; Le Page du Pratz; Antoine François Laval; Louis Armand Baron de Lahontan; Jean Bernard Bossu; Brissot de Warville; Peter Esprit Radisson; Robert Rogers; Jonathan Carver; James Adair; Daniel Coxe; Thomas Hutchins; Andrew Ellicott; James Hall; and Alexander Mackenzie. These were the very works in which the Mississippi was simultaneously described as an extraordinary geographical feature and imagined as a cultural icon in its pre-American phase (indeed, sometimes literally dreamed up by influential frauds like Hennepin and Lahontan). Many stood as warnings: the relics of lost empires, damaged reputations, and wasted opportunities. Jefferson's fascination with these books meant that he became, in Allen's words, "the most knowledgeable American insofar as the geographical lore of the trans-Missouri region was concerned."[16]

"INTEREST REGULATES THE PASSIONS OF NATIONS"

Self-interest was General James Wilkinson's guiding credo—"and he who attributes a different motive to human affairs," he wrote in his *Expatriation Declaration,* "deceives himself or seeks to deceive others." Jefferson was the most knowledgeable theoretician of Louisiana and the trans-Mississippi West, but the greatest exponent of practical, Mississippi realpolitik was General Wilkinson. What Jefferson imagined, Wilkinson knew. For John Seelye, the general was the Mississippi made flesh, a "turbid flood that draws tribute from the entire western region, only to destroy the lands it passes through on its way to New Orleans." Less vituperatively, Jefferson and Wilkinson combined to personify the spirit of the American Mississippi at this watershed moment: the former, as mind and soul; the latter, as body and heart. Upon his arrival in the West in 1784—the "seething and confused ferment" of the river frontier, to borrow William Davis's phrase—Wilkinson swiftly assessed the scene. It was this ability to gauge the spirit of the Mississippi territory, complemented by strident rhetoric and a protean nature, which made Wilkinson a pivotal figure in the river's history. His career was paradigmatic of the secret history of the Mississippi. Numerous imperial plots came and went; Wilkinson and the river abided. What exactly Wilkinson planned over the decades is unclear, and he evidently changed course as circumstance dictated. But that there were schemes and intrigues is apparent, and behind them all stood the dream of a breakaway western empire aligned with the Mississippi.[17]

Wilkinson reached the Mississippi in 1786. His career had already taken Mississippi-like detours. Having served under Benedict Arnold in the Revolutionary War (along with Aaron Burr), and having been implicated in the "Conway Cabal" to remove Washington, he arrived in Kentucky in 1784—"just another merchant who had come west to make a fortune," in Buckner Melton's words. Wilkinson ingratiated himself sufficiently to take a prominent position in the Kentucky conventions that were concerned with the separation of Kentucky from Virginia and Kentucky's freedom of access to the Mississippi. What was the world that Wilkinson arrived in? Partisan feelings ran high, and anger about the social, economic, and political limbo of the West dominated. Alongside those who sought only statehood for Kentucky, there were some who saw their future in a total break from the Union, and perhaps a few who sought an allegiance with Spain to actualize such an outcome. Access to the Mississippi, denied them since 1784, was the central issue. As Henry Adams described the situation: "The entire population, both free and slave, west of the mountains, reached not yet half a million; but already they were partly disposed to think of themselves, and the old thirteen states were not altogether unwilling to consider them, the germ of an independent empire, which was to find its outlet, not through the Alleghanies to the seaboard, but by the Mississippi River to the Gulf."[18]

Back in Virginia, Jefferson expressed his worries: "I fear [. . .] that the people of Kentucky think of separating, not only from Virginia [. . .] but also from the confederacy." Bodley argued that "probably no one in Kentucky thought of a separation from Virginia without her consent, since that consent she had willingly given." Regardless, thanks to James Wilkinson the atmosphere existed on all sides to make such an outcome at least seem possible. By playing both sides of the river against the other, he attempted to steer his own precarious course to the Gulf. As he described in his *Memoirs*: "these circumstances, produced my first voyage to New Orleans, with a view to promote my own fortune, and to benefit my fellow citizens, by awakening the Spanish government of Louisiana, to a just sense of its interests, and thereby to effect the commercial intercourse, which was indispensable to the western country."[19]

In April 1787, Wilkinson loaded a keelboat with "tobacco, hams and butter" and set out for New Orleans. How he eased his passage downriver is unclear; bribery was undoubtedly crucial. Bodley suggests that Wilkinson let Spanish governor Esteban Miró believe that his arrest would provoke war; Hay and Werner conclude that he ingratiated himself by "deploring" the "recent seizure of Spanish subjects at Vincennes" by George Rogers Clark. Certainly, Clark seems to have been the focus of much of Wilkinson's scheming. Presumably seeking his own preferment, Wilkinson is believed to have been the author of anonymous notes that accused Clark of having his own agenda in the West: "Clarke is playing Hell. He is raising a regiment of his own [. . .] is eternally drunk, and [. . .] a stroke is meditated against St Louis and Natchehez." As Bodley noted, "almost any wild story about a western army invading Louisiana would find ready belief [. . .] in Congress." Regardless, somehow Wilkinson arrived in New Orleans in July—with a cargo that inaugurated the rapid growth of commerce on the Mississippi.[20]

While in New Orleans, Wilkinson took the opportunity to make contact with Governor Miró, apparently in the hope of securing his own Mississippi monopoly. In September 1787, he presented the governor with his "Memorial." First, Wilkinson outlined the history of the Kentucky people: "the unanimity of the reports upon the fertility of the soil and healthfulness of the climate in the territory of Kentucky given by all those who had explored it, fixed the attention of people of all classes and conditions upon the western country." The western settlements were "already powerful and on account of their nature, irresistible." But the Kentuckians had been cut off from navigation of the Mississippi—"the fountain from which they must hope for future relief and comfort." To promote a free Mississippi, according to Wilkinson, they were "working to separate themselves from the American Union." They were faced, Wilkinson attested, with two choices: *an amicable arrangement with Spain, or hostilities with the help of Great Britain.*"

What, according to Wilkinson, should "the policies of Spain [. . .] be at this critical juncture"? When "we cast our eyes on the country East of the Mississippi," Wilkinson pondered: "Does it not [. . .] strike the most limited intellect that he who closes the only gate by which the inhabitants of this extensive region may approach their neighbours in pursuit of useful intercourse, opposes this benevolent design? Is not the Mississippi this gate? The privation of its use takes away from us Americans what nature seems to have provided for their indispensable convenience happiness." Only Wilkinson could follow such an assertion with a claim for his own monopoly. To the Spanish, he offered the vision of Kentucky's secession, her dependence on Spain, and the creation of a buffer zone. (As he astutely informed Miró, "Spain ought to consider the navigation of the Mississippi as one of the most precious jewels of her crown.") To the Kentuckians, he tried to promise the Mississippi. For Wilkinson himself, there was to be "an *exclusive* privilege of trading" at New Orleans, as "this would make [his fellow Kentuckians] envy his good fortune and leave the Union in order to share it." The status quo was what Wilkinson truly desired. He accompanied his "Memorial" with his "Expatriation Declaration," secured his right of deposit, and a Spanish stipend.[21]

Truly protean, Wilkinson simultaneously used his position in the Kentucky conventions to give voice to the frustrations of the West. This influence culminated in the sixth Kentucky convention of November 1788. Wilkinson read out a heavily doctored version of the "Memorial," which he claimed to have presented to Governor Miró. He told Miró the same: "I submitted to its examination my original memorial," for which he received "the unanimous thanks of that body." His guiding hand, and his ability to gauge the spirit of the times, can be seen in the particular emphasis given to the Mississippi in the convention. The *Kentucky Gazette* reported that, "Mr. Wilkinson, from the committee appointed to draught an address to Congress, requesting immediate & effective measures to be taken, to obtain the navigation of the river Mississippi, reported that the committee had taken the matter into consideration, and prepared an address, which he read in his place." Gilbert Imlay—an inhabitant of Kentucky at the time of the sixth convention, a friend and business associate of the general, and just embarking on his own Louisiana projects—included the work as a provocative opening to his *Topographical Description of the Western Territories of North America:* "this petition contains sentiments so pure, and so manly, that I think there cannot be a better idea conveyed of their dispositions and manners, than by inserting it at full length." More moderate voices won the day in Kentucky. It was awarded statehood in 1792. But the Mississippi remained a central western cause. When the Democratic Society of Lexington questioned its senator, John Edwards, in 1794, its first question asked insistently: "What progress was made [. . .] to obtain the free use of the Mississippi, and what was the issue of the negotiations on the subject?"[22]

* * *

Wilkinson was not an isolated case. Plots and rumors of plots, labyrinthine in their complexity, raged throughout the Mississippi Valley at the close of the eighteenth century. The French had never given up on the chance of an American empire focused around the river, and were the first to make a move toward that end. In 1792, the Genet conspiracy embroiled numerous prominent figures (including Jefferson) in an attempt to detach the Mississippi Valley from the rest of America. A French agent was active in Kentucky as early as 1785, and French ambitions in Louisiana stretched back as far as 1762. In 1792, an anonymous French report stated that the inhabitants of Louisiana were all "Frenchmen or Anglo-Americans" who were "sworn enemies of Spaniards who in truth do not oppress them, but constrain their industry and trade." Resentments were still felt about the "barbarous manner" in which the Spanish, under Alejandro "Bloody" O'Reilly, had taken possession of the colony; the garrisons at New Orleans and Natchez were weak; and the Anglo-Americans—"robust, enterprising, good hunters"—"have been making overtures secretly to the French Minister at Philadelphia to engage us to relieve them of the Spanish yoke." The anonymous agent felt, moreover, that the cooling of Revolutionary ardor in the East meant that some of "the most informed and influential men among them, far from desiring the independence of Louisiana, have not even made vows for the liberty of navigating the Mississippi." He therefore felt sure that an insurrection in "Louisiana promises successes most immediate, most certain, and least expensive."[23]

These anonymous speculations were in tune with the thoughts of the Girondists —powerfully placed in the French Revolutionary Convention in 1792—and their leader, Brissot de Warville. Brissot had already made his own journey to the American West and had felt the quickening pulse: "they all expect that the navigation of the Mississippi becoming free, will soon open to them the markets [. . .] But the question to be solved is, whether the Spaniards will open this navigation willingly, or whether the Americans will force it." Either way, the settlers were "determined to open it by good will or force; and it would not be in the power of Congress to moderate their ardour." At that time he was convinced that "the present union will forever subsist." In 1792, full of revolutionary fervor and encouraged by his American friends, Brissot reversed that decision. The expatriate circle that surrounded Thomas Paine in Paris was vital in influencing nascent French plans. Paine himself "sympathised warmly with the project of the Kentuckians to expel the Spanish from the Mississippi." At his home (one of Madame de Pompadour's old mansions), Brissot met Joel Barlow and Gilbert Imlay. In addition, Paine was in correspondence with his Revolutionary War comrade Dr. James O'Fallon—George Rogers Clark's brother-in-law and "business" associate. All were involved in French imperial designs on the Mississippi. As so often in the river's antebellum history, land speculation was the key.[24]

Joel Barlow, poet and statesman, had already been implicated in one of the most notorious land schemes of the early West. The Scioto Land Company, through a combination of incompetence and immorality, sold around fifty thousand acres of land in the southern Ohio country to six hundred French emigrants, mostly Royalists looking to escape the Revolution. The land, named Gallipolis, was worthless, highly vulnerable to Indian attack, unhealthy, and not even legally theirs. When Volney traveled through the Mississippi Valley in the 1790s, he visited the "forlorn" Gallipolis. He was shocked to find only about eighty of the original six hundred immigrants, and was startled by their "thin pale faces, sickly looks, and anxious air." For Barlow, and all those who dealt in western lands, the opening of the Mississippi was essential to the value of their holdings. But the Mississippi had symbolic resonance, too. In a public address Barlow gave at Yale College in 1781, the Mississippi appeared as an image of sublime mystery, beckoning America to uncover its secrets: "Lands yet unknown and streams without a name [. . .] Where Mississippi's waves their sources boast, / Where groves and floods and realms and climes are lost." A document in the French Foreign Affairs' archive recommended Barlow—"un véritable ami de la liberté"—for a position on the Louisiana committee.[25]

Gilbert Imlay remains best known as the man who drove Mary Wollstonecraft to the brink of suicide, but Imlay was also a Revolutionary veteran who, like many of his comrades, had moved beyond the Alleghenies to Kentucky in 1784. Imlay's land speculations were even more convoluted and dubious than Barlow's, driving him into continual games of cat and mouse with sheriff's summonses and court writs. As it had for Barlow, the Mississippi also entered Imlay's imaginative world. Imlay's *A Topographical Description of the Western Territories of North America* (1792) and *The Emigrants* (1793), an epistolary travel account and a sentimental novel, both offered powerful, millennial visions of the West: "Everything here assumes a dignity and splendour I have never seen in any other part of the world," he enthused in his *Topographical Description*. "Here an eternal verdure reigns [. . .] Every thing here gives delight; and, in that mild effulgence which beams around us, we feel a glow of gratitude for the elevation which our all bountiful Creator has bestowed upon us." For Imlay, the true heart of the Revolutionary spirit ("reason and humanity") would beat not in Paris, and not in the newly established federal capital in Washington, but westward in the (secessionist?) Mississippi Valley. Its veins would be the Western Waters:

We shall pass through the Mississippi to the sea—up the Ohio, Monon-gahala and Cheat Rivers, by a small portage, into the Potowmac [. . .] from the northern lakes to the head branches of the rivers which run into the Hudson's bay—[. . .] and from the sources of the Misouri into the Great South Sea. Thus in the centre of the earth, governing by the laws of reason and humanity, we seem calculated to become at once the emporium and protectors of the world.[26]

This vision was given a fictional spin in *The Emigrants*. With the same watch-words and aspirations—"reason and humanity"—Captain Arl—ton establishes Bellefont, a utopian community for his Revolutionary comrades, situated on the Ohio near Louisville. With the aid of the benevolent General W——— (mod-eled on Wilkinson), Bellefont is founded to "extend the blessings of civilization to all orders of men." The issue of a liberated Mississippi was therefore a topic close to Imlay's heart. "Whoever are possessed of this river," he predicted, "must in time command that continent." Imlay wrote two encouraging papers to the Committee of Public Safety, and apparently intended to take an active part in whatever Louisiana insurrection was planned by the French, complaining to Brissot in April 1793 that "he had not yet received official authorisation for the Mississippi expedition."[27]

One conspirator certain to take an active part in "l'expedition du Missisipi" was George Rogers Clark, languishing back in America. Clark had already had his own moment of Mississippi glory in 1778, when he captured Kaskaskia and Vincennes in the Revolutionary War. Clark's victories in the Northwestern Ter-ritories helped to establish the Great Lakes as the northern boundary of the United States. Jefferson was certainly aware of Clark's preeminence in the West. In 1783, he wrote to Clark expressing his fears that the British were contemplat-ing an exploration of "the country from the Missisipi to California." Though the British claimed that this expedition was "only to promote knolege," Jefferson was "afraid they have thoughts of colonising into that quarter." Accordingly, "some of us have been talking here in a feeble way of making the attempt to search that country," and though it came to nothing, Jefferson made an offer to Clark that his brother William would later fulfill: "how would you like to lead such a party?"[28]

Yet Clark's star was not long in the ascendance. Defamed by Wilkinson and refused any of the expenses that he had invested in his northwestern cam-paign, Clark looked across the Mississippi, to the Spanish, for new land and new opportunity (like Daniel Boone, who became a Spanish official in 1799, or James Bowie's father, settling a few miles across the river in Tywappity Bottom, soon to be Missouri). Two plans for an autonomous river community within Spanish jurisdiction, like Imlay's imagined Bellefont, were almost formulated—one near the mouth of the Yazoo River and present-day Vicksburg, the other opposite the mouth of the Ohio in present-day Missouri. Neither materialized. Finally learning in November 1792 that his claims in the Virginia courts had been rejected, Clark's thoughts turned to the French. In the background of these machinations—perhaps generating them—was the Irish adventurer Doctor James O'Fallon, Clark's brother-in-law in 1791. O'Fallon's own intrigues with the South Carolina Yazoo Company, the Spanish, and the ubiquitous Wilkinson concerning projected Mississippi colonies were tortuous and obscure.[29]

Either way, O'Fallon and Clark, apparently unaware of the plans being prepared by the Girondists and expatriate Americans in France, formulated a scheme for the military conquest and separation of Louisiana in the latter months of 1792. In essence, Clark's letter described that for three thousand pounds sterling (to cover expenses), he would muster a force of 1,500 men who would expatriate, become French citizens, and march on New Orleans. The plan, written by O'Fallon but signed by Clark, was sent to the French authorities care of O'Fallon's friend Thomas Paine. Paine wrote back in February 1793. The general's "offers and propositions" had been "recd. by the Provisionary executive Council of the Republic with satisfaction [. . .] The Georgia Grants [. . .] will be confirmed to the companies that shall have been assistants in the expedition." Most tellingly, Paine had checked the suitability of Clark's character for the forthcoming enterprise with an eminent correspondent: "Mr Jefferson's private sentiments respecting him" had favorably convinced Paine to "excite every exertion" that he could on Clark's behalf. So, early in 1793, the Girondists, Thomas Paine, Gilbert Imlay, Joel Barlow, and George Rogers Clark were poised on the brink of an extraordinary filibustering expedition along the Mississippi against the Spanish—apparently with Jefferson's foreknowledge.[30]

And yet: the plan that was formulated by the French from these disparate elements —sweeping in its magnitude—was entrusted in large part to Charles Edmond Genet, minister plenipotentiary of the French Republic to the United States. Brissot had personally chosen Genet to (echoing Jefferson's phrase) "promote the extension of the Empire of liberty." Central to this was the French concern to "open the Mississippi to the inhabitants of Kentucky, [and] deliver our brothers in Louisiana from the tyrannical yoke of Spain." Genet arrived in Charleston early in April 1793. "Almost from the first," in Harry Ammon's words, "he alienated the President and even rendered the support of his friends difficult." Washington, steering a course between Britain and France, was committed to a policy of neutrality. Genet's privateering against the British, his attempts to fit out a ship, the *Petite Democrate,* for an assault on New Orleans—compounded by his threats to defend the rights of France by appealing to the people against the president—essentially doomed French plans before they had even begun. The fall of the Girondists, particularly the loss of Brissot (guillotined in October), removed much of the impetus of Genet's expedition.[31]

Still, Jefferson's relationship with the plot, particularly with Genet, was significant. Jefferson's own record of a provocative meeting with Genet in July is illuminating in regard to his attitude about an insurrectionary Louisiana. He attended the meeting "not as Secy. of state, but as mr. Jeff." Genet outlined his plans, and Jefferson recorded his reaction: "I did not care what insurrection should be excited in Louisiana." His only concern was to maintain apparent American neutrality in the matter, warning Genet that "enticing officers & souldiers from Kentucky to go against Spain, was really putting a halter about their necks." In Genet's version of events: "Mr Jefferson [. . .] made me understand that he thought a little spontaneous interruption could advance the matter" of an American "entrepot below New Orleans."[32]

Their mutual interests were stronger still, and they focused around a French botanist. While Genet was plotting, André Michaux was sponsored by the American Philosophical Society to explore the headwaters of the Missouri River and the possibilities of a transcontinental water route (Meriwether Lewis, then eighteen, volunteered to lead the expedition). A subscription paper to raise funds for his journey attracted both Washington and Alexander Hamilton as donors. Jefferson's instructions to Michaux emphasized that the exploration of the Missouri was the "fundamental object of the subscription," followed by the discovery of the "shortest and most convenient route of communication between the U.S. & the Pacific ocean." Genet had other ideas, seeing in Michaux a perfect "Agent of the Republic of France to the inhabitants of Kentucky, Louisiana, and Illinois" to help him "break the chains of the inhabitants of Louisiana." Genet even urged Michaux to befriend and revolutionize any Native tribes he encountered, encouraging them "to make common cause with us to free our Louisiana brothers [. . .] who groan in the fetters of the tyrants." After his meeting with Genet, Jefferson knew about Michaux's double role. Again his support was tacit, since he changed Michaux's letter of introduction to Governor Shelby to note that Michaux was "one having the good opinion of Genet."[33]

As Michaux set off for Kentucky, Genet reached the apotheosis of his grandiose, continental dreams, declaring to the French authorities, "I am arming the Canadians to throw off the yoke of England; I am arming the Kentuckians, and I am preparing an expedition by sea to support the descent on New Orleans." The plot finally collapsed. Destined for the guillotine back in France, Genet was allowed to remain in America, and he settled down with Governor Clinton's daughter. George Rogers Clark faced the end of his public career, more expenses he would never meet, and a wait of more than a decade before brother William would once again attach glory to the family name. Fauchet, Genet's successor, issued a proclamation in March 1794 terminating all plans for military adventure in Louisiana. Though the Genet plan concluded with a whimper, it echoed through the years. The aura of conspiracy was indelibly tied to the river's imperial role and would never truly leave it (just as the river frontier later proved a fertile breeding ground for filibustering dreams in the Floridas, Texas, and Cuba). The threat of a secessionist Louisiana remained, amplified by the ongoing concern about the possible retrocession of the territory from Spain to France after their alliance in 1796. Both Britain and the Anglophile Federalists harbored their own hidden hopes for Mississippi domination.[34]

The most notable was the conspiracy that crystallized around William Blount, former governor of the Southwest Territory, Tennessee senator, and a land speculator of note. The financial panic of 1797 damaged the value of such investments, and the increasing likelihood of French possession of the Mississippi meant that the price of land in the Mississippi Valley plummeted further. Blount turned to international conspiracy with the British as a means of saving his personal fortune. The plan, though never refined to the level of the Genet conspiracy, or as well connected, would have involved an attack on "New Madrid and the Red River silver mines of Spain [. . .] by Northwestern volunteers with British aid from Canada" and a simultaneous assault "under Blount [. . .] by Southwesterners and Indian allies against New Orleans." A British fleet would provide support at New Orleans, and Britain would claim Louisiana. New Orleans would be a free port, and navigation of the Mississippi would be open to all. These plans were either optimistic or fantastical, and they soon collapsed. Then again, at "the conspiracy's height, one of Blount's chief henchmen found the new senator dining with General Wilkinson and Vice President Jefferson"— although this may have been a Federalist rumour.[35]

Alexander Hamilton harbored his own plans for military glory along the Mississippi, and, according to Arthur Whitaker, "threw himself heart and soul into the plan of conquest in 1798 and 1799." Whatever his differences with Jefferson, the two were united in their desire for the imperial river. In 1790, he wrote to Washington outlining his belief that "when we are able to make good our pretensions, we ought not to leave in the possession of any foreign power the territories at the mouth of the Mississippi." In 1802, he could honestly assert, "I have always held that the unity of our empire, and the best interests of our nation, require that we shall annex to the United States all the territory east of the Mississippi, New Orleans included." As the XYZ Affair further worsened the relationship between the United States and France, the call for war, especially among Federalists, grew more insistent. War with France would almost inevitably mean war with Spain—and therefore, attractively, the possible seizure of Spanish territories in America. In September 1799, as chief of "all the forces on the Mississippi River," Hamilton planned to "descend the stream like lightning" (as Washington expressed it) with the cooperation of the British fleet. The plan progressed no further, stymied by a lack of funds and support, the failure of the French to declare war, and even Republican accusations of possible military dictatorship. Dry thunder, not lightning, marked these filibustering ambitions.[36]

"EVERY EYE IN THE UNITED STATES IS NOW FIXED ON THE AFFAIRS OF LOUISIANA"

In 1800, American fears were realized: Spain restored Louisiana to France. Jefferson dispatched Robert Livingston to Paris in August 1801 as the new minister to France; he was joined by James Monroe (returning as minister extraordinary following the new closure of the Mississippi) in April 1803. The crisis was succinctly described by Alexander Hamilton: "since the question of independence, none has occurred more deeply interesting to the United States than the cession of Louisiana to France." As Jefferson wrote to Livingston, "Every eye in the United States is now fixed on the affairs of Louisiana." Madison encapsulated the western position: "the Mississippi to them is everything [. . .] It is the Hudson, the Delaware, the Potomac and all the navigable rivers of the Atlantic states formed into one stream." Unlike 1784, the import of this Mississippi closure and its effect on the destiny of America were widely felt. Early in 1803, Charles Brockden Brown, frustrated by the apparent lack of action, voiced the feelings of many by calling for "war on the Mississippi": "the acquisition of the Spanish province is, at once, easy, desirable, necessary and just." Brown blasted Jefferson and his diplomatic endeavors, describing him as: "a weak visionary, timorous and irresolute: whose hand is well enough qualified for the nice adjustment of quadrants and telescopes, but far too feeble and unsteady for managing the helm of government."[37]

International tensions ran high—but almost without cause. Spain had not been too reluctant to bargain away its soured Louisiana dreams to Bonaparte: "Between ourselves," the Spanish foreign secretary wrote to an agent in Paris, "Louisiana costs us more than it is worth." Napoleon's aspirations for an empire that would move through Santo Domingo and, in Henry Adams's words, "roll on to Louisiana and sweep far up the Mississippi," did come tantalizingly close to fruition—but the failure of the French to wrest Santo Domingo from Toussaint-Louverture removed much of his desire for the river. External, though not unrelated, international events decided the Mississippi's imperial fate. Yet the ministerial efforts of Livingston and Monroe should not be underestimated. The radical policy of Louisiana Purchase, rather than conquest, had been formulated in the closing months of 1802. Thomas Paine, still concerned with the free navigation of the Mississippi for Americans, wrote to Jefferson on Christmas Day 1802. He suggested that since the French treasury was empty, "suppose then the government begin by making a proposal to France to repurchase [. . .] Louisiana [. . .] A monied proposal will, I believe, be attended to." Jefferson wrote back the very next day, affirming that he already intended to purchase what territory he could.[38]

Livingston and Monroe set to serious work in late 1802, and their diplomatic efforts produced some of the most startling visions of the post-Revolutionary Mississippi. In an effort to secure Louisiana, they were continually at pains to denigrate the river and its colonial utility. James Madison invited Louis Pichon, head of the French legation in Washington, to his office in January 1803. He was keen to point out, Pichon recorded, that "New Orleans had no sort of interest for [France]." Equally, the United States "had no interest in seeing circumstances rise which should eventually lead their population to extend itself on the right bank [of the Mississippi]." The river would be the borderline between France and the United States. If not, it would be the uncomfortable borderline between East and West America, for "no colony beyond the river could exist under the same government." Whatever separate "empire" lay across the Mississippi, Madison assured the French, it would have in its bosom "germs of collision with the East."[39]

Robert Livingston, frustrated by his task, deconstructed the river even further. Stonewalled by French diplomacy, he composed the memoir "Whether it will be advantageous to France to take possession of Louisiana?" and circulated it "in such hands as I think will best serve our purpose." For George Dangerfield, this essay "aimed a dagger at the heart of the Bonapartist empire." Primarily, its arguments were economic. Rather than providing a market for French manufactures, a colonist would in fact "consume so much less in America than he would have done in France," for having next to "nothing to give in exchange, he can

32

furnish little from the parent country." More than this, Livingston argued, the country itself was hostile to colonization. What of "the hardships, expenses, and loss of lives" that would inevitably be the result of a Mississippi empire? It was "a marshy country" with a "warm climate" plagued by the "inroads of savages, the insurrection of slaves, the insubordination of troops, and the abuses of officers when far removed from the superintending eye of the Sovereign."[40]

Most of all, Livingston attacked the Mississippi. Livingston knew that "an idea prevails that the commodities of France can, by means of the Mississippi, find their way into the western part of the United States." This, however, demonstrated "perfect ignorance of the navigation of that river; and of the wants of the inhabitants." French wines, a symbolically telling example, "are ill calculated for so warm a climate as they must pass through to arrive in the Western States." Moreover, they were "worse suited to the palates or purposes of the inhabitants; both of which are better adapted to their own liquors, cider, beer, whisky, and peach brandy." The only French goods that might be introduced were "silks, cambrics, and other light articles of luxury." Even those "will never pass by way of the Mississippi." Why? The "navigation of the Gulf" was dangerous; "passage up the river against the current" was "slow and expensive"; and accordingly, the "great improvements that are daily making in the inland canals and roads, will always carry these [. . .] on cheap and easy terms." To be sure, "even England, with all her enterprise, her right to the navigation of the Mississippi [. . .] has never ventured to send her commodities by that channel." If, on the other hand, France was to cede Louisiana to the United States, then the opposite would result. While reserving the right of entry and deposit at New Orleans, France could keep on good terms with America—a valuable market for French exports—and maintain her other colonies.[41]

Dangerfield asserts that this memorial "made little impression on Bonaparte when it first came under his eyes." Nonetheless, France agreed to the purchase. François Barbé-Marbois, Livingston's opposite number in the Louisiana negotiations, had lived in America at a time when the previous controversy about navigation of the Mississippi had dominated the national scene, and he well appreciated the "value placed on [. . .] free navigation." Accordingly, he more than doubled the price quoted by Napoleon for all of Louisiana. While Barbé-Marbois may not have been fooled by Livingston's disingenuous critique of the river, perhaps the memoir did have some effect. Declaring his intentions "with the greatest regret" to Barbé-Marbois and Talleyrand, perhaps some echo of Livingston's arguments may be discerned in Napoleon's decision: "I think of ceding it to the United States. I can scarcely say that I cede it to them, for it is not yet in our possession. If, however, I leave the least time to our enemies, I shall only transmit an empty title to those republicans whose friendship I seek. They ask of me only one town in Louisiana; but I already consider the colony as entirely lost; and it appears to me that in the hands of this growing Power it will be more useful to the policy, and even to the commerce, of France than if I should attempt to keep it."[42]

On the Fourth of July 1803, it was widely reported (probably with an anonymous, preemptive prompt from Jefferson himself, to ensure that the announcement fell on an auspicious date) that the United States had purchased the entirety of Louisiana from France at the cost of $22.5 million. The Mississippi was an American river and, almost twenty years after the first Spanish closure of the river in 1784, open for trade. In just under six decades it would close again, on the outbreak of Civil War. Within that brief window—a human life span imposed upon a giant of nature—the river would rise to the high-water mark of its cultural and economic ascendancy. There was, as the *Washington National Intelligencer* proclaimed, "widespread joy [. . .] at an event which history will record among the most splendid in our annals." (It was Wilkinson who was given the honor (alongside Governor Claiborne) of "the reception of the province of Louisiana from the French Prefect Laussat," as well as the governorship of "Upper Louisiana.") Not all were enthused. The Federalists were wary of sectional supremacy: for Thomas Pickering, it was "the purchase of an immense territory which we did not want [. . .] and at such a price." Fisher Ames, a Massachusetts Federalist, ambivalently predicted: "We were confined within some limits. Now, by adding an unmeasured world beyond that river, we rush like a comet into infinite space." To commemorate the event, John L. Boqueta de Woiseri produced one of the first images of New Orleans and the Mississippi. It was a fitting mélange of components: part pastoral, part river view, part urban scene, part promise of things to come. An American eagle unfurled a banner over the town: "Under my wings every thing prospers." A copy hung in Monticello.[43]

At the moment that it became an American river, the Mississippi was in economic and social flux. Before 1790 the principal crops on the Lower Mississippi had been tobacco, indigo, and rice. Spanish royal purchases of Creole tobacco were slashed in 1791; the indigo crop failed in 1794. The profits from wheat, corn, and timber were insufficient. Finally, therefore, it was to cotton and sugar that planters turned, crops that would provide the basis for the Mississippi's economic explosion. In 1802, still in the early years of its cultivation, the cotton exported from New Orleans was valued at over $1 million. By 1860, 1,915,852 bales of cotton were transported down the Mississippi. The great artery of the nation, that key component of Jefferson's Empire of Liberty, was now destined to be the principal river of American slavery. The "growth and expansion into the Old Southwest," as William Davis has outlined, "required vast cheap labor." Slavery would proliferate, and not solely in agriculture. As Thomas Buchanan has recently calculated, the steamboat economy that would soon emerge itself claimed an increasing proportion of slave labor until "by mid-century, about 2000 to 3000 slaves" worked in the industry at any one time—alongside their "1000 to 1500" free black colleagues. "The Mississippi Valley," wrote Frederick Jackson Turner, "rejuvenated slavery, had given it an aggressive tone characteristic of Western life." Here were the seeds of sectional conflict—very different from the secessionist fears proliferating along the river at the turn of the nineteenth century—set to grow alongside cotton in the antebellum years.[44]

The boom was stimulated by Eli Whitney's invention of the cotton gin in 1793. Greater industrial developments followed. The wedding of steam and the Western Rivers was a consummation devoutly wished for in the West. Thomas Paine was said to have "spoken of just such a means of locomotion in 1778." As early as 1784, it was already western doctrine. John Filson wrote with great expectation about "the newly invented mechanical boats" of James Rumsey. In 1785, Rumsey himself wrote to Washington with his own prediction: "boats of passage may be made to go against the current of the Mesisipia [. . .] from sixty to one hundred miles per day." Imlay presented the matter as a fait accompli in his *Topographical Description*, writing that "boats must be worked up [the river] with steam and sails"—steam being a matter about which "there can be no doubt of [. . .] success."[45]

In 1819, the frontispiece to Charles Mead's *Mississippian Scenery* (1819) pictured what might be seen as the nuptials of the longed-for union. In this pastoral hymn to "the chief of Floods," Ceres, Roman goddess of fertility, agriculture, and motherly love, wanders in "sylvan shade" on the banks of the Mississippi. Ceres gazes out to the river, where a rudimentary steamboat is clearly visible, the only symbol of human progress in an otherwise primordial vision of "spontaneous verdure." This is not a rude industrial interruption into a bucolic idyll (even if the steamboat would often be figured in that role). This machine is the perfect complement to the bounty of Ceres' garden. Without their marriage, the divine promise of "the western wilds" would be forever denied. Of course, Mead's heroic pastoral is supremely, ridiculously Jeffersonian, especially for 1819. Instead of plantations, Mead envisaged "plough-boys in the fields"; instead of cotton, sugar, and slavery, it was grain that dominated his vision.[46]

As well as guaranteeing the extension and continuation of slavery, the revolutionary rise of the steamboat had other casualties. Before its successful application, dozens attempted to harness the power of steam for motive power. Most notable was John Fitch—an adopted son of the West following spells as an armorer, a winter at Valley Forge in the Revolution, and a disastrous flatboat journey on the Ohio that ended in shipwreck and Indian captivity. Fitch's fascination with the Western Rivers was evidenced in the "Map of the Northwest" that he planned, engraved, and printed himself (using a cider press) while a deputy surveyor in Kentucky—for his "own amusement," as he described it, to "keep the Ideas of the country in." The finished product, covered in winding waterways, was as captivating and eccentric as its creator. Fitch's vision of the Mississippi beckoned America as a desideratum so powerful that it could not be contained within the bounds of cartography and burst beyond the limits of his map, pushing outside its borders.[47]

For Fitch, steam became an obsession in 1785. Selling his map to provide sustenance and fund the project, Fitch traveled to New York to petition Congress with his ideas. "The Machine," as he described it in the third person, "he has made to facilitate the internal Navigation of the United States, adapted especially to the Waters of the Mississippi." Given the prevailing attitude of the East, at this moment, toward navigation along the Spanish-controlled water, his petition fell on deaf ears. Lacking the polish and connections that would ensure Robert Fulton's success, Fitch struggled to find support. In his desperation, and with a keen awareness of the geopolitical situation, he even attempted to interest the Spanish in his passion, and accordingly "was nearly sucked into the [. . .] maelstrom being stirred up by General Wilkinson." His attitude toward the Western Waters took on the rhetoric of divine inevitability favored by Wilkinson and Imlay: "great advantage will accrue [. . .] to the Mississippi and Ohio Rivers, where the God of Nature knew their Banks could never be traversed with Horses, and has laid in a store of fuel on their Head Waters, sufficient to last for the latest ages." In 1791, a federal Board of Patent Commissioners, headed by Thomas Jefferson, gave a patent to Fitch for his invention of the steamboat, but awarded one to Rumsey too, and failed to give Fitch any superior claim. After a peripatetic spell through France and England, Fitch ended up back in the West, in Kentucky, on the Ohio—where he killed himself in 1797.[48]

In the year of Fitch's suicide, Robert Fulton arrived in France. At the age of thirty-two, he had been an artist, a canal builder, an inventor: success had proved elusive. Eventually, he would bring steam to the Mississippi. Fulton established himself at Madame Hillaire's boardinghouse on the Left Bank and soon immersed himself in the expatriate American community, including some of the remaining members of the Genet conspiracy. Some he came to know intimately. He embarked upon a relationship with Ruth Barlow, alone in Paris while Joel, still thriving in France, acted as a special ambassador to Algeria. Whatever the nature of the relationship between Fulton and Ruth, it grew to encompass Joel when he returned to France. The three, in an impenetrable ménage, set up house together, first in a Left Bank hotel, later (October 1800) in a sprawling mansion purchased cheaply from a dispossessed French aristocrat. What Barlow described as the "happy trinity" proved profitable for Fulton. Most valuable would be the contacts that Fulton made at Barlow's social gatherings. The circle had changed somewhat since the time of the Girondist plans for Louisiana. Volney, back from his American travels, had joined the circle; so too had the Montgolfier brothers. Thomas Paine was still a friend. One other newcomer was Robert Livingston, attempting to prize Louisiana from the French grip. As well as trying to secure the Mississippi for America, Livingston had also unsuccessfully sought a steamboat partnership since 1796. Early in 1802, at a party in Joel Barlow's mansion, he met Robert Fulton.[49]

Whatever arrangement they came to on that night in 1802, their partnership was swiftly established. Fulton was as eager for Livingston's patronage as Livingston was for the talents of this "most ingenious young man." Together, they would go on to promote an invention that would revolutionize the Mississippi. As early as January 1803, Fulton expressed this ambition, even though the immediate application of his steamboat was to be on the Hudson. He wrote to the French Conservatory of Arts and Trades: "My first aim in busying myself with this was to put it in practice upon the long rivers of America where there are no roads suitable for haulage." When Napoleon—who had already clashed with Fulton over an abortive submarine—eventually heard about their steamboating successes in July 1803, he lamented, enigmatically, that it had come to his attention "too late to permit it to change the face of the world."[50]

For the moment, the Mississippi was far away. On August 9, 1803, with Livingston looking on, Fulton steamed against the current of the Seine for about a mile at about the speed of three miles per hour. The *Journal des débats* reported that the journey was "un succès complet et brillant." Exactly four years later, Fulton made his inaugural voyage on American waters. In August 1807, he steamed "one mile up the East River." To spectators, the *North River* was "a monster moving on the waters, defying the winds and tide, and breathing flames and smoke." For Fulton, one thought was uppermost: "everything is completely proved for the Mississippi, and the project is immense." In his annual message to Congress in 1806, Jefferson hopefully acknowledged that "new channels of communication will be opened between the States." This would ensure that "the lines of separation" between old and new, East and West, "will disappear, their interests will be identified, and their union cemented by new and indissoluble ties." The steamboat would immeasurably contribute to such a desire.[51]

"SAVAGE GROVES, AS YET UNINVESTIGATED BY THE TRAVELLER"

Once the Mississippi had become an American river it was of great importance to make it seem like one. As Jefferson well knew, the pantheon of names associated with the exploration and colonization of the Mississippi were Spanish, French, and British. As Timothy Severin has described, explorers were considered "a rare and exotic breed," and the American public was "eager to create its [own] explorer-heroes." Accordingly, Edgar Allan Poe, in an anonymous, straight-faced hoax, created the fictional Julius Rodman. He lived "in hermit fashion, on the banks of the Mississippi" and, Poe pretended, was "*the first* [. . .] to cross the gigantic barriers of that immense chain of mountains." The American public, in such written accounts and on the ground itself, traveled in the footsteps of its explorer heroes.[52]

As the *Freeman's Journal* made clear in 1782, the mystery surrounding the Mississippi and its tributaries contributed greatly to its romantic appeal. The Mississippi: "from a source unknown collecting his remotest waters, rolls forward through the frozen regions of the north, and stretching his extended arms to the east and west, embraces those savage groves, as yet uninvestigated by the traveller, unsung by the poet, or unmeasured by the chain of the geometrician." For Jefferson, the urge to explore westward had been instilled in his childhood when his father, Peter, joined a number of his fellow Virginians in chartering the Loyal Land Company in 1749. The Reverend James Maury, Jefferson's schoolmaster, recorded that their ambitions stretched further than the stated "discovery and sale of western lands": "some persons were to be sent in search of that river Missouri, if that be the right name of it, in order to discover whether it had any communication with the Pacific Ocean; they were to follow the river if they found it, and exact reports of the country they passed through." The inherited lure of the Northwest Passage, the promise of the Passage to India, could not be easily shaken: Thomas Jefferson repeatedly attempted to complete what Peter Jefferson had help to conceive—abortively, with George Rogers Clark, in 1783, and fantastically, in 1786, with John Ledyard and his attempt to travel from Moscow, across the Bering Sea to West Coast America, and thence on foot to

Washington. (Ledyard was arrested in Siberia by Catherine the Great's troops. He later died in Egypt, planning an expedition to the sources of the Nile.) By the time that Michaux's transcontinental expedition collapsed in 1793, Jefferson's interest—or patience—with such schemes seems to have undergone a temporary suspension.[53]

Nonetheless, Jefferson's library constantly provided him with inspiration. Perhaps the most important volume was Jonathan Carver's record of his Mississippi adventures. Carver served in the French and Indian Wars, gaining his promotion to the rank of captain. He had a passion for exploring and for the Mississippi, predicting that the river "will enable [its] inhabitants to establish an intercourse with foreign climes" and become "powerful and opulent." In 1766, he met Robert Rogers in Boston. Robert Rogers was a popular hero of the Seven Years' War. He wrote well-circulated books (and a play) about the trans-Mississippi, particularly *A Concise Account of North America* (1765), and was obsessed with the promise of a Northwest Passage. Rogers had failed to gain funding for his own voyage of discovery. When Carver "offered his services as an explorer and cartographer" to him, Rogers happily assented, while offering Carver little practical support. Carver's journey—projected toward the Northwest Passage via the source of the Mississippi—was hampered by conflict between the Sioux and the Chippewa, a lack of supplies, and accusations that Rogers was planning some treasonous act in the Mississippi Valley, perhaps a breakaway state. It proved a highly influential piece of exploration nonetheless. His *Travels through the Interior Parts of North America,* first published in 1778, appeared at a propitious time and went through over forty editions. It was, as Allen notes, "a fundamental part of early nineteenth-century American geographical thought" (and not only was an influence on Jefferson but also inspired the likes of Schiller and Byron). This fame was also a product of controversy. Poverty-stricken in London, Carver sold his manuscript to a publisher. With or without his knowledge, his original account was embellished with a series of fantastical stories (many culled from previous fakers like Hennepin and Lahontan). This simultaneously increased its romantic appeal but cast doubt on its very real geographical provenance. Carver died destitute, trying to finance further exploration in 1780.[54]

By 1803, Jefferson's presidency and American possession of the Mississippi finally allowed the long-anticipated transcontinental adventure to commence. Jefferson instructed Meriwether Lewis on June 20, 1803, that he was to "explore the Missouri" to see whether he could find a "practicable water communication across the continent for the purposes of commerce." The Mississippi featured as an important stepping-stone in the journey, a psychological border—a transitional moment from East to West. On November 13, 1803, Lewis and Clark reached the Mississippi. Lewis was immediately "siezed [*sic*] with a violent ague which continued about four hours." When they pulled into the river on November 19, their troubles only increased. Struggling against the current, their keelboat moved upriver at little more than one mile per hour. They reached Kaskaskia on November 28; St. Louis (or Cahokia, directly opposite on the American side) was reached in early December. On the brink of the unknown, imagined West, Lewis and Clark set up winter camp on the Mississippi. There was plenty to do. Clark took time to note that, "I send to the Missouries water for drinking water, it being much Cooler than the Mississippi." Lewis, armed with a questionnaire, sought out those seasoned travelers whose knowledge would be the most useful. As the *Quarterly Review* remarked, the party was not "amused by such tales as were told to Hennepin" and "did not expect to meet with the Spirits and Pigmies"— but there remained "enough to excite imagination in the wide region before them." At 3.30 in the afternoon of May 21, 1804, "under three Cheers from the gentlemen on the bank," the expedition moved into the Missouri, leaving their Mississippi limbo, and the known world, behind.[55]

Jefferson diligently oversaw the Lewis and Clark expedition from inception to departure; Zebulon Pike's 1805 mission to the Upper Mississippi, on the other hand, was a military affair, envisaged and executed under the auspices of General Wilkinson. At the same time that Wilkinson dispatched Pike to the source of the Mississippi, he came close to destruction in his involvement with the Aaron Burr "conspiracy"—the last clandestine vision of a Mississippi empire, and the only scheme, save the thwarted British invasion in 1815, that threatened the river once it was in American hands. What Burr planned is unclear. Opinion, then as now, differed. In form, Burr's conspiracy may have been similar to the Mississippi plots of Clark, Genet, or Blount in its conception of a breakaway state centered around the river—except, of course, that Burr relied not on an opposing colonial power like France or Britain, but on the desire and determination of the settlers along the Mississippi themselves. Certainly, Burr was greeted with warm enthusiasm when he began his lengthy tour of the West in 1805. Soon, however, as Milton Lomask has described, rumors began to circulate "connecting the colonel's travels with traitorous machinations." In March 1806, General William Eaton warned Jefferson of a prospective "insurrection, if not [. . .] revolution, on the waters of the Mississippi." Jefferson—now an old hand at such matters— "said he had too much confidence in the [. . .] attachment of the people of that country to the Union, to admit any apprehensions"; or, at least, so he told Eaton. Whatever Burr's plans might have been, General James Wilkinson was centrally involved, as he was in their unmasking. In October 1806, Wilkinson claimed that he received a fateful letter that Burr had composed three months earlier. "A numerous and powerful association," Wilkinson dramatically warned Jefferson, "extending from New-York through the Western states, to the territory bordering on the Mississippi, has been formed with the design to levy and rendezvous eight or ten thousand men in New Orleans"—where they were headed with the "utmost possible velocity."[56]

Wilkinson claimed that Burr had described the "plan of operation" in a secret cipher that they used to communicate: "[We will] move down rapidly from the falls on fifteenth November, with the first 500 or 1000 men in light boats [. . .] to be at Natches between the 5 and 15 December [. . .] then to determine whether it will be expedient in the first instance to seize or pass by [Baton Rouge]." The truth of this communication was called into question almost immediately. Wilkinson "was forced to acknowledge that he had forged at least parts" of the letter. Lomask has highlighted the "tissue of absurdities" outlined in the correspondence, and the probability that "the letter [Wilkinson] was deciphering was not written by Burr but by Dayton," a co-conspirator and childhood friend of Burr. Yet it is still clear that Burr planned something on the Western Waters. According to Roger Kennedy, Burr was simply attempting to colonize the Bostrop Tract on the Ouachita River in Spanish territory, and he "had every reason to believe that his colonization project [. . .] had the support of Wilkinson and the acquiescence of Jefferson." For Kennedy, the unmasking of the "conspiracy" was political expediency on Jefferson's part, capitalizing on "rumor-induced fever" to "permit him to deal with his rival." Alternatively, Lomask has concluded that the objective of Burr's conspiracy was a filibustering invasion of Mexico, to commence at the announcement of war with Spain: "illegal [. . .] but it was not a betrayal of, or separation from, Burr's own country. It was not treasonable." Regardless, Burr was never found guilty of treason. In 1806, the truth was less important than rumor, and the shadows of his supposed conspiracy persisted. He took flight, dressed as a common boatman.[57]

In the middle of these machinations, Zebulon Montgomery Pike was sent to find the headwaters of the Mississippi. The Louisiana Purchase had made the journey symbolically valuable. As Henry Whiting outlined in 1844, it "would more fully develop the geography of the country; would open the great avenue to the north-western trade, thus far exclusively in the hands of the British [. . .]; and would manifest, in a palpable way, both to the Indian tribes there, and to the foreign traders among them, that the United States were the sovereigns of the country, and intended to be respected as such." It would have the additional benefit of focusing "attention on the disputed boundary dividing the Louisiana Purchase from Canada." This American "explorer-hero"—for all his shortcomings—would provide the newly expanded country with the resonant prize of the river's head. Pike, in Seelye's words, "was Lewis' antithesis"; as one of his earliest biographers noted, he "was not qualified to act in any of the scientific departments." Nonetheless, Pike's journey came at the right time to capture the public imagination. Jefferson, though not Pike's mentor in the way that he had been to Lewis, was also interested in the objectives of the journey. In a letter to William Dunbar in March 1804, Jefferson stated his intention to "charge the Surveyor-general N. of Ohio, with a survey of the Mississippi from its source to the mouth of the Ohio, and with settling some other interesting points of geography in that quarter."[58]

Therefore, on July 30, 1805, Wilkinson ordered Pike "to proceed up the Mississippi with all possible diligence." Lewis and Clark's journey—capped with the lonely tragedy of Lewis's suicide on the Natchez Trace, the boatman's highway—was epic; Pike's expedition up the Mississippi (as with any Wilkinson endeavor) had the potential for broad burlesque. Throughout his journey, Pike benefited from the assistance of fur trappers and traders, American and Canadian, who already inhabited the area; finally, beset by hardships, Pike negotiated an agreement whereby Grant of the Canadian fur-trading North-West Company ushered the party from trading post to trading post, seeing them off in the morning on each day's voyage of discovery, then welcoming them in as they slowly progressed.[59]

Together, with the rest of the party following, Grant and Pike made their way to Leech Lake, arriving there on February 1, 1806. This was where the voyage ended, eighty miles from the river's true source, but closer than any official party had traveled up the river before. Pike adjourned to Hugh McGillis's North-West Company headquarters on the shore of the lake. There he recorded the announcement in his journal: "I will not attempt to describe my feelings on the accomplishment of my voyage, for this is the main source of the Mississippi." His feet were "so much swelled that I was not able to wear my own clothes." While recuperating, he settled down with some symbolically resonant reading material: Volney's *Travels through Egypt and Syria,* wherein he would have contemplated another river whose true source remained hidden. "The Egyptians," Volney wrote and Pike would have read, "have always professed, and still retain, a religious veneration for the Nile"; but for a European, never "will these troubled and muddy waters have for him the charm of transparent fountains and limpid streams."[60]

Pike's journey was not quite over. On February 16, at Leech Lake, Pike addressed a gathering of the Sauteaux Indians. "Brothers," Pike declared, "I was chosen to ascend the Mississippi to bear to his red children the words of their father." He had great news to tell them, an alternative reading of recent river history: "A few months since the Spaniards shut up the mouth of the Mississippi, and prevented the Americans from floating down to the sea. This your father, the President of the United States, would not admit of. He therefore took such measures as to open the river, remove the Spaniards from both sides of the Mississippi to a great distance on the other side of the Missouri." In Pike's story, the germs of future conflict were evident. It would not be just the Spaniards who were removed from the Mississippi. Jefferson wrote to William Henry Harrison, the governor of Indiana Territory, as early as February 27, 1803, that "the Indians [. . .] will in time either incorporate with us as citizens of the U.S. or remove beyond the Mississippi." If any tribe were "foolhardy enough to take up the hatchet," then the result would be "the seizing of the whole country of that tribe and driving them across the Mississippi." This prophecy would come to pass, writ large, in the space of just thirty years.[61]

In 1806, however, Pike's expedition, according to Hollon, "awakened considerable interest in the Upper Mississippi Valley." Publication was key. What would eventually become the official record of his journey was brought to the public's attention in Jefferson's sixth annual message in December 1806 (an address much concerned with the position of the Mississippi in national life). Having paid tribute to Lewis and Clark, Jefferson noted: "Very useful additions have also been made to our knowledge of the Mississippi by Lieutenant Pike, who has ascended to its source, and whose journal and map, giving the details of the journey, will shortly be ready for communication to both houses of congress." Pike's journal of his Mississippi voyage was not published until 1810. In the interim, he carried out another mission for Wilkinson (a dramatic journey into Spanish territory that saw his arrest) that further increased his profile. By 1810, the public had only received Patrick Gass's record of the Lewis and Clark expedition, not the official account, and were hungry for reports of the West. This partly explains the popularity of Pike's book. The widespread fascination with the Mississippi itself must have accounted for the numerous (American, English, French, German, and Dutch) editions of the journal—the first American successor to the works of Marquette, Hennepin, Carver, and others that Jefferson had amassed and absorbed over decades; the first true American explorer-hero. As Joel Barlow optimistically predicted in his *Columbiad,* in 1807:

> Proud Mississippi, tamed and taught his road,
> Flings forth irriguous from his generous flood
> Ten thousand watery glades; that, round him curl'd,
> Vein the broad bosom of the western world.

But in its forthcoming role in American life, the Mississippi would seem far from tamed.[62]

2

Frontier

Jackson and the "Half-Horse, Half-Alligators"

The Mississippi! The great big rollin', tumblin', bilin', endless and almost shoreless Mississippi! There's a river for you! I don't care what John Bull may say, or any other ruffle-shirted fellow [. . .] I tell you the United States is a great country! There ain't nobody else but Uncle Sam as could afford such a river as that!
Spirit of the Times, 1844

Half horse, half alligator, a touch of the airth-quake with a sprinkling of the steamboat!
JAMES KIRKE PAULDING, *Lion of the West,* 1830

When Andrew Jackson died on June 8, 1845, testimonies poured in. For the compiler of a collection of memorials to Jackson, the general presented "one of the most striking examples, recorded in history, of a man rising from the humble walks of private life to the most exalted station in the world." Speaking in Pennsylvania, Washington McCartney felt that Jackson "entered heart and soul into the great movement of his age" to "imbody the true spirit of his nation." On the Mississippi, in Natchez, a different note was struck. Dr. Samuel A. Cartwright felt inadequate to the task of describing Jackson's role in national life. Speaking in the spiritual home of the boatmen who were so intimately connected to Jacksonian life on the Mississippi, he felt a sharper focus was appropriate: "let it be my humbler task to call to mind those occurrences in the great hero's life which more particularly connected him with the people of Mississippi." He might have said the people of the Mississippi, but the intent was the same. Cartwright expressed a crucial truth: throughout his life, Andrew Jackson was intimately connected with the river, its people, and its destiny.[1]

Whatever claims were made for Jackson as an embodiment of the national spirit, they were more true for the Mississippi; or rather, Jackson's closeness to the heart and soul of the nation was a direct result of his closeness to the Mississippi. His was the era of steam and the cultural rise of the common man. Throughout the period over which the first western president's influence reached, the Mississippi moved from preindustrial agrarianism, through flush times, to steam-driven economic powerhouse; emigration grew exponentially. Culturally, the Mississippi achieved a new prominence in national life, as both a symbol of the frontier and the West, and a breeding ground for national icons who came to be seen as potent representatives of the American spirit. Through the rise of Jackson; through the development of western writing by the likes of Timothy Flint and James Hall; through popular representations of Davy Crockett, Mike Fink, and the half-horse, half-alligator boatmen; through navigation aids and emigration guides; and through the growth of southwestern humor, the Mississippi and its avatars, to use Carroll Smith-Rosenberg's phrase, "danced charismatically across the male Jacksonian imagination." Their rise was coterminous with Jackson's; one spurred on the other, and both were grown from Mississippi mud. Marked by its particular brands of masculinity, violence, noise, sentiment, and humor, the adolescence of the American Mississippi was fiercely Jacksonian.[2]

Andrew Jackson himself was inaugurated early into the mysteries of the Mississippi. Turning away from an orphaned and subsequently dissipated youth of drinking and gambling in North Carolina, Jackson shifted his sights westward. He reached Nashville in October 1788, the nascent town that marked the terminal of the Natchez Trace, the legendary boatman's highway. Nashville had been founded eight years earlier and had a population of approximately three hundred. The young public prosecutor boarded with the widow Donelson, one of the town's first settlers. While there he met Rachel, the youngest Donelson daughter (also twenty-one), who was estranged from her jealous and violent husband Lewis Robards. At that moment, the couple were attempting to begin their marriage again. Jackson's arrival at Mrs. Donelson's establishment soon terminated the rapprochement. Robards's jealousy was directed toward the new arrival. Declaring that Jackson was "too intimate with his wife," Robards left for Kentucky.[3]

What happened next? According to the official account given by Jackson's friend John Overton in 1827 (when Jackson was running for president), late in 1790 Rachel was in fear that Robards would return to Nashville and force her to follow him to Kentucky. She determined to go to Natchez to stay with friends and family. Jackson helped escort her there. The party floated down the Cumberland, Ohio, and Mississippi rivers to the Spanish town—a journey that Jackson knew well. Jackson returned to Nashville. Hearing that Robards had obtained a divorce in the summer of 1791, Jackson returned to Natchez, where the two were married. Unofficially, evidence exists to suggest that as early as January 1790, "Jackson and Rachel went to Natchez together [. . .] and at least by the summer of that year entered into an intimate relationship"—perhaps even a bigamous marriage. In 1845, Cartwright's eulogy noted with pleasure (employing a riverine metaphor): "here in Natchez, fifty-four years ago, a kind Providence [. . .] gave him a pilot in pious woman's form." Not all saw the union in such a light. Jackson's great Tennessee rival, John Sevier, sneered in 1803, "I know of no great services you have rendered the country, except taking a trip to Natchez with another man's wife."[4]

Jackson already had other connections to Natchez. As early as 1789 he was visiting the Mississippi town, possibly with an eye to emigration. Taking to the Western Waters in the role of boatman, Jackson traveled to Natchez with trade items like "cotton, furs, swan skins and feathers for bedding, lime, pork, beef, boats and slaves." Like many frontiersmen, he understood "that the Cumberland settlements could not prosper without free passage of the Mississippi." He was certainly drawn into the orbit of the Spanish conspiracy, writing a letter of recommendation for a Spanish merchant acting as a courier between Governor Miró and the settlers in February 1789: "He wishes you to write to the Governor," Jackson wrote to Brigadier General Daniel Smith, an important figure in the Cumberland settlement, "informing him of the desire of a commercial treaty with that country [. . .] I hope you will consider it well."[5]

Alongside Rachel, the most important influence on Jackson's relationship with the Western Waters entered his life in 1791. Jackson met William Blount soon after he arrived in the Territory. Blount was the driving force behind Tennessee's admission to the Union in 1796, just as he was responsible for Jackson's election to Congress as the first representative for the new state. Jackson's close connection to this "complete political animal" brought with it allegiances that might have proved embarrassing to other men. Jackson was too occupied in Congress, and with failing finances, to have taken an active role in Blount's dismal conspiracy. Nonetheless, Jackson was vociferous in defense of his mentor, and in defense of the plan itself and its ambition to fully open the Mississippi and New Orleans. As Remini described, "Jackson was particularly eloquent in conjuring for western minds what might have been accomplished for them had the conspiracy succeeded." After receiving news of the Louisiana Purchase, Jackson happily wrote to Jefferson: "on the Joyfull event of the cession of Louisiana and New Orleans, every face wears a smile and every heart leaps with joy." In 1804, he took to flatboating again, establishing a trading firm seven miles from Nashville. Alongside running a dry goods store, boatyard, tavern, and even a racetrack, Jackson and his partners sent the bartered goods they received in payment down to Natchez, where they were sold for the New Orleans market. Land speculations continued. With John Overton, he purchased land on the fourth Chickasaw Bluff. This long-coveted spot would eventually become Memphis.[6]

When Aaron Burr arrived in Nashville on his fact-finding tour of the West in 1805, he was a houseguest of the Jacksons. This was an honor. Burr was one of the most important Americans to have crossed the Appalachians, certainly to reach frontier towns like Nashville. His duel with Hamilton caused little disapprobation in Tennessee—rather, as Melton argues, the killing of "the great Federalist enemy" on the field of honor only increased the West's approval. Jackson the duelist certainly did not care, and warmly welcomed both an old friend of the now-deceased William Blount and a personal friend from his own spell in Congress. He held a ball in Burr's honor. Jackson, now a Spanish-hating expansionist, also listened eagerly to Burr's plan and provided him with a flatboat to continue his journey to the Mississippi. Quite what Burr told him of his plans is unclear. Perhaps Burr simply talked of his intention to "oust the hated Spaniard" from Western and possibly Eastern Florida and even Mexico. Jackson himself later wrote that "plans [. . .] had been named of settling new countries, of Punishing the Dons, and adding Mexico to the United States." When ugly rumors of treason started circulating, Jackson feared that he had been told "mere coverings to the real designs." He wrote letters of warning, including one to Jefferson. Remarkably, perhaps uniquely, Burr managed to change Jackson's mind and convince him that there was nothing treasonous about his plans. Burr returned to Nashville, and Jackson accepted his pledge of allegiance and delivered Burr's order of boats and provisions for the descent of the Mississippi.[7]

Jackson stood by Burr as he had stood by Blount. Testifying to Burr's innocence in June 1807, Jackson also delivered "a spectacularly incoherent speech to a curious crowd clustered on the Virginia capitol steps [. . .] denouncing Thomas Jefferson and James Wilkinson." This ensured Jackson a spell in the political wilderness. By 1812, the Jacksons were reestablished, living the life of successful southern planters. Then, on Friday, June 18, a messenger was dispatched from Washington: Billy Phillips, a young Tennesseean (who had ridden Jackson's famous horse, Truxton, in "a heat race for the largest purse ever heard of west of the mountains"), sped along the Wilderness Road to Nashville, then down the Mississippi to New Orleans, announcing war.[8]

"I AM AN ALLIGATOR; HALF MAN, HALF HORSE"

While Jackson was experiencing the vicissitudes of life on the Western Rivers, a uniquely American mode of existence had grown up on the Mississippi; its colorful representatives had already begun to penetrate popular culture, a process that the coming war would only compound. Looking back in *Astoria* (1836), Washington Irving described the "singular aquatic race that had grown up from the navigation of the rivers": "the hectoring, extravagant, bragging boatmen of the Mississippi [. . .] possessed habits, manners, and almost a language, peculiarly their own [. . .] their consequence and characteristics are rapidly vanishing before the all-pervading intrusion of steamboats." The boatman of the Western Rivers flourished in the presteamboat era. It was a heterogeneous breed, especially in the years preceding the American advance. The majority were French Canadians, although Spaniards and other assorted Europeans were in evidence, as were Native and black boatmen. Anglo-Americans took their place in such a mélange. After 1784, though Spanish closure of the river slowed the process, they rose to dominance. Andrew Jackson's business dealings confirm Elizabeth House Trist's impressions: the river frontier was more fluid than the lines of officialdom. The Spanish needed American goods; accordingly, they filtered through. In Natchez, Jackson dealt with transplanted, expatriated Americans. Trade developed steadily in the years before 1795—to such an extent, that it provided bargaining power in the negotiations that resulted in the Treaty of San Lorenzo. After that agreement, the Mississippi was officially open to trade; the western boatman prospered. The Kentuckian was master of the scene. (This appellation had no real geographic specificity. Any American working on the Mississippi would have accepted the title in its half-horse, half-alligator, frontiersman sense. The Creole population along the river, unconcerned with American geographical niceties, fostered this. Mothers disciplined their children with the phrase, "toi, tu n'es qu'un mauvais Kaintock!" [You're nothing but a naughty little Kentuckian!])[9]

Stratification soon became evident. Michael Allen has identified four distinct types of boatman. Merchant navigators were businessmen. Some traveled on the rivers themselves, some commissioned others to do the work. Andrew Jackson was a merchant navigator who fulfilled both roles. (The Devol family of Marietta—one of whom found notoriety as a Mississippi gambler—were famous merchant navigators.) Farmer flatboatmen used the Western Waters to transport their cargo to market. (The term "flatboat" was given to any rudimentary craft, often homemade, that was designed to survive one trip downriver.) They made up 90 percent of river craft in the early nineteenth century. At its destination it would be broken up and sold for firewood. In the presteam years, its crew walked home.[10]

The mythologization of the western boatman was directed at the final two groups: the common hand, and the agent boatman. The term "professional" gives too great a sense of order to these boatmen's lives, but these were the men who engaged in work on the Western Waters as a means of existence—precarious, indigent, and itinerant. Their work was sporadically hard, but wages were high for peripatetic boatmen, "generally exceeding, sometimes by twice, the prevailing rate for labor." The vessel most associated with these professionals was the keelboat; its operation was the greatest testament to their skill, even though it never "flourished in great number" and was displaced by the steamboat. The keelboat was more sophisticated than the makeshift flatboat, with a rounded hull built around ribs and a pointed bow—resembling a more conventional sailing ship. "No employment," Flint concluded, "can be imagined more laborious, and few more dangerous, than this of propelling a boat against the current of such a river."[11]

T. B. Thorpe described the arduous process that was undertaken, he felt, by "men more remarkable than any other that ever lived": "From fifteen to twenty hands were required to propel it along. The crew, divided equally on each side, took their places upon the 'walking-boards,' extending along the whole length of the craft, and, setting one end of their pole in the bottom of the river, the other was brought to the shoulder, and with, body bent forward, they *walked* the boat against the formidable current." This technique was augmented by bushwhacking (manually dragging the boat along with the help of greenery on the bank), cordeling (tying a rope around a tree, and pulling the boat forward), even rowing and sailing if circumstances allowed. These professional boatmen, fighting a daily war of attrition against the inexorable river, dominated the cultural Mississippi as it rose to national prominence.[12]

For Richard Dorson, this was the period in which "an indigenous American folklore" began to emerge. Almost as soon as the boatman took his place on the Western Rivers, he became the subject of "a yeasty corpus of anecdotal legends that floated up and down the river cities of the Ohio and Mississippi." For Thorpe, the boatmen's "exaggerations, physical and mental" gave rise to "the most genuine originality we can claim as American character." Henry Adams later echoed this: the "Mississippi boatman and the squatter on Indian lands" were "the most distinctly American types then existing, as far removed from the Old World as though Europe were a dream." As Constance Rourke described, "the freer ways of the water" meant that the boatman "emerged more quickly as master of his scene than did the backwoodsman." Yet the stories told about the boatmen had little time to ferment; the move from oral to printed lore was almost immediate. For folklorists like Richard Dorson, this is a problem: it is impossible to prove that the motley boatmen deserve the status of folk hero in the strictest sense of the word. And for a historian like Michael Allen, trying to piece together the real lives of Mississippi boatmen, the prominence of the romanticized myth obscures "the flesh-and-blood boatmen." In Jacksonian America, however, the myth was all-important.[13]

All pre-1815 descriptions of the boatman are particularly valuable. In 1804, Meriwether Lewis, waiting for the spring to usher in his westward journey along the Missouri, attended a horse race in Cape Girardeau. His fellow racegoers, while not explicitly identified as boatmen (though a number of them must have been), were of the same stock and displayed the same characteristics that soon dominated discussion of the boatmen: "uncivilized backwoodsmen [. . .] they are almost entirely emegrant from the frontiers of Kentuckey & Tennessee, and are the most dessolute and abandoned among these people; they are men of desparate fortunes."[14]

The first significant account of Mississippi boatmen came in Christian Schultz's *Travels on an Inland Voyage* (undertaken in 1807 and 1808, published in 1810). The boatman stepped out of Schultz's narrative and onto the national stage fully formed in the important particulars. A popular oral mythology of the boatman was already in evidence: Schultz had "heard [. . .] many unfavourable stories concerning the character of the Kentucky sailors." Accordingly, he shipped with French Canadian boatmen. After contact with the Kentuckians on his journey downriver, Schultz found them "rough" but "a more amiable class of citizens, than they have been represented to be." He formed a "good opinion" of the "Kentucky sailors in general." More generally, the boatmen's habits warranted comment. The gambling and bawdy establishments of Natchez provided "no trifling luxury" to the "Mississippi sailor." Returning to the flatboat early in the morning, Schultz disturbed four "copper-coloured votaries of the Cyprian queen" who had "undertaken to enliven the hours of our [. . .] crew." Hearing "some very warm words" passing between "some drunken sailors, who had a dispute respecting a Choctaw lady," Schultz recorded the words of their argument. He might have filled "half a dozen pages with the curious slang," but chose to select "a few of the most brilliant expressions by way of sample":

> One said, "I am a man; I am a horse; I am a team. I can whip any man *in all Kentucky*, by G-d." The other replied, "I am an alligator; half man, half horse; can whip any *on the Mississippi* by G-d."

The boasting, gambling, drinking, whoring, fighting, and elaborately self-actualizing anthropomorphic boatman had been established as a literary archetype, and as a vivid representative of the New World.[15]

In 1812, with war on the horizon, a correspondent from New Orleans informed the *Salem Gazette* of a significant shift in the boatman's language, indicative of an important shift in the world of the boatman, and life on the Mississippi in general. While "half-horse, half-alligator" had "hitherto been the boast of our up-river countrymen when quarelling," the *Gazette* described, momentous events of the previous year had shifted their emphasis: "A few days ago two of them quarreled in a boat at Natchez, when one of them [. . .] declared that he was a *steamboat.* His opponent immediately followed him, swearing he was an *earthquake* and would shake him to pieces."[16]

As the boatmen's boasts demonstrated, 1811 was a momentous year for the Mississippi. The Great Comet was visible in western skies. An unexpected rise in the river led to flooding, destruction, and disease. A slave revolt, involving hundreds, took place north of New Orleans: plantations burned along the Mississippi, and retribution was bloody. And finally, steam reached the river. Nicholas Roosevelt was a partner in the Mississippi Steamboat Navigation Company with Robert Fulton and Robert Livingston. They held the monopoly for steam travel on the Western Rivers. The plans that had been formed in Paris almost a decade earlier finally came to fruition. Roosevelt's steamboat, optimistically named *New Orleans,* set out on October 20. When it arrived in Louisville under cover of darkness, some sleepy inhabitants thought that the Great Comet had fallen into the Ohio. At Louisville, Roosevelt's wife gave birth to the couple's second child (conceived on an earlier exploratory flatboat journey) in the cabin of the *New Orleans.* After entering the Mississippi, just below the mouth of the Ohio, a fully manned canoe of Chickasaws tried to race alongside the vessel. They were soon left behind. As Lydia's brother recorded, "with wild shouts" they "turned into the forest from whence they had emerged."[17]

On December 15, 1811, the powerful New Madrid earthquake was the Mississippi's last convulsive attempt to stave off the yoke of steam power. English botanist John Bradbury was in his keelboat: "in the night [. . .] I was awakened by a most tremendous noise, accompanied by so violent an agitation of the boat that it appeared in danger of upsetting [. . .] immediately the perpendicular banks, both above and below us, began to fall into the river in such vast masses, as nearly to sink our boat." The *New Orleans* weathered the beating and even managed to pick up a load of cotton in Natchez—a symbolically momentous achievement. When Roosevelt steamed into New Orleans in January 1812, the union of craft and river was played out on board the boat. A minister from Natchez married the engineer to the boat's maid. Comet, pestilence, and earthquake; birth, marriage, commerce, and seemingly inevitable demise: in a year of revolution, the steamboat dramatically announced its presence on the river. Fulton confidently relayed events to Joel Barlow: the "Mississippi [. . .] is conquered." But in truth, the matter of conquering the Mississippi was an international issue that had been revived: when the *New Orleans* passed Mr. Weldon's farm above Cincinnati, the farmer and his two sons, startled by the arrival of the steamboat, ran along the river bank: "'The British are coming down the river,' they cried. 'The British are coming!'"[18]

THE BATTLE OF NEW ORLEANS

Congress and the nation divided along roughly regional lines in their enthusiasm for the War of 1812. While New England and New York voted against the hostilities, the declaration of war was cheered from Pennsylvania to the Mississippi. The conquest of the Floridas loomed large in the imagination. In truth, the nation was ill-prepared for the conflict: "both America and Great Britain waged it in great confusion and finally concluded it inconclusively." In the North, a three-pronged American attack was unleashed on Canada, limped along, and ended in defeat. (Zebulon Pike died a hero at the Battle of York; General James Wilkinson failed ignominiously, was relieved of his command, but, as ever, was cleared by an official inquiry.) The War of 1812 became a succession of debilitating American losses, including the humiliating burning of Washington, offset only by small naval victories. In the South, things were different—and Andrew Jackson was a large part of that difference. Through the Creek War, his sortie into Spanish Florida, and, of course, the Battle of New Orleans, Jackson became a national hero. The alligator-horses basked in his reflected glory.[19]

In the three years from 1812 to 1815, Andrew Jackson sought military glory at almost any price. Madison had not forgotten Jackson's slurs at the time of the Burr trial, or his support for Monroe, and was at pains to deny Jackson a commission. Fortunately for Jackson, William Blount's half brother, Willie, was the new governor of Tennessee. Blount went against the administration's implicit wishes and commissioned Jackson as the major general of the volunteer force that was ordered to New Orleans to assist General Wilkinson's defense of the city. Jackson mustered 2,071 volunteers and meticulously oversaw their preparations; on November 14, 1812, he addressed the volunteers who had rendezvoused in Nashville. The river was at the heart of his rhetoric: "Every man of the western country turns his eyes intuitively upon the mouth of the Mississippi [. . .] Blocked up, all the fruits of his industry rot upon his hands; open, and he carries on a commerce with all the nations of the earth. To the people of the western country is then peculiarly committed, by nature, herself, the defence of the lower Mississippi. At the approach of an enemy in that quarter the whole western world should pour forth its sons to meet the invader and drive him back into the sea. Brave volunteers, it is to the defence of this place, so interesting to you, that you are now ordered to repair." The force departed for New Orleans on January 7, 1813. Thomas Hart Benton was commanding one of the three regiments, and wrote that it was "impossible to describe [. . .] the enthusiasm with which the men committed themselves to the stream."[20]

Thirty-nine days later, the flotilla reached Natchez, having traveled down half-frozen rivers. Jackson found letters from Wilkinson waiting for him, insisting that he remain in Natchez and stay away from New Orleans. A letter from the secretary of war followed: "the causes embodying and marching the Corps under your command having ceased to exist, you will on receipt of this letter, consider it as dismissed from public service." Furious at the dismissal, certain that he would not disband or deliver his men to General Wilkinson, Jackson turned back toward Nashville. Though not the expected military glory, a different renown attached itself to the march home. Without official funding or supplies and with 150 men listed as sick, Jackson's force of will ensured that tidy military columns stretched along the Natchez Trace. By the time they arrived back in Nashville less than a month later, Jackson was a great general in his men's eyes. He was Old Hickory.[21]

The Creek War finally gave Jackson a military target, and, according to Remini, it crystallized an ambition that would drive him through the coming years: "to eliminate all foreigners along the southern frontier as a necessary prelude to the systematic destruction of the Indian menace and the territorial expansion of the American nation." Jackson led his troops to a crushing victory. "We [. . .] shot them like dogs," attested Davy Crockett, who was there as one of Jackson's volunteers. When claiming land from the conquered Creeks at the Treaty of Fort Jackson, the general wrote to Colonel John Williams that he sought to "extend our settlements to the Mississippi to cut off all communications of the Southern tribes with that of the North, and give to our citizens perfect safety in passing through their country." It was the beginning of work that would be completed years later. At the end of 1814, after Jackson's detour through Mobile and Pensacola in Spanish Florida (turning British invasion away from those Gulf routes), New Orleans beckoned.[22]

The commander of the British Gulf force, Vice Admiral Cochrane, was clear in his ambitions for the planned invasion, and the river was central: "I have it much at heart to give them a complete drubbing before Peace is made [. . .] and the Command of the Mississippi wrested from them." He set sail from Jamaica, bound for New Orleans, on November 26, 1814. Andrew Jackson rode into New Orleans on December 1, accompanied by volunteers and militiamen from Kentucky and Tennessee. Local merchant Vincent Nolte described them as a "feeble force" who "had no idea whatever of military organisation and discipline." Nonetheless, they would help produce an unexpectedly glorious climax to a dispiriting war. A miscellaneous force undertook the defense of New Orleans, perhaps the most racially varied "American" military force ever, a vivid representation of the diverse people of the Mississippi. American, French and Spanish Creole, free Black, slave, Choctaw Indian, and even Baratarian pirate troops defended New Orleans from the British invasion. There were, of course, tensions among the troops. The French felt that the Americans would have little allegiance to the defense of their newly acquired territory; Jackson was loathe to work with the Baratarian pirates; no one trusted the free men of color. And yet, they fought together. Following an exchange of artillery early in the New Year, the British marched on the city on January 8. The disparate American force held off eight thousand British soldiers. The Chalmette battlefield was bloody: the British suffered over two thousand casualties, the Americans fewer than one hundred.[23]

Andrew Jackson's victory at New Orleans was a personal triumph that ignited a moment of unifying national celebration. Jefferson wrote to Lafayette: "I am glad [. . .] that we closed our war with the *éclat* of New Orleans [. . .] The cement of this Union is in the heartblood of every American." The victory was entirely associated with the Mississippi, now a potent symbol of American victory and unity. Mr. Troup of Georgia, addressing the House of Representatives, felt that the battle was "a fit subject for the genius of Homer," and pictured "the yeomanry of the country [. . .] committing themselves to the bosom of the mother of rivers." On February 25, 1815, in celebration of Jackson's victory, the *Washington National Intelligencer* printed a poem by "P." entitled "The River Mississippi." A millennial victory ode addressed to the "sire of floods," it refigured Jackson's victory over the British as the passing of fluvial supremacy from the Thames to the Mississippi, and proudly positioned the river as "the glory of our wide domain!"[24]

After the Mississippi, and next to Jackson, it was the frontiersmen who emerged as the popular heroes of this victory. Historically, their role has been uncertain. Jackson arrived in New Orleans with a force of 1,500 frontiersmen. More Kentucky troops arrived in the city on the evening of January 2; but as Jackson wrote to Monroe the next morning, of the 2,300 militiamen who made the trip downriver, "not more than one third of them are armed, & those very indifferently." When the British advanced on New Orleans on the eighth, the American front line was composed of 3,569 troops: 2,100 of those "could fit the frontiersman category." Undoubtedly, other factors were crucial to victory: Jean Lafitte's Baratarian bombardment and ammunition supply; the front-line duties of the free men of color, the Choctaw Indians and the New Orleans volunteers; the home-front support. America needed American heroes, however, and Jackson and the linsey-woolsey frontier force provided a perfect contrast to the routed Redcoats.[25]

Jim Girty, a boatman who achieved some fame as a popular hero, always claimed to have been empowered to raise a company of boatmen by Jackson, to have been commissioned captain, and to have fought at Chalmette. There is no evidence for this, and Leland Baldwin was circumspect about the role of boatmen in the battle: "Probably there were not very many flatboatmen [. . .] since only five flatboats had arrived in December, 1814." One famous boatman was certainly present: Henry Miller Shreve had been a keelboatman, but by 1815 he was an evangelist for steam. The most important opponent of the Fulton-Livingston monopoly, he would later go on to clear the Western Rivers of many navigational obstructions. At the Battle of New Orleans, Shreve provided Jackson with invaluable help. In the famous steamboat *Enterprise,* he fetched supplies, ran the British blockade, and repulsed the British forces. According to William Petersen, "this daring feat was loudly acclaimed by Jackson and his troops; and Shreve was the hero of the hour." A Fulton boat, the *Vesuvius,* was pressed into service but ran aground.[26]

The war clearly had an important effect on river life. Throughout the war the supremacy of the British navy meant that, "New Orleans' customary Atlantic routes broke [. . .] and its merchants turned to the [traditionally] expensive interior waterways." The upstream Mississippi trade was therefore boosted. In the peace that followed, the river trade grew more prosperous than ever. For the itinerant young men who had lately served their country, life on the river seemed an attractive proposition. Claudius Cadot was one such veteran who "went on the river to follow keel boating for the purpose of raising money to buy a piece of land. Keel boating on the river was the only place where a man could go to earn money at all." In truth, while the boatmen may not have been veterans, the veterans became boatmen.[27]

Regardless, a popular print commemorating the victory showed that the alligator-horse Kentuckian was immediately taken up as the popular hero of the battle. A horrified John Bull asks, "what the devil are you?" In reply, a beastly American boasts in fine boatman style: "half Horse half Alegator, and have the prettiest Sister, the surest Gun, & the best Knife [. . .] if you run against me, you run against a Snag!" By 1834, a humorous vernacular biography of Jackson by Seba Smith (writing as Major Jack Downing) portrayed the frontiersmen as the established heroes of the hour, descending the Western Rivers like a force of nature:

"afore you could say Jack Robinson the troops from Louisiana, Kentucky, Tenesee, Ohio and other places, the real screamers, who cou'd 'grin the bark off a tree, look a panther tu death, stand three streaks of lightning without dodging' [. . .] was aflote on the Ohio and Missippi in a flash."[28]

The most important step in this association, and for the boatman's popular ascendance, came in 1822 with the first performance of "one of America's most popular songs": "The Hunters of Kentucky (or The Battle of New Orleans)," a ballad composed by Samuel Woodward celebrating victory in 1815. It was performed most famously by Noah Ludlow. The song contained a familiar description of the Kentuckian troops—"ev'ry man was half a horse, / And half an alligator"—and thus introduced the alligator-horses of the Mississippi to a national audience. It had a powerful effect on the boatmen themselves. Noah Ludlow premiered the song to a receptive New Orleans audience: "I found the pit, or parquette, of the theatre *crowded full* of 'river men'—that is keel-boat and flat-boat men. There were very few steamboatmen. These men were easily known by their linsey-woolsey clothing and blanket coats. [. . .] I dressed myself in a buckskin hunting shirt and leggins, which I had borrowed of a river man [. . .] I presented myself before the audience. I was saluted with loud applause of hands and feet, and a prolonged whoop, or howl [. . .] The whole pit was standing up and shouting. I had to sing the song three times that night before they would let me off." Dressed in the clothes of a boatman, performing before boatmen, Ludlow celebrated a popular victory that, in truth, had only a little to do with boatmen. The enormous success of Ludlow's first performance continued along the river and spread throughout the country (until Ludlow was sick of the song that followed him "like some evil genius"). Years later, the song had an important second life: Andrew Jackson used the ballad as his campaign song in the election of 1828. John William Ward quotes an "anonymous student" of the 1828 election who has asserted that "'The Hunters of Kentucky' had much to do with arousing sentiment [for Jackson]." The Mississippi and her valiant boatmen helped Jackson—the alligator-horse president—to steam into the White House.[29]

"AN USEFUL AND NECESSARY GUIDE"

Emigration was vital to the Jacksonian Mississippi: following the War of 1812, what had been a steady drip became a flood. In 1790, the census found one hundred thousand Americans in the Mississippi Valley; by 1830, four million lived across the Alleghenies; by 1848, "the aggregate population, of all the States and Territories bordering on the navigation of the Ohio and Mississippi is eight million four hundred and thirty seven thousand." Though significant numbers emigrated in the presteam era—and continued to use flatboats to reach their destinations well into the age of steam—in large part, the emigration explosion was a result of the steamboat. Writing in *Hunt's Merchant Magazine and Commercial Review* in 1841, James Lanman explained its significance: "Steam navigation colonized the West! It furnished a motive for settlement and production by the hands of eastern men, because it brought the western territory nearer to the east by nine-tenths of the distance [. . .] Steam is crowding our eastern cities with western flour and western merchants, and lading the western steamboats with eastern emigrants and eastern merchandise. It has advanced the career of national colonization and national production, at least a century!"[30]

The multitude of new travelers on the Mississippi constituted a ready readership for printed material on the river. The first key texts were navigation aids, a product of the presteam era. The earliest, and most influential, was Zadok Cramer's *Navigator*. Cramer was a crucial figure in the cultural development of the West. In 1800, he opened what Wade describes as "the most famous book mart in the West, advertising over eight hundred titles." Cramer spotted a gap for what he felt would prove "an useful and necessary guide." As Charles Dahlinger narrates, he "daily saw swarms of immigrants pass through [Pittsburgh] [. . .] who lingered there attempting to learn, not only about navigating the rivers, but of the country to which they were bound. He proposed to furnish the information and set about collecting data [. . .] venturing upon an almost uncharted sea." *The Navigator* was born. Published from 1802 to 1824, "that famous book" (as Timothy Flint described it) was seminal.[31]

Cramer accompanied those traveling down the river from inception to journey's end. "The first thing to be attended to," Cramer made clear, "by emigrants or traders wanting to descend the river, is to procure a boat"—and "be careful that the boat be a good one." He assisted with the tribulations of river navigation ("Must not go too near the Iron Banks, there being an eddy near the shore under them"). Then he celebrated eventual arrival, "after an irksome passage of between five and six weeks": the moment when the "navigator [. . .] leaps upon shore with ecstasy [. . .] with elated heart and joyful countenance." Cramer was the first to provide rudimentary but detailed maps of the river's course, complemented by thorough textual descriptions of the river. Cramer's tone was reassuring, imperturbable, and conversational. As he described the bend of "General Hull's left leg": "It was formerly a dangerous and deceptive enemy; it is now harmless, providing you bear well to the left and keep a good look out." Little wonder that when Timothy Flint steered his boat into trouble: "Instead of running to the oar, we ran to look in the 'Navigator.'" Cramer's description of the river also allowed those who could not reach the Mississippi to experience the river, to know the river as a navigator did.[32]

Cramer's book—and its successor, Samuel Cumings's *The Western Pilot*—served another valuable service, circulating important moments of Mississippi history and culture. Cramer's constant updates of *The Navigator,* based often, as he acknowledged, on "the goodness of others to detect [. . .] errors" and provide "observations," meant that his version of the Mississippi, like the river itself, was always in flux. In 1807, Cramer published the first account of the Lewis and Clark expedition—Patrick Gass's journal. The 1808 edition of *The Navigator* contained another report on the journey, and on the Missouri and Columbia rivers. After 1811, Cramer recorded the effects of the New Madrid earthquake and the "concussions of the earth." One of his informants may have been Nicholas Roosevelt, who made Cramer's acquaintance in Pittsburgh during the construction of the *New Orleans.* Roosevelt relied on *The Navigator* for his journey to New Orleans (and Cramer welcomed the party into Natchez, since he was there in December 1811, "hoping to find a cure for his consumption").[33]

Cramer was indeed a steam enthusiast. In the 1814 edition of *The Navigator,* he excitedly informed his manifold readers about the "new mode of navigating our western waters." He reported that the *New Orleans* had made "the clear gain of 20,000 dollars for the first year's labour." In Cramer's enthusiastic account, the steamboat became an almost supernatural phenomenon and a clear example of "that happy kind of superior genius" innate in Americans: "It will be a novel sight, and as pleasing as novel to see a huge boat working her way [. . .] without the appearance of sail, oar, pole, or any manual labour about her—moving within the secrets of her own wonderful mechanism, and propelled by power undiscoverable!" He was no less sanguine about predicting what effect this "wonderful mechanism" would have on the West:

> This plan if it succeeds, must open to view flattering prospects to an immense country, an interior of not less than two thousand miles of as fine a soil and climate, as the world can produce, and to a people worthy of all the advantages that nature and art can give them, a people the more meritorious, because they know how to sustain peace and live independent [. . .] the vast riches of the bowels of the earth, the unexampled advantages of our water courses, which wind without interruption for thousands of miles, the numerous sources of trade and wealth opening to the enterprising and industrious citizens, are reflections that must rouse the most dull and stupid.[34]

Cuming's *Western Pilot* provided its readers with a different kind of extraneous matter: literature. Cumings introduced a wide audience—who (though they purchased a dollar copy of a river navigator, a Bible, perhaps a *Crockett Almanac*) were unlikely to invest in further literary matter—to seminal cultural moments in the river's antebellum life. Based in Cincinnati, he did not have to look far for suitable sketches. He found a wealth of material from the Cincinnati school connected to Daniel Drake's literary salon, the Buck-Eye Club, and the Semi-Colon Club. When Morgan Neville's sketch "The Last of the Boatmen," was published in 1828, it was immediately picked up by Cumings and ran in the 1829, 1832, and 1834 editions of *The Western Pilot*. His choice of material was judicious. Alongside Neville, Cumings selected the two major Cincinnati voices whose concept of the West, and the Western Rivers, was defining. Timothy Flint and James Hall were largely responsible for the flowering of literature across the Alleghenies. Their conception of the West (like Cramer's) met on one important idea: whether travelogue, geography, or fiction, it ran "along the rivers."[35]

Timothy Flint was no alligator-horse, but as an itinerant missionary in the West he spent a great deal of time floating on the Western Waters. After the end of the War of 1812, following a turbulent pastorate in Massachusetts, Flint was appointed to missionary work in the states of Ohio and Kentucky. The peripatetic decade that followed provided him with a wealth of knowledge and experience. His first important thoughts on the Mississippi appeared in a work that was part travelogue and part memoir. *Recollections of the Last Ten Years in the Valley of the Mississippi* (1826) recounted Flint's western odyssey—from missionary, to farmer, to the head of a small college, to convalescent, and, finally, to man of letters. His transformations were often traumatic, and the role of the Mississippi in the narrative reflected his changing fortunes. At first, the river represented the promise of the West. Flint—more vividly than any other antebellum writer—felt the romantic pull of this "ultima Thule." Upon the arrival of his family at the "far-famed Mississippi," the "novelty and freshness of everything" "revived those delightful images of youth, the spring-time of existence." Soon, however, "illusion" gave way to "sad reality." Flint saw emigrants to the West, expecting a "land of milk and honey," massing at Cincinnati. They were "wretchedly furnished [. . .] unusually sickly [. . .] Many suffered, died, and were buried by charity." Flint's own family was struck by tragedy. Trapped on the river, lashed by the weather, unable to progress, and running out of provisions, Mrs. Flint went into labor on the second Chickasaw Bluff: "the babe staid with us but two days and a half, and expired [. . .] We deposited the body of our lost babe—laid in a small trunk for a coffin—in a grave amid the rushes."[36]

Somehow, Flint's optimism survived. Beginning his *Recollections* in a flatboat, Flint's last journey was by steam. Though seriously ill, Flint marveled at the rate of advancement: "We had come on average more than an hundred miles a day, against the whole weight of the Mississippi current [. . .] We are certainly making great strides in luxury." This was the tone that pervaded Flint's later works on the Western Waters. His ambitious *Condensed Geography and History of [. . .] the Mississippi Valley* (1828, with numerous reprints and revisions) was a reference work that attempted to synthesize all known information on the West—intended for both "stay-at-homes in the East and [. . .] prospective emigrants." Its description of the Mississippi—"No thinking mind can contemplate this mighty and resistless wave, sweeping its proud course from point to point, curving round its bends through the dark forests, without a feeling of sublimity"—was made famous by its inclusion in *The Western Pilot*. Most interesting, though of less importance to posterity, was his novel *George Mason, The Young Backwoodsman [. . .] A Story of the Mississippi* (1829). Like a prototype Horatio Alger hero transplanted to the Mississippi, George Mason works his way to wealth, but not in the way that his dead Jeffersonian father—enchanted by the "bucolic romances of Imlay and Chateaubriand"—had predicted on his family's removal to the West. Instead, reflecting the changing nature of the river frontier, George turns from yeomanry to commerce, making hats to sell to the "card-playing people, and the vain women" traveling on passing steamboats. He swiftly climbs through western society, first clerking on a steamboat, then piloting it ("his cherished purpose"), and finally owning half of a boat. Flint's varied works provided many writers with their vision of the Western Waters.[37]

James Hall was no less influential. Like Flint, he encouraged the nascent literature of the West. Hall was primarily concerned with the cultivation of polite fictions. As he wrote in later life, "I have always held and imposed as a rule on myself, that a writer [. . .] should imagine a modest woman, or a sober-minded well bred gentleman to be looking over his shoulder." A world away from other important Jacksonian literary representations of the Mississippi—the vernacular roughness of the *Crockett Almanacs* or the *Spirit of the Times*—Hall's work was nationally recognized (for a time, second only to Irving's).[38]

Hall's conception of the Western Rivers was even more forward facing than Flint's. Flint's conception of progress was, *George Mason* excepted, "consistently pre–Industrial Revolution"; Hall's work was rhapsodic about industry and commerce. His last published work, *The West: Its Commerce and Navigation* (1848), was a prolonged hymn of praise to "the liberal spirit of commercial enterprise" and its agent, "the application of steam power to the purposes of navigation." His first major work had been equally concerned with the Western Waters and "the fruits of [. . .] American enterprise." *Letters from the West* (1828), in essence a sentimental tour along the Ohio, remains of interest because of Hall's romantic firsthand account of boatmen. In his description, the "half horse and half alligator" men were in communion with "coarse" frontier muses: "It is amusing to see poetry [. . .] like a good republican [. . .] dressed in rags and limping upon crutches [. . .] she becomes the most quaint, ingenious, entertaining little imp imaginable." All the boatmen were rude poets: "some rows up but we rows down, / All the way to Shawneetown"; "Pappy" was their acknowledged laureate. Establishing one of the iconic images of flatboating, Hall described Pappy's role: "While others worked, he would sit for hours scraping upon his violin, singing catches, or relating merry and marvellous tales."[39]

Ironically, for one so concerned with the industrial growth of the Western Waters, Hall's most extraordinary vision of the Mississippi was specifically concerned with the dangers of progress and emigration. "Three Hundred Years Hence" was a rudimentary work of science fiction that envisaged the Mississippi Valley in 2130. St. Louis in 2130 initially seems little different from St. Louis 1830, except in industrial scale: "How glorious was the sight presented by 'THE GREAT FATHER OF WATERS!' A forest of masts lined both shores, for miles, and every flag of Europe waved at the mast head of the steam ships that ploughed its waters. I entered the city by one of the iron bridges that spanned the river [. . .] St. Louis, in the interior of the most fertile region of the globe, far exceeded, in wealth and population, the largest city of the eastern hemisphere." The narrator is gratified to see such progress, and to witness "that employment and sustenance was afforded to so numerous a population [. . .] I remembered with exultation, that I had warmly advocated every plan [. . .] to induce emigration to the west." That satisfaction is soon destroyed. In the growing darkness, mobs start to assemble, and a cry for "BREAD!" rises up at factory gates. Rampant industrialism has left the people "squalid with hunger and rage" and at the mercy of "obnoxious" employers. Martial law is evoked, and battle ensues. The narrator is accidentally taken for an insurgent and put to death—only to wake in the bucolic paradise, the "wildness," of 1830. Though the symbolic value of Flint and Hall's Mississippi came from its progression from frontier to industry, the river's "wildness" still retained a powerful charm—as further evidenced by the rise to prominence, sentimentally tinged, of the river frontier's most famous cultural sons. "This was the Heroic Age itself," as Thoreau concluded, having seen a moving panorama of the Mississippi, "though we know it not, for the hero is commonly the simplest and obscurest of men."[40]

"THE CELEBRATED, AND SELF-CREATED, AND NEVER TO BE MATED, MISSISSIPPI ROARER"

Morgan Neville, the man responsible for the popular rise to cultural prominence of legendary boatman Mike Fink, was an associate of James Hall; he was the dedicatee of Hall's *Letters*. Though not as prolific as his friend, the brief sketch that Neville produced in 1828 arguably had the greatest influence on the Jacksonian cultural conception of the Mississippi. The year that Jackson ascended to the presidency was the year that the popular fascination with the Mississippi boatmen coalesced into one iconic figure. Neville's "The Last of the Boatmen" (1828) was the first extended literary treatment of the definitive alligator-horse, the king of the keelboatmen, Mike Fink. After a century and a half in the New World, and almost a half century of independence, "Americans began to center their folk invention upon themselves." Mike Fink was the first uncommon common man to occupy a central cultural role in America—a folk hero "to frontier squatters and Eastern shopkeepers alike."[41]

Neville's story was not the first portrait of Fink. In 1821, Alphonso Wetmore, a young army paymaster posted to the Mississippi, wrote a play for the St. Louis Thespians. *The Pedlar* was a landmark: a panorama of regional types including the Yankee Pedlar, the Backwoodsman, the Revolutionary Veteran, and the Emigrant, all based on "Wetmore's own experiences [. . .] oral lore, and his reading in newspapers." Taking his place in this cavalcade was the Boatman. Wetmore's stage directions make it clear that he appeared in the boatman's unofficial uniform, "with red shirt and tow trousers on—a little drunk, singing soundings." The Boatman boasts that he is a "steamboat." He rough-and-tumbles with the Backwoodsman and demands more Monongahela whisky: "for a *picayon* I can get happy as a lord; and for a *bit,* dead drunk." In the very last line of the play, an aside for the river-town audience, the Boatman is named as Mike Fink. Two years later, the real Mike Fink was dead. This occasioned his second appearance in print. Fink, the real-life keelboatman, had quit the Western Waters and had signed up as a fur trapper with the famous Ashley-Henry expedition up the Missouri (three fellow members were mountain men Jim Bridger, Jedediah Smith, and Hugh Glass). The *Missouri Republican* reported on July 16, 1823: "By a letter received in town from one of Gen. Ashley's expedition we are informed that a man by the name of Mike Fink well known in this quarter" had been "shot [. . .] dead."[42]

In the same year as Fink's cameo in *The Pedlar,* the figure of the boatman was put to a very different literary use in General William O. Butler's poem "The Boatman's Horn" (originally "The Boat-Horn"), published in the *Western Review* in 1821. Butler was a Kentuckian who had fought with Jackson at New Orleans and later served as Jackson's aide. Butler's poem—"famous in its day"—was an elegy to lost childhood. Its narrator wanly remembers "boyhood's joyous days" and the "soft numbers" blown by "every simple boatman": "each pulse to nature true, / And melody in every tone [. . .] As if to charm from storm and wreck / The boat where all his fortunes ride!" Butler's sentimental interpretation of the boatman found an eager audience, and influenced the interpretations that followed, including Neville's.[43]

Neville, the grandson of two Revolutionary War generals, grew up along the Ohio in Pittsburgh. In 1806, he had responded to Burr's western call to arms. With thirteen of his colleagues from the Pittsburgh Academy, he "started down the river" on the way to "the rendezvous of Burr's troops at the mouth of the Cumberland." The force was apprehended by the Virginia militia, at the island of co-conspirator Harman Blennerhassett. In Neville's words, it was "a moment of visionary speculation," and Burr was "an adventurer—himself the dupe of others." In later years, Neville edited the *Pittsburgh Gazette* before moving to Cincinnati. When James Hall was seeking contributors for his influential miscellany, *The Western Souvenir,* Neville provided numerous sketches. Hall's collection was subtitled *A Christmas and New Year's Gift for 1809;* it was a ladies' book, textually sentimental and paratextually lush. The volume was an attractive duodecimo, "bound in forest-green silk [. . .] adorned with green end papers and neat gold lettering." Such was the setting for the most influential Mike Fink story.[44]

Neville began "The Last of the Boatmen" with an extended meditation on the development of the West: "the sublime power and self-moving majesty of a steam boat [. . .] in five years has enabled us to anticipate a state of things which, in the ordinary course of events, it would have required a century to have produced." Claiming intimate knowledge of the famous boatman, "familiarly known to me from my boyhood," Neville's portrait of Mike Fink drew on an extraordinary range of cultural reference points: Fink "presented a figure that Salvator [Rosa] would have chosen from a million as a model for his wild and gloomy pencil." Fink was "Herculean"—but he was also like "Apollo," and "he might have been a Roland," or "the favourite of the Knight of the Lion-heart," and "he would have ranked with the Morgans and Putnams" of the Revolution. He might even "have passed for the principal warrior of some powerful tribe." And to his enemies, he was "Rob-Roy."

Mike Fink "stood an acknowledged leader" amongst the boatmen. He was "celebrated on the rivers of the West" as "the hero of a hundred fights, and the leader in a thousand daring adventures." According to Neville, Fink began his career as a Scout—"a body of irregular rangers, which was employed on the Northwestern frontiers of Pennsylvania" for the purposes of Indian fighting, spying, and hunting. At this time he "acquired a reputation for boldness and cunning." When the Scouts were no longer needed—following General Wayne's victory at the Battle of Fallen Timbers and the Treaty of Greenville—their "erratic mode of life" had "unfitted them for the pursuits of civilized society." Those that didn't turn Indian became "boatmen, then just becoming a distinct class." Neville knew that the life of a boatman was not just uncivilized but "calculated to destroy the constitution and to shorten the life." But he also recognized that it had an unmistakable charm: "sons abandoned the comfortable farms of their fathers, and apprentices fled from the service of their masters," such was the "captivation in the idea of 'going down the river.'" In 1828, Neville concluded, such times were past. According to Neville, Mike Fink was "the correct representative of a class of men now extinct [. . .] The period of their existence was not more than a third of a century. The character was created by the introduction of trade on the Western waters; and ceased with the successful establishment of the steam boat." Fink, so an old acquaintance informed Neville, "could not bear the hissing of steam," could not become a pilot, and, unlike many of his old colleagues, could not settle down to farm: "With Mike Fink expired the spirit of the boatman."[45]

Other accounts of Mike Fink acknowledged their debt: Timothy Flint commended the "vivid and admirable portrait"; Charles Cist praised Neville's "graphic pen" and noted that it had "given celebrity to Mike Fink." It was the most widely published of the Fink stories, thoroughly penetrating antebellum culture. Its appeal was based in its resonant combination of oral folklore, sentiment, nascent western humor, the forward-looking rhetoric of western development, and classical association. Resigning the boatman to the past amplified his romantic appeal. It allowed western writers to draw a line under the frontier era of their youth, simultaneously lamenting the passing of the preindustrial pastoral river. The presteam boatman, writers felt, was of a different breed, almost mythical in his abilities.[46]

In truth, though the steamboat profoundly affected the keelboat trade, it in no way banished presteam boatmen from the Mississippi. As Louis Hunter described, "keelboats lingered on for decades"; they worked on smaller rivers and at times of the year when steamboats found it difficult to run. They "figured in the commercial statistics of Pittsburgh as late as 1868." As for the flatboat, the steamboat never truly displaced it. Its demise was concurrent with the downfall of the steamboat and the river trade as a whole. Flatboat arrivals in New Orleans peaked in 1846–47, at circa 2,792—up from 598 in 1814. By 1856–57, that number had declined to 541, still a significant element of Mississippi life. If anything, the steamboat stimulated the flatboat trade, since it provided boatmen with a more comfortable and convenient return journey. The deck of the steamboat became a surrogate flat or keel. *Baird's Emigrant Guide* romantically described boatmen taking deck passage in 1832. One might have seen a "half-horse, and half-alligator Kentuckian boatman, swaggering and boasting of his prowess [. . .] one is sawing away on a fiddle all day long; another is grinding a knife or razor; here is a party playing cards, and in yonder corner is a dance to the tune of a jew's harp."[47]

Many of the most important western writers of the day turned their hand to a Mike Fink story, contrary in their judgment of the boatman but consistent in the presentation of his essential characteristics. Alongside Neville, Flint, and Cist there stood T. B. Thorpe, John S. Robb, J. M. Field, Emerson Bennett, Friedrich Gerstäcker, and Ben Cassedy. As Constance Rourke noted: "the sad noisy sentiment mounted through twenty years or more. The exploits of Fink were still being celebrated during the 50s by the western almanacs." In fact, as Blair and Meine have shown, Fink stories proliferated most widely in the 1840s and 1850s, dropping off abruptly when sectional conflict came to dominate the national scene. For Rourke, the king of the keelboatmen was "a Mississippi river-god, one of those minor deities whom men create in their own image and magnify to magnify themselves." In terms of mythological precursors, perhaps the often-felt influence of Egypt is discernible, and Fink was a manifestation of Sebek, the Egyptian half-man, half-crocodile god of the Nile. The son of the goddess of warfare, Sebek represented the respect and fear that the river commanded. Sebek was believed to have created the Nile and to control the river, and was thus associated with its fertility; he was related to the power of the Pharaoh; and, like the Nile crocodiles, he was ferocious and quick, and associated with the dead. Evidently, Fink contained multitudes, and resonated strongly with Jacksonian America's conception of itself. Neither did his spirit expire with him. As Captain Jo Chunk—purportedly quoted in the *Crockett Almanac for 1839*—asserted: "there ain't a boatman on the river, to this day, but what strives to imitate him."[48]

Mike Fink was not the only popular frontier figure to have an important connection to the Mississippi River. First a follower of Jackson (in the Creek War and in Congress); then an opponent (in part, because of Jackson's policy of

Indian removal); finally, a hero at the Alamo—Davy Crockett's life and mythology were deeply connected to the waters of the Mississippi. As a character in the *Crockett Almanac for 1839* addressed him: "Are you the feller that makes them allmynacks about crusing after panthers and snakes and swimming over the Mississippi?"[49]

In the years before he went to Congress, living in West Tennessee by the Obion River close to where it fed into the Mississippi, Crockett knew the river frontier intimately. Like Jackson, he even took to the Mississippi as a merchant navigator. He attempted to transport "two boats and about thirty thousand staves" to New Orleans by flatboat, but he and his inexperienced crew were soon "bad scared" by the river. The boats, lashed together, were unwieldy; worse, "a fellow had to go ahead whether he was exactly willing or not [. . .] Here we had about the hardest work that I ever was engaged in, in my life." The craft "went broadside full tilt against the head of an island." Crockett was only just saved from drowning. His escape route was a small porthole, and he ended up 'skin'd like a rabbit [. . .] even without shirt or hide." Such a lucky rebirth was enough for him to declare the experience "the last of my boats, and of my boating." Disaster precipitated his emergence into public life.[50]

Though his time as a flatboatmen was less then auspicious, the river featured prominently in Crockett's political career and was vital to the persona that he cultivated for the stump. At the same time that "The Hunters of Kentucky" rang out for Jackson, Crockett went one step further and appropriated the boatman's vernacular for his speeches, claiming that he could "wade the Mississippi" and "carry a steam-boat on his back." Crockett and his rise to prominence captured the public's imagination. The river itself was politically prominent during his time in Congress, particularly in his split with Jackson. Crockett was the only member of his delegation to challenge Jackson's desire to make the Mississippi the borderline beyond which peaceful Native tribes from Mississippi, Alabama, Tennessee, and Georgia would have to pass forever. In direct opposition to the president, he unsuccessfully tried to advocate the allocation of funds to improve navigation along the Ohio and the Mississippi. "The people of this country," he warned, directly attacking the party machine surrounding Jackson, "like the humble boatsman on the Mississippi, ought to begin to look out for *Breakers!*"[51]

All along the river frontier in the early 1830s, the talk was of Crockett. In December 1831, while traveling along the Mississippi as part of the tour that would lead to his writing of *Democracy in America*, Alexis de Tocqueville arrived in Memphis (recently platted on Jackson's old landholding, with a population of just six hundred). De Tocqueville noted disapprovingly in his journal, conflating already established fiction with fact: "two years ago the inhabitants of the district of which Memphis is the capital sent to the House of Representatives in Congress an individual named David Crockett, who has had no education, can read with difficulty, has no property, no fixed residence, but passes his life hunting, selling his game to live, and dwelling continuously in the woods." (Remarkably, just a week later, de Tocqueville boarded a steamer bound for New Orleans. A fellow passenger was another potent icon of Jacksonian democracy. Returning from his time in the wilderness, on the brink of another extraordinary Texan career, de Tocqueville drew the following sketch of Sam Houston: "Mr H. is a man of about 45; the disappointments and labours of all kinds that have accompanied his existence have as yet left only a light trace on his features [. . .] everything in his person indicates physical and moral energy.")[52]

As important as the river was to the real-life David Crockett, its prominence in the myth making that immediately surrounded him was evident. When J. K. Paulding wrote the important drama *The Lion of the West* in 1830, it was popularly believed that Nimrod Wildfire, the titular backwoodsman, was a stage version of Crockett. The actor most associated with the role, James Hackett, had already established a reputation for playing frontier types in William Moncrieff's *Monsieur Mallet; or, my Daughter's Letter* (1829). Playing "Jeremiah Kentucky" in Moncrieff's play, Hackett had already proclaimed the famous boast: "half-horse, half-alligator, with a touch of the steamboat, and a small taste of the snapping-turtle." Before he performed *The Lion of the West* in London in 1832, however, Paulding wrote to Hackett disingenuously denying the similarity between Crockett and his fictional frontiersman, but revealing more profound connections between Crockett and the river: "take care [. . .] to let it be known that it is not intended to represent the character of a Kentucky Gentleman, or of Kentuckians generally, but of a particular class, originally Mississippi boatmen." An examination of Nimrod goes some way to supporting Paulding's statement. During the play he exclaims a familiar boast: "half horse, half alligator, a touch of the airth-quake with a sprinkling of the steamboat!"[53]

It was, however, in the *Crockett Almanac(k)s* from 1835 to 1856 that the mythologization of Crockett, and his symbolic connection to the spirit of the Mississippi, was most profound. As Franklin Meine highlighted, "the Mississippi plays an important part: stories about life on the river for the first time bring into focus the role of the River in the vast panorama of the frontier [. . .] its significance in the everyday life of the frontiersman." More than a backdrop for stories of frontier life, the river imagined in the *Almanacs* began to take on the transformative powers already hinted at in the new American breed of the half-horse, half-alligator. The polar opposite of the polite western myth making of Flint and Hall, the *Crockett Almanacs* imagined an exuberant, enchanted, and amplified river frontier that figured prominently in the Jacksonian imagination.[54]

Perhaps inspired by Crockett's disastrous flatboat dunking, *Almanac* writers often pictured Crockett naked in the Mississippi itself (like a backwoods nymph or a Greco-Roman river god). The small and simple woodcuts that complemented the texts managed to evoke a Mississippi that seemed truly epic. They were the first significant attempts at a visual representation of the river. On the cover of the 1836 *Almanack,* Crockett bestrode the river like a New World Colossus on stilts—whiskey barrel suspended from his waist, gun strapped to his belt, the river stretching away to either side. Inside the *Almanack,* the inhospitable river and its animal spirits got the better of him. A powerful catfish "whirled my canoe round and round like a car-wheel on a railroad [. . .] I went souse into the water." The metaphysical quality of this sketch of a backwoodsman and his inhospitable environment was amplified in the *Almanack* for 1837. Instead of one extraordinary catfish, the whole of Mississippi creation descended upon Crockett. The sketch began admiringly: "Of all the rivers on this airth, the Mississippi beats all holler. Many a tough time have I had in swimming across its turbid waters." Having shot three geese, Crockett jumped into the water to retrieve them—but without his customary coating of "skunk's grease," he attracted the unwanted attentions of a wolf, a bear, and a "river calf." With a little help from some sharp-shooting steamboat passengers, Crockett managed to beat them off: "I was invited on board, but as there was ladies on board, I did not like to appear in a state of nature, so I dove under the boat and swam ashore."[55]

By 1839, Crockett did not even need a raft: "I was laying asleep on the Mississippi one day, with a piece of river scum for a pillow, and floating down stream in rail free and easy style." The mystic hints of Crockett's river experiences filtered throughout these annual publications in stories about boat races, boatmen, alligators, the Battle of New Orleans, the odd "riproarious fight on the Mississippi" —the amplified world of the Jacksonian river. They spoke, in Dorson's terms, "with the brash and strident voice of Jacksonian America." Many of the stories, like Fink's, were filled with "anti-intellectualism, chauvinism, and racism." But in their conception of the Western Waters, the *Crockett Almanacs* wove enchantments. A story like "A Kentucky Team" (illustrated under the title "The Way They Travel in the West") imagined a magic river-world of supernatural possibility: "Thar is sum folks that makes much of their figgers and larning and owl sorts of inventions, and I spose when they got their steemboates and railroads a going they thort they war going to upset the world rite off and make the sun rise by steem [. . .] they ar only a sampling compared to what Bartholomew Grithard did last fall [. . .] I see the waters of the Mississippy in wuss pother than the Pukes at the election [. . .] Bartholomew bauled out to me to hold fire, for the two varmints [alligators] was tackled up and harnist to his bote, and he war driving 'em down stream." In the rough-and-rowdy world of the *Crockett Almanacs,* the alligator-horse could become his own magnificent natural steamboat.[56]

As the Jacksonian years waned, and as the frontier gave way to increasing industrialization, the attention that was lavished on the iconic presteam boatman was transferred to the men who worked the steamboats. The captain and the pilot became river kings, almost aristocratic in their bearing. As Flint wrote in 1829, "there are but few personages, entitled to higher and more heart-felt homage than the captains of steam-boats." The steamboat engineers inherited the characteristics of the alligator-horses. This hierarchy was apparent in a story published in 1846, "The Steamboat Captain Who Was Averse to Racing." The captain was "a noble fellow." On the inaugural voyage of his "magnificent new steamer," the grand gentleman sent out "Gilt-edged covers [. . .] accompanied with invitations to 'see her through,' upon her first trip down the river." Below decks, such finery was absent. The engineer was responsible for keeping the boat in one piece, providing the steam and the vernacular. As he replies to the captain's desire for extra racing speed, with a gesture to the "crow-bar [. . .] braced athwart the safety valve" and the melting solder running down "the connection pipe": "I rayther think she moves *some* as it is."[57]

The celebration of the steamboat engineer as a repository of the alligator-horse spirit reached its zenith in a poem written after the Civil War by John Hay, one of Lincoln's private secretaries. Published in Hay's *Pike County Ballads* in 1871, the enormously popular "Jim Bludso" mixed melodramatic sentiment with frontier vernacular. Jim, the engineer of the *Prairie Belle,* "were n't no saint"— "them engineers / is all pretty much alike,— / One wife in Natchez-under-the-hill / And another one here, in Pike." But when the *Prairie Belle* explodes, Jim bravely holds the boat steady until all the passengers are safely off:

> He were n't no saint,—but at jedgment
> I'd run my chance with Jim,
> 'Longside of some pious gentlemen
> That wouldn't shook hands with him.
> He seen his duty, a dead-sure thing,—
> And went for it thar and then;

And Christ ain't a going to be too hard
On a man that died for men.[58]

The steamboat revolution also slowly removed the emigrant from the flatboat and the keelboat; it was not much of an elevation. Deck passage (where all were crowded together in the open air, close to the waters of the Mississippi) was the dominant mode of emigrant travel. Just as Cramer answered the need of those emigrating along the Western Waters in the presteam years, others attempted to write for those traveling on the deck. Gone were concerns with navigating the river. Steamboat life brought new problems. J. M. Peck's guide, for example, was written "to answer the pressing call [. . .] made for information of these Western States." All guides were keen to point out the benefits of settlement along the river, even the romance of steam travel. Very rarely did they reflect the Mississippi experience of most immigrants. John Regan, who emigrated from Scotland to Illinois in the 1840s, wrote at length about his experiences in his *Emigrant's Guide to the Western States of America*. Having "eagerly pored over [. . .] books descriptive of the promised land" before his departure, Regan reached America via the gateway of the Mississippi: "The huge and resistless river [was] underfoot [. . .] while the loud bellowings of the breathing engine resounded through the primeval forest in a tone which promised to carry the dominion of man through all its recesses;—all these combined to fill the soul with such feelings as make one rejoice that he also is one of that vast fellowship whose mission it is to fill up the western plains with the arts, industries, and improvements of eastern lands." Rhetoric was one thing, reality another. Having seen deck passengers "gnawing a huge piece of beef off a square biscuit," Regan enquired where they had obtained it. A friend "told me he had got it from the men in the steamboat, who had more of it than they could consume, and were much amused to see with what a good appetite the emigrants demolished the remains [. . .] which they were in the habit of throwing overboard."[59]

The *View of the Valley of the Mississippi: or the Emigrant's and Traveller's Guide to the West* (1832) also blurred the realities of emigrant steamboat life. The cabin was curtly off-limits to deck passengers: there "you will find ladies and gentlemen of various claims to merit." Despite that, the author tried to evoke the experience of life on deck with delight and sentiment: "there is every thing that may be called *human*,—all sorts of men and women, of all trades, from all parts of the world." From the "half-horse and half-alligator Kentucky boatman," to the man "sawing away on his wretched old fiddle," to the "party *playing cards*" and those dancing "to the sound of the Jew's harp." There may even be a few "trying to demean themselves soberly, by sitting in silence or reading a book." But the distractions of "the wondrous tale and horrible Indian story," the free circulation of "the bottle and the jug," the incessant "boisterous and deafening laugh" were "sufficient to banish every vestige of seriousness, and thought, and sense."[60]

In their journey to the Mississippi—to the heartland of the supposedly classless Jacksonian democracy—immigrants would have found the steamboat a rude and very visible stratification along the lines of wealth. For Lee Benson, the "Jacksonian Democracy concept" was "*invented*"; for Edward Pessen, "not equality but disparity of condition was the rule in Jacksonian America [. . .] [it] witnessed no breakdown of a class society." To Mississippi immigrants traveling in the age of steam, such criticisms would have rung terribly true. As William Petersen described, those who traveled on the deck risked "poor food and wretched accommodations, sickness, suffering, and death." Steamboats carried cholera along the river. A German deck passenger, one of the few to record his experiences, warned those of his fellow countrymen who were "not obliged to save a few dollars" to "avoid this Trojan belly into which the poor are packed like herring."[61]

By and large, the affluent passengers comfortably housed in the cabin were only concerned with those on deck as a vivid example of local color. Alternatively, they followed the "intelligent English traveler," quoted by the Rev. J. P. Thompson, in deploring "the vagrant pioneers of the West" and their practices of "gambling, drinking [. . .] licentiousness" and "constant swearing." Matilda Houstoun, traveling on the Mississippi in the late 1840s, recorded an attempt by cabin passengers to ameliorate the "cruel and tyrannical manner in which the Germans and Irish on board were treated." Having approached the captain and addressed their points to him, he "made the following *humane* reply: Well, by ——! if they don't like it they may just go ashore and be ——, nobody wants 'em to stop here." As the passengers turned to leave, one spoke out: "Well by ——! cap'em, if them wause *niggers,* you daren't treat 'em as you do the poor devils."[62]

"HURRA FOR THE BIG BAR OF ARKANSAW!"

The frontier era of life on the Mississippi was coming to a close, but its final, and most potent expression was still to come. The steamboat cabin was a compelling mixture of urbane modernity and the rude frontier, a forum where social interaction took on a fluidity that retained productive friction. It was a microcosm of Jacksonian America. While excluding those experiencing the travails of the deck, it brought together disparate elements of the democratic experiment—with no little awareness and pride. With exuberant enthusiasm, Timothy Flint described the assorted social pleasures of a Mississippi steamer:

> An Atlantic cit, who talks of us under the name of backwoodsmen, would not believe, that such fairy structures of oriental gorgeousness and splendor [. . .] had ever existed in the imaginative brain of a romancer, much less, that they were actually in existence, rushing down the Mississippi, as on the wings of the wind, or plowing up between the forests and walking against the mighty current "as things of life," bearing speculators, merchants, dandies, fine ladies, every thing real, and every thing affected in the form of humanity, with pianos and stocks of novels, and cards, and dice, and flirting, and love-making, and drinking, and champagne.

All American life was there. For T. B. Thorpe, the typical steamboat crowd presented "more than is anywhere else observable in a small space, the cosmopolitanism of our extraordinary population." In a biography of his brother—the famous western Whig orator and lawyer Seargent Smith Prentiss—George Prentiss evoked precisely the social excitement of Mississippi steam travel in its golden age: "No small portion of his time was passed in the floating palaces which enliven the bosom of this majestic river. Aside from the calls of business, there was an excitement and variety in this mode of existence, which agreed well with his disposition. He was generally known on the river; and everybody that did not know him, was anxious to make his acquaintance, or at least to get a glimpse of him. The steamboats between Vicksburg and Natchez were to him little more than ferryboats, upon which he was perpetually flying to and fro."[63] In 1838, William T. Porter, the editor of the weekly sporting journal the *Spirit of the Times* (founded in 1831), embarked upon a research trip down the Mississippi. He met with some of his correspondents and spent time conversing in the sort of heterogeneous steamboat cabins described by Flint and Prentiss. The particular "stressing of local realism and folklore" in the *Spirit,* the most influential journal in the proliferation of nascent southwestern humor sketches of Jacksonian life on the Mississippi, dated from that excursion. Storytelling, as Blair has noted, was "particularly well adapted to travelers by [. . .] boat." The enforced companionship of the steamboat cabin was the perfect setting for the exchange of yarns and tall tales, both impersonal and expressive of some shared truth. A framing device, where, for example, "an author would indicate [. . .] he had listened to the story he told [. . .] on a steamboat on the Mississippi," or establish that setting before embarking on a vernacular narrative, was a common formula for a humorous sketch.[64]

The early and undisputed masterpiece of steamboat sketches was T. B. Thorpe's "The Big Bear of Arkansas," first published in Porter's *Spirit* in 1841. Thorpe moved to Louisiana in the late 1830s and settled in Feliciana Parish on the Mississippi. As a writer, a painter, and an adopted member of the planter class, Thorpe's life revolved around the river. To one friend, he even looked like "an embodiment, in semi-human form, of a thick fog on the Mississippi, at half past three in the morning to a man who has just lost his last dollar at poker."[65]

Thorpe's "Big Bear" is set on board a Mississippi steamboat, a place where "the heterogeneous character of the passengers [. . .] can scarcely be imagined by one who has never seen it with his own eyes"; passengers find themselves "associated with men from every state in the Union" and "every portion of the globe." A "desperate gambler" rubs shoulders with members of the "half-horse and half-alligator species of men." But for Thorpe's polite narrator, the character of Jim Doggett presents another matter: "a loud Indian whoop" emanates from the bar; snatches of familiar boasts filter through: "'Hurra for the Big Bar of Arkansaw!'" [. . .] 'horse' [. . .] 'screamer' [. . .] 'lightning is slow.'" Finally, Jim Doggett "took a chair, put his feet on the stove, and [. , .] passed the general and familiar salute of 'strangers, how are you?'"

The style and characterization of a Fink or a Crockett is readily apparent in Thorpe's protagonist. Doggett is a backwoodsman, his vernacular an abrupt contrast to the exaggeratedly ornate language of the narrator. Something about the newcomer "won the heart on sight"; his "perfect confidence in himself was irresistibly droll." But Doggett is a man with a worried mind. His account of a recent trip to New Orleans hints at the changing nature of the river frontier. Doggett laments, "I am thrown away in that ar place, and useless." The "gentlemen" called him "*green*": "well, perhaps I am, said I, *but I arn't so at home.*" Thorpe's narrator asks Doggett for a "description of some particular bear hunt"; Doggett agrees.

At this point in the story, Doggett takes complete narratorial control. His description of the hunt—though less than half of the total length of the story—is the most remarkable part of the sketch. From a workaday frontier tale, Doggett's yarn enters the metaphysical. In bear hunts, Doggett is "*numerous.*" The essentials of a bear hunt are simple: "It is told in two sentences—a bar is started, and he is killed." But one bear hunt still "puzzles" him. When Doggett first saw the marks left by this particular big bear, "I couldn't believe it was real." Numerous hunts in pursuit of it were unsuccessful. The "bar finally got so sassy, that he used to help himself to a hog off my premises." The disappointment consumed Doggett: "missing that bar so often took hold of my vitals, and I wasted away [. . .]

I would see that bar in every thing I did: *he hunted me,* and that too, like a devil, which I began to think he was." Doggett determined (echoing Crockett) "to catch that bar, go to Texas, or die." This is Doggett's description of what happened next:

> Well, stranger, on the morning previous to the great day of my hunting expedition, I went into the woods near my house, taking my gun and Bowie-knife along, just *from habit,* and there sitting down also from habit, what should I see, getting over my fence, but *the bar!* Yes, the old varmint was within a hundred yards of me, and the way he walked *over that fence*—stranger, he loomed up like a *black mist,* he seemed so large, and he walked right towards me. I raised myself, took deliberate aim, and fired. Instantly the varmint wheeled, gave a yell, and *walked through the fence* like a falling tree would through a cobweb. I started after, but was tripped up by my inexpressibles, which either from habit, or the excitement of the moment, were about my heels, and before I had really gathered myself up, I heard the old varmint groaning in a thicket near by, moaning like a thousand sinners, and by the time I reached him he was a corpse.

A careful reading is needed to appreciate the mixture of pathos and bathos, sublime and ridiculous, epic and farce, that combine in the denouement. On the day before his planned expedition, Doggett thinks that he has prepared thoroughly for all eventualities; the big bear finds him squatting in the woods with his trousers round his ankles. Managing to stand up and shoot the bear, Doggett trips over his underwear. He finds the bear dead in a copse. This unexpected climax leaves Doggett troubled: "I never like the way I hunted, and *missed him.* There is something curious about it, I could never understand—and I never was satisfied at his giving in so easy at his last." Doggett uncertainly concludes that the bear must have been "an *unhuntable bar, and died when his time come.*"[66]

Similar sketches would follow, but Thorpe's sketch marked the cultural peak of the Jacksonian backwoods hero. Thorpe's poetic use of vernacular was one of the most delicately handled examples of colloquialism at a time when voluble Jacksonian oratory echoed in the literature of the frontier and, in Constance Rourke's words, "public speech burst forth in a never-ending flood." (As one western politician said of his garrulous rival, for example, the only thing he hadn't pledged his constituents was his assurance "that the Mississippi run upstream one half the year and downstream the other for the benefit of the river trade.") The influence of Thorpe's sketch of life on the Jacksonian Mississippi—on Melville, on Twain, on Faulkner—is evident. Jim Doggett was the apotheosized alligator-horse, the Jacksonian spirit incarnate, who infiltrated river writing long after his noisier colleagues had faded from the collective memory.[67]

Jackson presided over the era of the Mississippi's greatest commercial and cultural expansion—a time when the river was the West, the symbol of the frontier, the breeding ground for alligator-horses who were intimately connected to the spirit of the times. He did not forget the river. He was responsible for one of its most profound imperial realignments: as an ignominious borderline between "savagery" and "civilization." Though Thomas Jefferson had raised the idea of Indian removal across the Mississippi at the time of the Louisiana Purchase, Jackson was driven by the ambition throughout his presidency. Soon after his accession to the presidency, it was not the Trail of Tears that Jackson envisaged, but a trans-Mississippi paradise. (Remini insists that Jackson "firmly believed" that his policy was driven by a desire to "get the Indian to a place of safety [. . .] west of the Mississippi River.") "Say to the [Indians]," Jackson wrote, "beyond the river Mississippi where a part of their nation have gone, their father has provided a country, large enough for them all, and he advises them to remove to it. There, their white brethren will not trouble them [. . .] and they can live upon it, they and all their children as long as grass grows or water runs in peace and plenty." Steadily, inexorably, tribes were forced beyond the river.[68]

The Black Hawk War, fought in 1832, was the final attempt by the Sauk and Fox Indians to reclaim their Illinois land (lost in an 1805 treaty that they disputed). Early in April 1832, Black Hawk crossed the Mississippi "in a warlike manner." The insurgence was short-lived. Help failed to materialize from either the British or the Illinois. Black Hawk later wrote, "Our only hope to save ourselves, was to get [back] across the Mississippi." But it was on the river that many of Black Hawk's party perished. On the first of August, several of the retreating canoes, filled with women and children, drifted downriver to a position where Captain Throckmorton was waiting with the steamboat *Warrior*: "As we reached them, they raised a white flag [. . .] but we were too old for them. [. . .] we let slip a six-pounder loaded with canister, followed by a severe fire of musketry." The rest of the retreating force fared little better. Driven into the river by General Henry, he "opened a disastrous and terrible fire upon the poor wretches who were struggling with the waves of the Mississippi."[69]

The policy of removal was fulfilled in 1838: Georgia militiamen rounded up the Cherokee Nation and transported them, packed into railroad cars and onto steamboat decks, across the Mississippi. Of the sixty thousand Indians removed beyond the river in its new capacity as borderline, fifteen thousand are estimated to have died in transit. The role of the river in the exodus had a grim climax in October 1837. The steamboat *Monmouth,* on its way up the Mississippi to New Orleans, was full to capacity when "she collided with another steamship and was cut in two; 311 of the Indians on board were killed"—the worst disaster on the antebellum Mississippi. Only nine thousand Indians remained in the East without treaties requiring their removal across the river. De Tocqueville witnessed a moment of this historical movement. An "agent of the American government" employed the steamboat on which he traveled to New Orleans to transport sixty-seven Choctaws to Arkansas: "it is a singular fate that brought us to Memphis to watch the expulsion, one can say the dissolution, of one of the most celebrated and ancient American peoples [. . .] In the whole scene there was an air of ruin and destruction, some thing which betrayed a final and irrevocable adieu."[70]

Jackson's political conception of the river frontier ended in tragedy for the native tribes; his personal relationship with the Mississippi also soured. Financial worries, compounded by his spendthrift adopted son, Andrew Jackson Jr., plagued the ex-president in his final years. The Panic of 1837 temporarily put an end to flush times along the river. In 1838, at the high price of $20 an acre, Jackson Jr. purchased a 1,200-acre plantation named Halcyon in Coahoma County, Mississippi—right next to the river. This investment initially seemed promising. Two years later, Jackson inspected the property en route to the celebrations marking the silver jubilee of the Battle of New Orleans. Jackson had taken to the rivers for the final time. This once-familiar journey was rendered strange and painful by the freezing conditions and his precarious health.[71]

When he inspected Halcyon, he was pleased with what he found. He liked its location, and wrote to his daughter-in-law Sarah that alongside cotton, supplying steamboats with wood could make "a great deal of mony." According to his (inflated) calculations, ten slaves could cut twenty cords of wood a day, worth thirty dollars "in cash." Leaving the plantation in the care of its overseer, Jackson boarded the steamer sent by the State of Mississippi to take him to Vicksburg, thence New Orleans. His arrival in the city was timed for the exact day of the auspicious anniversary. When the four-steamer convoy arrived in the city on January 8, 1840, thirty thousand spectators lined the levee. The procession moved slowly along Canal Street. A celebration at the St. Charles Theatre was marked by a poetical address by Joseph M. Field (soon to be the author of a Mike Fink serial in the *St. Louis Reveille*). The quarter century that had passed marked not only the anniversary of the battle: it represented the unassailable Americanization of the river. Both America and the Mississippi had grown into adulthood, and their adolescence had been firmly Jacksonian. But for Jackson, the alligator-horse who made it to the White House, that Americanization never quite felt secure. The site of his famous victory was often in his thoughts. Jackson "fretted over the possible loss of New Orleans," particularly in his later years, when the question of Texas (and its possible alliance with Great Britain) was pressing. He could still see the shadows of military fantasies and imagined an invasion force marching through Arkansas and Louisiana, ready, he wrote, to "throw our whole west into flames that would cost oceans of blood [. . .] to quench."[72]

The celebrations in New Orleans were a bright moment in an otherwise gloomy decline. Halcyon was a persistent victim of the capricious Mississippi. Years of bad weather commenced in 1838: incessant rain, overwhelming flood, hard frosts. In 1844. Parker, the overseer, described in a distressed torrent of words the devastating floods that ruined crops and killed livestock: "There was not one inch of land out of the water on the highest part of the walnut ridge they run skifts and canoes over the highest parts of the ridge the water over our cotton everywhere was from one to six feet deep our levees is washed down and washed up some places it seems to have washed up by the roots and other places covered up in the deposit [. . .] I have been over the plantation in a canoe since I came home." No full crop was ever harvested from Halcyon. Jackson Jr. sold it off piece by piece to meet debt payments. The last of the river property was sold in 1849. Water—whether Mississippi floods or the dropsy that swelled his body—dominated Jackson's final years as it had determined the course of his life.[73]

Speaking to Dr. William A Shaw, who visited Nashville in Jackson's last years, the ex-president reminisced about the vicissitudes of his life. He quoted Shakespeare (Brutus, in *Julius Caesar*): "there is a tide in the affairs of men, / Which, taken at the flood, leads on to fortune." After pausing, he murmured, "that's true, sir, I've proved it during my whole life." But he knew that a Mississippi flood rarely promised fortune. Just before his death in June 1845, the river frontier of his youth now industrialized and "civilized," Jackson recited a couplet from memory that provided him with some comfort in his last days. Who knows what memories its repetition provoked?

> When thro, the deep waters I call thee to go,
> The rivers of wo shall not thee overflow.[74]

Tom rescues Eva from the Mississippi. From Harriet Beecher Stowe,
Uncle Tom's Cabin (London: C. H. Clarke, 1852), 125.

John L. Boqueta de Woiseri, *A View of New Orleans Taken from the Plantation
of Marigny* (1803). Courtesy Historic New Orleans Collection.

Frontispiece to Charles Mead's *Mississippian Scenery* (Philadelphia: S. Potter, 1819).

A keelboat, from *Harper's New Monthly Magazine* 12, no. 67 (December 1855).

John Bull Making What He Calls a Demonstration on New Orleans (1815).
Courtesy American Antiquarian Society.

Col. Crockett's Method of Wading the Mississippi (Crockett Almanac for 1836).

Crockett Coming to the Surface after His Fight with a Cat-fish (Crockett Almanac for 1836).

Ben Harding Falling in with Col. Crockett (Crockett Almanac for 1839).

The Way They Travel in the West (Crockett Almanac for 1840).

The Belvidere, from Richard Griffin's *The Domestic Manners of the Americans* (Glasgow: Richard Griffin, 1836).

Explosion of the Moselle, from *Lloyd's Steamboat Directory and Disasters on the Western Waters* (Cincinnati: J. T. Lloyd, 1856).

George Caleb Bingham, *The Jolly Flatboatmen* (1846). Manoogian Collection.
Image © Board of Trustees, National Gallery of Art, Washington.

George Caleb Bingham, *Lighter Relieving a Steamboat Aground* (1846–47).
Courtesy White House Historical Association (White House Collection).

The Machinery for Banvard's Panorama, from *Scientific American* 4, no. 13 (December 16, 1848).

Dr. Dickeson Excavating an Indian Burial Mound, from the *Panorama of the Monumental Grandeur of the Mississippi* (1850). Courtesy Saint Louis Art Museum.

Massacre at Fort Rosalie, from the *Panorama of the Monumental Grandeur of the Mississippi* (1850). Courtesy Saint Louis Art Museum.

Henry Lewis, *Keokuk, Iowa* (1854–57) from Henry Lewis's *Das Illustrirte Mississippithal* (Düsseldorf: Arnz, 1857).

Henry Lewis, *Vicksburg, Mississippi* (1854–57) from Henry Lewis's *Das Illustrirte Mississippithal* (Düsseldorf: Arnz, 1857).

Seth Eastman, *Cassville, Wisconsin, in 1829* (1848). Courtesy Saint Louis Art Museum.

Seth Eastman, *20 Miles below the Mouth of the Ohio* (1847–49). Courtesy Saint Louis Art Museum.

Alfred Waud, *Natchez-on-the-Hill, from the Marine Hospital,* from *Harper's Weekly* 10, no. 498 (July 14, 1866).

Selection from *Arrowsmith's Panorama of Western Travel* (designed for exhibition in England), from *Harper's New Monthly Magazine* 18, no. 103 (December 1858).

F. E. Palmer, *The Champions of the Mississippi* (Currier and Ives, 1866).

Canada Bill Throwing Monte from George Devol, *Forty Years a Gambler on the Mississippi* (Cincinnati: Devol and Haines, 1887).

The Crescent City Sport, or *Gabe Ganderfoot's Mississippi Man-Hunt,* no. 843 (New York: Beadle and Adams Dime Library, 1894).

Samuel Clemens, age 14. Courtesy of the Mark Twain Project, Bancroft Library, University of California–Berkeley.

3

Travel and Tourism
Europeans on "This Foul Stream"

If I had a pocketful of money, I think I should go down the Ohio & up & down the Mississippi by way of antidote to what small remains of the Orientalism—(so endemic in these parts)—there may still be in me, to cast out, I mean, the passion for Europe by the passion for America.
RALPH WALDO EMERSON to Margaret Fuller, 1841

Looking southward from this point, we had the satisfaction of seeing that intolerable river dragging its slimy length and ugly freight abruptly off towards New Orleans [. . .] never, I trust, to see the Mississippi more, saving in troubled dreams and nightmares.
CHARLES DICKENS, 1842

Writing about his travels along the Mississippi in 1828, Italian explorer Giacomo Beltrami succinctly described the changes that had recently swept along the river: "what used to be a journey is a *promenade*." Beltrami was qualified to comment. In 1823, he had been a passenger on the *Virginia*, the first steamboat to make its way along the Upper Mississippi to Fort St. Anthony in Minnesota. The pioneering voyage of the *Virginia* compounded the transformations begun by the introduction of the steamboat in 1811—for the economic and political life of the Mississippi, but also, profoundly, for the nature of travel itself. The revolutionary power of steam changed the river, particularly the Upper Mississippi, from a threatening frontier along which travel was largely a matter of necessity, to the setting for a burgeoning tourist trade.

Writing in 1841, the same year that Emerson imagined the Mississippi as an antidote to the last vestiges of the Old World in America, celebrated Native American portraitist George Catlin called for the creation of a "Fashionable Tour" featuring the Mississippi: "This Tour would comprehend but a small part of the great, 'Far West'; but it will furnish to the traveler a fair sample, and being a part of it which is now made so easily accessible to the world, and the only part of it to which *ladies* can have access, I would recommend to all who have time and inclination to devote to the enjoyment of so splendid a Tour, to wait not, but make it while the subject is new, and capable of producing the greatest degree of pleasure." Catlin wrote presciently: by 1841, tourism along the river was burgeoning; travel narratives, many by women tourists, had already begun to circulate defining representations of the Mississippi to a wide audience; soon, canonical sights and established itineraries would intercede and dilute the relationship between the tourist and the river.[1]

As the presence of Beltrami indicates, European tourists—often internationally prominent, and eager to publish accounts of their adventures on the river— were in many ways the most influential travelers to encounter and interpret the antebellum Mississippi. Indeed, Catlin's call for a "Fashionable Tour" of the Mississippi was itself evidence of an abiding European cultural influence. Jacksonian America rendered the river as a glorious symbol of a burgeoning young nation. As a result, the Mississippi had a magnetic pull for tourists from the Old World seeking to understand the New—only to repel most of them when they were faced with the reality of its representative waters and the social microcosm of the steamboat cabin. While Emerson and Catlin were, in their separate ways, celebrating the river, Charles Dickens was enduring his own odyssey on what he and many others felt to be a "foul stream." The clash of Old World aesthetics and New World landscape, though crucial, was only one element in the difficulties that many travelers encountered on the river. Jacksonian American largely skirted over the more ambiguous meanings of the Mississippi, but the European tourists who reached its muddy waters confronted the realities of democracy and slavery, and their own attitudes toward them, head-on.[2]

In a western steamboat, contact with "the great experiment" of democracy was at its most vivid. Fellow passengers—gamblers, roustabouts, alligator-horses, slaves, and slaveholders, and, worst of all, spitters—tested European travelers' preconceptions of America, sometimes to destruction. For as Melville described, "Here reigned the dashing and all-fusing spirit of the West, whose type is the Mississippi itself." The likes of Mike Fink and Davy Crockett were the boisterous sons of the Mississippi; in response, European tourists frequently cast themselves in the role of scolding nannies. Some were able to find a more sympathetic communion with the river. Either way, for many of them, for both good and ill, the Mississippi stood as their defining experience of America. It was their resonant accounts of the river, devoured and dissected in the New World as much as the Old, that were most alive to the Mississippi's symbolic qualities as an artery of the Jacksonian nation.[3]

"THE MEDIUM OF A TRANSLATION"

Though the relative speed and comfort of steam had made the river more amenable to travel, the Mississippi still presented many problems for its early tourists. The river seemed impossible to classify within existing aesthetic criteria.

Whether European or American, antebellum tourists were often strongly influenced by the model standards of travel that had been established on the European Grand Tour, and, particularly, the attendant landscape aesthetics of the eighteenth century. As Lynne Withey has described, "American and European travellers shared a common cultural tradition that encouraged them to seek out particular kinds of landscape and describe them with a common vocabulary." Culture and landscape were the central tenets of Grand Tour travel, so that, for example, "Grand Tourists entered Italy with expectations of its grandeur drawn from a variety of literature, tourists' pamphlets and poetry." Itineraries became established and were rigorously followed; the "*topoi*" of each city— "view-points, famous monuments and favourite panoramas"—were marked out for special interest. The aesthetic strictures of the Grand Tour, especially the concept of the picturesque, furnished the traveler with "a subtle psychological protection" when "exposed to daunting and often disorientating landscapes." But when transplanted to America, this "protection" became more of a curse than a blessing. These aesthetic criteria deeply informed the reaction of tourists to the Mississippi and vividly coloured their representations of the river. For European travelers, inevitable comparisons between Old World and New led to friction—sometimes uncomfortable, sometimes productive.[4]

The dominant aesthetic ideas of the picturesque and the sublime, crucial to tourism, were developed and refined in the eighteenth century. Though the sublime was antecedent to the picturesque, the later concept first gained prominence for travelers. It inaugurated, as Carl Paul Barbier has described it, a "frame of mind" that involved a "direct and active relationship with the natural scenery." In its initial popular conception, in the works of William Gilpin, the picturesque in nature was simply that which aspired to the quality of a painting—a landscape by the likes of a Claude Lorrain or a Salvator Rosa. It seems likely that the average traveler intuitively felt the concept rather than intellectually understanding it. Accordingly, works like *The Tourist's Grammar* (1826) were produced to provide the fashionable traveler with a convenient and systematic guide to the elements of landscape that could rightly be termed picturesque. The section titled "Water" may explain many of the problems that tourists encountered on the Mississippi: "A river of which the stream is buried between two high banks, is dismal [. . .] A sluggard, silent stream, creeping heavily along altogether, has a gloom which no art can dissipate, no sunshine disperse [. . .] The curvatures of rivers ought to be small [. . .] The banks of rivers should be varied, otherwise they are dull and monotonous." The psychological element of the picturesque was equally important, especially the theory of "association" developed by Archibald

Alison. In 1790, Alison linked the "emotions" produced by a landscape to the "interesting associations" (whether historical, literary, artistic, or musical) that it evoked—associations of which the Mississippi, in the early years of the nineteenth century, seemed bereft.[5]

It may be assumed that the sublime—with its appreciation of that which was immense, awesome, and overwhelming—provided a more amenable aesthetic approach to the Mississippi. Niagara Falls, for example, provided tourists with an archetypically sublime experience; travelers were thrilled with the "psychological impact" and "pleasurable terror" created by the "the astonishing height, enormous volume, stupendous force and eternal sound of the Falls." Dickens, famously, was driven to rapture by the roaring water: "how near to my Creator I was standing [. . .] what Heavenly promise glistened in those angels' tears." The Mississippi, as ever, was another matter. Though it was undeniably big, its enormity did not fit well into any of the established definitions of the sublime. As Edmund Burke, its most significant theoretician, wrote, "Greatness of dimension, is a powerful cause of the sublime." But of the three possible extensions (length, height, and depth), "length strikes least." Unlike Niagara, the enormous length of the Mississippi had to be experienced in time as well as space. The sublime therefore proved equally problematic as a solution to the successful aesthetic appreciation of the river.[6]

All antebellum tourists would have been well versed in, or at least influenced by, these concepts. This led to a crisis of terminology. On the Mississippi, the vocabulary traditionally employed to capture a landscape was often redundant and frequently inappropriate. Many travelers were left with Ida Pfeiffer's dissatisfaction: "this is a grand thing to think of at first, but after a few days one gets tired of the perpetual monotony." And as a despairing American noted in 1830, "we have no word to distinguish this *river* from the Cam or the Isis"; American nature, he lamented, was experienced "through the medium of a translation." All travelers were forced to experience a river which had outgrown the terms at their disposal. To appreciate the environment that they encountered, therefore, they were required to rethink their existing notions of landscape aesthetics—a process that many swiftly abandoned. Tourists frequently rejected the Mississippi in favor of more traditionally picturesque rivers. "Nothing could be more beautiful," wrote Frances Trollope, "than our passage down the Hudson [. . .] as I thought of some of my friends in England, dear lovers of the picturesque."

And yet the influence of the picturesque was felt beyond the merely visual. Though bereft of cultural associations, and much that was conventionally picturesque, the Mississippi seemed nonetheless to force tourists to the ultimate conclusion of the psychology of the picturesque—as Wylie Sypher has described it, to "a way of seeing the world emotively [. . .] until the contour of a landscape becomes the image of one's consciousness." Or as Emerson had it, "Nature always wears the colors of the spirit." In precisely this way, the most significant antebellum tourist accounts transformed the Mississippi into something more than a river: it became the image of a traveler's emotive reaction to America as a whole.[7]

Margaret Fuller argued that an American "passing in a boat from one extremity of the Mississippi to another [. . .] observing every object on the shore as he passed, would yet learn nothing of universal or general value, because he has no principles, even in hope, by which to classify them." Apparently less inclined to publish lengthy travel accounts of their own country, and more familiar with cultural interpretations of the river that appeared in the Jacksonian press, Americans more frequently described their encounters with the Mississippi in magazine sketches, or journals, or brief letters home now largely lost and unpublished. This was the case for as eminent an American as Emerson. When he eventually embarked on his much-anticipated journey along the Mississippi in 1851, there was no resulting account of his travels except in private correspondence.[8]

Ephemeral, personal accounts of travel on the river, not polished for publication, still provide vivid pictures of antebellum life. Caroline Hale, for example, wrote to her sisters from New Orleans in March 1844: "the water varies from a mile to a mile and a half in width is deep and rapid, if a man falls in, [repeating an oft-told Misqissippi story] he is lost beyond doubt, the under current is so strong. When our Stevadoor fell in, no one moved to save him, he never rose again. The water is very muddy but after it has been purified it is the most delightful water to drink I ever tasted." Mr. J. Burt Jr. wrote to his wife and children in 1862, from the steamer *Mississippi:* "I wish you could have been with us as we sailed along, but as you was not, follow me in your thoughts as I describe it, not as wide as it is from the factory over to Fair Haven but as we sail along we can see hear [*sic*] and there a house built of rough boards with straw roofs [. . .] as we get farther along up the river you can see some pleasant places." Such American accounts were not, however, engaged with the imaginative transformation of the Mississippi into a more resonant symbol. It was European tourists, with plenty of fixed principles, looking to analyze, dissect, and define a strange New World, who found something far more significant in its waters than mud.[9]

In the antebellum years, the Atlantic was a busy thoroughfare. The volume of European accounts of America was such that as early as 1836, Richard Griffin published *The Domestic Manners of the Americans; or, Characteristic Sketches of the People of the United States,* a popular miscellany of travel writing that sought to *"exhibit the Americans* AS THEY ARE" through the words of "the most sensible, most extravagant, most liberal, and most prejudiced of our travellers." In his introduction, Griffin noted: "Nothing can be more contradictory than the descriptions of AMERICAN MANNERS, published abundantly of late [. . .] It is difficult, beyond conception, for those who wish to ascertain the real state of American society."[10] Europeans flocked to witness, in Frances Trollope's words, "the great experiment [. . .] now making in government" across the ocean. Their accounts achieved much popularity—European interest in America and its institutions was almost surpassed by American interest in what these visitors wrote. Though travelers from Europe had been visiting and critiquing their experiences in the New World for centuries, 1830 marked a watershed moment for Jacksonian America. The publication of Basil Hall's *Travels in North America* led, in Trollope's words, to "a moral earthquake"—only surpassed by her own travel account. Wildly popular, and highly controversial, Hall prefaced the flood of antebellum European travel accounts taking stock of America at the time when it had become markedly different from the Old World. At times critical of what he found on his travels, Hall's account seemed a monstrous betrayal of the hospitality and trust he had received in American homes. He set the corrosive tone—in his case, more perceived than actual—that characterized many of the accounts that followed. As James Kirke Paulding wrote in an unpublished description of the Mississippi, he had received his "impressions [. . .] from the race of Smellfungus Traveller of the John Bull School, who go about as it were like roaring Lions, seeking who they may devour, and who libel a nation for a bad road or a bad dinner." Or, as Eliza Steele complained in her own account of the Mississippi, part of her *Summer Journey in the West* in 1840, "My information [. . .] had been taken from foreign tourists, and [. . .] was far from truth."[11]

Within the pages of Richard Griffin's travel miscellany, for example, the Mississippi appeared in three extracts that presented the rather derogatory picture of life on the river that had already become characteristic in European accounts: Fanny Trollope's critique of her fellow steamboat passengers; Tyrone Power's description of Chapman's floating theater; and Frances Kemble's secondhand reportage of steamboat mores: "He told me sundry steamboat stories that made my blood curdle; such as, a public brush, a public comb, and a public *tooth-brush.* Also, of a gentleman who was using his own tooth-brush,—a man who was standing near him said, 'I'll trouble you for that article when you've done with it.'" In Griffin's compilation, this story appeared without the even more telling footnote that Kemble appended to its appearance in her *Journal of a Residence in America:* "this happened on board a *western* steamboat, I beg to observe, if it happened at all."[12] But such horror stories were only half the picture. As much as the Mississippi soon came to represent social and physical discomfort, it also held a different sort of promise. On its first page, Griffin's miscellany featured a woodcut of the *Belvidere,* the "large and handsome boat" which carried Frances Trollope up the Mississippi. The picture of the *Belvidere* was a copy of Auguste Hervieu's gloomy engraving for Fanny Trollope's work. The copying process, and the new context, transformed the image into an emblem: beset by perils (the threatening snag in the foreground, the choppy water) and surrounded by an all-encompassing humanity (the crowded deck and cabins), the steamboat exudes a spirit of adventure, of a journey to the unknown, of an experience very unlike anything that could be found elsewhere. Such was America, and such was the Mississippi, to its European visitors in the nineteenth century.[13]

That experience, however, was swiftly and inevitably mediated by the intervening gauze of other travel narratives. From the moment that Frances Trollope became aware of Basil Hall's infamous success ("the book was read in city, town, village, and hamlet, steam-boat and stage-coach"), the business of writing about America became self-reflexive and intertextual. Some travelers, undoubtedly, followed the advice that a New York publisher gave to Harriet Martineau: "Trollopize a bit, and so make a readable book." Frances Kemble—celebrated actress, sometime plantation bride, and memoirist—never did reach the Mississippi in her far-flung and well-documented life, yet her correspondence demonstrated the profound impact that European travel narratives had on readers, and each other. Before embarking on a steamboat journey in the East, Kemble feared "rather an awful spectacle" because of "Vigne's account of the pushing, thrusting, rushing and devouring on board a Western steamboat." Vigne himself had relied on rumor and gossip for this account of travel on the Mississippi: realizing that he had no time for a trip down the river, he "was consoled by learning that the voyage is exceedingly tedious." Writing to Anna Jameson (herself a travel writer), Kemble noted that Harriet Martineau's book on America "has been universally read," and wondered whether it "has yet reached you." Two years later, she asked her correspondent, "Have you read Charles Murray's book about America? and how do you like it?" In 1840, Kemble was keen to praise Frederick Marryat's account for his "funny stories, some of them true stories enough." And in 1841, Kemble was "extremely curious" to see Dickens's *American Notes:* "if they are unfavourable, because his popularity as a writer is immense [. . .] his opinion will influence public opinion in England, and deserves to do so."[14] So what visions of the Mississippi did these travelers evoke for their antebellum audiences? To some extent, the answer depends upon the gender of the traveler in question.

"FEMALE PHILOSOPHERS ON [. . .] A VOYAGE OF DISCOVERY"

Throughout the antebellum years, travel writing by women was often treated with the sort of disdain that Anthony Trollope demonstrated toward his mother's landmark book, *Domestic Manners of the Americans:* "that was essentially a woman's book. She saw with a woman's keen eye, and described with a woman's light but graphic pen [. . .] But she did not regard it as a part of her work to dilate on the nature and operation of those political arrangements [. . .] Such a work is fitter for a man than for a woman." Henry Tuckerman, in his 1864 critique of American travel writing, echoed many commentators dismissive of female travelers and their accounts: "there are few situations in modern life more suggestive of the ludicrous, than that of a woman 'of a certain age,' professedly visiting a country for the purpose of critically examining and reporting it and its people." But female European travelers produced some of the most significant antebellum representations of the Mississippi. Not all of those women who reached America set out with, in Ida Pfeiffer's words, "an innate passion for travelling," or traveled for the purpose of philosophical examination, but many experienced and expressed the river more profoundly than did their male counterparts, particularly in their concerns about slavery. Men and women apparently sailed on different Mississippis. In spirit, antebellum female travelers were the descendants of the intrepid bluestockings who had, by the end of the eighteenth century, implicitly established the conventional criteria for female foreign travel.[15]

A sense of liberation had been at the heart of a Grand Tour excursion to the continent—liberation from conventional mores and morals, from the confines of the home, from parental or spousal influence. When female travelers turned their eyes across the Atlantic, the New World beckoned with new freedoms and new hopes. The implications and opportunities for women's literature were also profound. Travel provided subject matter, created a matrix of female letters and journals, and allowed women an expertise on a subject that could outrank any man's. The act of traveling and seeing a country firsthand validated female accounts: travel writing "presented a rare opportunity for Georgian [and, later, Victorian] women to articulate views on the world around them and their responses to it."[16]

Written five years before the arrival of the first steamboat on the Mississippi, the earliest tourist account of the Mississippi by a European woman was Priscilla

Wakefield's significant *Excursions in North America* (1806). It is an entirely appropriate starting point, since these *Excursions* were entirely imaginary. Wakefield—author, philanthropist, and educator—reflected the fashions of travel by producing three fictional travel accounts for children in which Mrs. Middleton and her family traveled the world: first Europe, then the British Empire. Then, as Wakefield described, Mrs. Middleton's son Arthur became "inflamed" with a desire to visit the land where "the rivers, the mountains, and forests are upon a grander scale than those in Europe." Wakefield, though a female author, used a male traveler to explore America—that world of "barbarities."[17]

Henry Tuckerman described Wakefield's book as "a favourite little work among the children on both sides of the Atlantic, half a century ago. It is amusing to revert to these early sketches, which have given to many minds, now mature, their first and therefore their freshest impressions of this country." Wakefield's account is highly significant since the picture of the Mississippi that it presented can be taken as a representative composite of the European image of the river at the beginning of the nineteenth century. For information and inspiration, Wakefield informed her readers, she had chiefly used the works of "Jefferson, Weld, Rochefoucault, Bartram, Michaux, Carver, Mackenzie and Hearn." Arthur's brief trip on the Mississippi in this formative work may go some way to explain the disappointments of so many later travelers on the river: "Many of the [New Orleans] inhabitants being ill of a pestilential fever, we decamped in haste, and having hired a boat, proceeded along the Mississippi to Manchac. During our row, we had leisure to admire this noble stream, which deserves the title of the Great Father of Rivers, that being the meaning of the word Mississippi. Every object that belongs to it bears the stamp of sublime grandeur. The banks rise high one above another, and are clothed with majestic trees." Seated comfortably in Tottenham, Wakefield was able to transform the Mississippi into a Grand Tour *topos*. The river became a "noble stream" suitable for boating excursions, and touched with a "sublime grandeur" that slotted the river into an established, Old World aesthetic mold. Later travelers to the river sought in vain for such a recognizable idyll.[18]

When steam eventually opened the Mississippi to tourism, a triumvirate of its earliest female travelers produced accounts of their individual struggles with the river that were miniatures of the larger cultural processes at work. Margaret Hall, Frances Trollope, and Harriet Martineau traveled in the late 1820s and early 1830s and experienced the infancy of the golden age of Mississippi steamboating. Trollope and Martineau were responsible for some of the most influential travel narratives of the antebellum years. Margaret Hall, on the other hand, was known in her day only as Mrs. Basil Hall, companion to her husband on his infamous journey. Her representations of the river went unpublished until 1931. As such, they were not subject to the strict editing that publication demanded. They form the lost side of a triangle linking all three women's narratives at this crucial moment in time and remain a fresh and frank record of her reactions, influenced throughout by the tastes and prejudices of the Old World. In many ways, her account of her struggles with the river may have been the most representative.

As a girl, Margaret Hall had traveled extensively in Europe. This, as Una Pope-Hennessey concluded, irrevocably set "the standard of life abroad" for the young tourist. She had been steeped in the aesthetic concepts that dominated travel in the early nineteenth century. As Margaret traveled through the New World in 1827 and 1828, she wrote home to her sister, Jane. In this correspondence her experiences found full expression. In Grand Tour style, Margaret was determined to find aspects of American culture and landscape to appreciate—however difficult, given her standards, that process was. The Hudson River and its valley was one of the rare locations that could boast the visual picturesque and an associative value bestowed on it by the works of Washington Irving and the art of the Hudson River school. When Margaret traveled in the region, she accordingly described it as "classic ground." The American Academy of Fine Arts in New York fared less well: "I suppose there was never anything seen in the way of arts less fine, such daubs to be sure [. . .] they think these vile things beautiful." The Mississippi, all along its great length, was largely bereft of associations. Margaret clung to the fact that Natchez was "the scene of a novel lately published by Chateaubriand [*Les Natchez,* 1827]." But though it may be expected that Margaret would have despised the Mississippi, this was not the whole case. Perhaps this was a reaction to the Americans who had warned her that a journey upriver would be "extremely monotonous": here was another opportunity for Margaret to prove the locals deficient in the rudiments of taste.[19]

When Margaret first saw the Mississippi, she could not match Basil's excitement: "[Basil] ran also, before returning to the house, to take a look at the Mississippi [. . .] I deferred my first visit to it till yesterday." When finally confronted with the river, Margaret's tourist training in the picturesque explicitly revealed itself. She assented that "its magnificence shows its claim to" the title of Father of Waters; "each successive view increased my veneration." She described an associated "feeling of awe" and even went as far as comparing the experience of gazing on the Mississippi to viewing that icon of the American sublime, Niagara. Taking to the river itself, the typical hardships of steamboat life were soon apparent: "the heat [. . .] the mosquitoes [. . .] the engine." But initially they proved insuf-

ficient to daunt her attempts to appreciate the landscape: "the temptation to remain on deck for the purpose of seeing the scenery on both sides of the river was
so great that we wore ourselves out by exposure to the burning sun." The Mississippi's flora and fauna, she felt, were often "of the most beautiful description."

Notably absent, however, was any imaginative elevation of this landscape.
Margaret's Mississippi remained simply a big river, not a greater symbol of something unique to, and expressive of, America. Her unhappy realization that "the
nice fine fields are the result of slave labour" was, perhaps, more connected to
her concern that it robbed the viewer of the picturesque "enjoyment in seeing
them," than it was evidence of abolitionism. Hall's time on the river, inexorably
bound by tastes suitable to another time and place, was ultimately fruitless, as
was any attempt that took such criteria as the sine qua non of travel. When Margaret eventually reached the comparatively picturesque Ohio, the relief she felt
is still palpable in the immediacy of her correspondence. The Ohio was "pretty"
and held "an air of great cheerfulness." Having left the Mississippi behind, she
could at last let the mask of the cultured, picturesque tourist slip, and vent her
real feelings about the river: "it was so flat and watery and swampy."[20]

Since Margaret's correspondence remained unpublished in its day, she was
spared the venom directed at her sister travelers. When an anonymous resident
of Baltimore burlesqued Frederick Marryat as "Captain Marry-it," Trollope and
Martineau were the recipients of much of his invective: "Miss *Martin-awe* was
too deaf to hear half the length of her nose—Mrs. Trollope could'nt see the
length of her pen—and the t'others wer either bribed by the hope of Yankee fa-
vour, or too partial to tell half what they seen [. . .] oh! Harriet Harriet, you false
deceptuous wench! [. . .] oh! for shame! your face, Mrs. Trollope!" Neither Frances Trollope nor Harriet Martineau was a typical tourist. Their time in America
contained very different personal investments. Margaret Hall judged America
according to her Old World standards and regarded American society with disdain; prejudice and assumption left her little room for interest in the merits or
failings of Jacksonian democracy. Trollope and Martineau were interested in
precisely that, and their Mississippi experiences reached a level that Hall's could
not. Both were intimately concerned with democracy and slavery, and their visions of the river took on the color of their conclusions. To borrow Andrew Dix's
phrase, their separate Mississippis transcended reality and entered the realm of
"metaphysical geography."[21]

A useful way into their contrasting visions of the river can be found in another brief description of the Mississippi by the prolific Frances Kemble. In the
preface to her *Journal of a Residence in America* (1835), Kemble apologized for

the limited scope of her travels: "[I] have had no opportunity of seeing two large portions of the population of this country,—the enterprising explorers of the late wildernesses on the shores of the Mississippi,—and the black race of the slave states [. . .] the one, a source of energy and growing strength, the other, of disease and decay in this vast political body." Writing in the abstract, Kemble imagined the Mississippi as both a channel of optimistic "energy" and the artery of slavery, "disease and decay"—one a symbol of change, transformation, and liberation, the other a symbol of stagnation, regression, and bondage. Trollope and Martineau took their places on different sides of this symbolic divide.[22]

Frances Trollope's expedition to the New World, contemporary with Jackson's first election victory, was beset by death, family difficulties, and financial worry. America was a beacon of hope. Fanny, accompanied by son Henry, daughters Cecilia and Emily, and exiled radical artist Auguste Hervieu, set sail from London in November 1827 (Anthony was left in England). The party was ultimately bound for a Utopian community led by famous abolitionist Frances Wright, and Fanny's expectations were high: "I expect to be very happy, and very free from care at Nashoba." Nashoba was dedicated to educating slaves as a precursor to emancipation, and Fanny traveled to the Mississippi, like many of the later European female travelers to the river, as a putative abolitionist. "I left England with feelings so strongly opposed to slavery," she wrote, "that it was not without pain I witnessed its effects around me." Arriving at the mouth of the Mississippi on Christmas Day, things seemed less auspicious, and grand dreams of emancipation soon dissipated. As Stephen Fender expressed it, at the liminal space marked by the imposing borderline of sea-blue and river-brown, it appeared that "Mrs Trollope came in through [America's] cloaca." Immediately the landscape seemed "utterly desolate." The ominous "murky stream" intruded upon her imagination. Dante, she felt, "might have drawn images of another Bolgia from its horrors." It seemed that she had crossed the Atlantic to find not the New World, but the underworld, a Mississippi purgatory: a new Styx, fatal to boats and humans alike, marked only by the mast of "a vessel long since wrecked [. . .] a dismal witness of the destruction that has been, and a brooding prophet of that which is to come."[23]

The boat steamed onward; apocalyptic visions compounded. Toppled trees descended the river, "roots mocking the heavens [. . .] like the fragment of a world in ruins"—or, perhaps, a vivid symbol of the social world turned upside down which Fanny would soon experience firsthand on a Mississippi steamboat. One vivid moment of identification stood out. At New Orleans, Fanny observed that the river was swollen and noted with distinct relish: "she was looking so mighty, and so unsubdued all the time, that I could not help fancying [. . .] farewell to New Orleans." In her fantasy of destructive power, the river became feminized. The effect was all too brief. Nothing prepared her for the difficulties of life on board a steamboat on the Mississippi. Fanny, exasperated by the conditions and company in which she found herself, warned unwary travelers who planned a journey on the river: "Let no one who wishes to receive agreeable impressions of American manners, commence their travels in a Mississippi steam boat; for myself, it is with all sincerity I declare, that I would infinitely prefer sharing the apartment of a party of well conditioned pigs."[24]

So much for Fanny Kemble's vision of a regenerative river. For Trollope, though bound for Frances Wright's radical Utopian community, America was riddled with the egalitarian disease that saw her "being introduced in form to a milliner." The Mississippi steamboat and the river itself were all-too-fitting symbols of this topsy-turvy society. There was no escape from either the "heavy horror" of the unceasingly level landscape or the "loathsome" leveled company of the steamboat. The world outside the cabin provided no relief. Rather than slavery, it was the "wretched inhabitants" visible on the banks of the Mississippi that caused Fanny the greatest despair. In Kemble's mind (and, of course, in the American popular imagination), backwoodsmen represented "a source of energy and growing strength" and a distinctive national type. For Trollope, they were the barely animated embodiment of the degeneracy that permeated the Mississippi. If the river seemed to corrupt those who traveled on board a steamboat— the incessant spitting, the appalling manners, the conversation—then those who lived by its "unwholesome banks" were, Fanny suggested, reduced to something not quite human. Living with "the assurance of early death," they appeared to be "squalid [. . .] unhappy beings" whose skin took on "a blueish white [. . .] ghastly hue." She had never "witnessed human nature reduced so low." Eventually, the Trollope party reached Memphis. Their journey to Nashoba was almost at an end. Worse disappointments were to follow. Ideologically, Fanny never recovered from the effects of her Mississippi journey. It had been a trial by fire that burned away her democratic spirit and, if not her abolitionism entirely, then at least her concern for practical emancipation. The river irreparably informed all of her American experiences to come.[25]

Harriet Martineau's radicalism was made of stronger stuff; the river was just as vital in her American journey. Martineau traveled to the New World in propitious circumstances: she toured as a financially independent woman and was welcomed as a fêted literary figure—meeting, among many other luminaries, Andrew Jackson himself. She arrived in New York on September 19, 1834, elated by "the early pleasures of foreign travel." New York bore "an air of gaiety" and felt akin to "a holiday dance." This renowned "little deaf woman at Norwich," as Lord Brougham had described her, had struggled with her health from a young age, but undaunted, ear trumpet in hand, she set out to experience America. This was not always easy, as even those who desired her acquaintance could feel, as the ubiquitous Fanny Kemble did, that her deafness was "some drawback to the pleasure of conversing with her": "as a man observed to me last night, 'One feels so like a fool, saying, "How do you do?" through a speaking-trumpet in the middle of a drawing-room.'" Martineau was a fellow traveler on what Joseph Reed has described as the "Unitarian-Transcendentalist-Abolitionist-Women's Rights Axis," and her radicalism garnered almost as much censure as Fanny Trollope's conservatism. Kemble, who "liked her very much indeed," did so only "in spite of her radicalism." Indeed, Martineau's journey to America was undertaken, in part, as a last-minute alternative to the Grand Tour of Europe. Her potent criticisms of despotism, serfdom, and injustice had made her unwelcome on the Continent. The abolitionist speech that she delivered at a Ladies' Anti-Slavery Society meeting had the same effect in America. Rather than recoiling from the democratic experiment in disgust like Trollope, Martineau found the New World lacking in the fulfilment of its egalitarian principles—the promise of which, remarkably, she was still able to locate in the waters of the Mississippi.[26]

Martineau knowingly brought an ambiguous pair of mythological resonances to bear on the river. In *Retrospect of Western Travel* (1838) she prefaced the chapter devoted to her experiences on the steamboat *Henry Clay* with two conflicting quotations, playing with already established dichotomies. The first was taken from an 1815 review of Lewis and Clark's *American Travels* in the *Quarterly Review*. In its original context, it referred to the "tales" that were told to "Hennepin and to Marquette, when they explored the Mississippi." In its new setting, it presented an abstracted Trollopian riverscape that blended both Christian and classical imagery: "That it was full of monsters who devoured canoes as well as men; that the devil stopped its passage, and sunk all those who ventured to approach the place where he stood; and that the river itself at last was swallowed up in the bottomless gulf of a tremendous whirlpool." But to counter this impression of a Mississippi journey that was equal parts pagan ordeal and New World *Odyssey,* she followed it with a passage from Virgil's ninth eclogue, a vision of a bucolic paradise, a fertile, bountiful, benevolent river:

> Hic ver purpureum: varios hic flumina circum
> Fundit humus flores: hic candida populus antro
> Immilet, et lentae texunt umbracula vites.

As Joseph Warton translated the passage in 1778:

> Here purple spring her gifts profusely pours,
> And paints the river-banks with balmy flow'rs;
> Here, o'er the grotto the pale poplar weaves
> With blushing vines a canopy of leaves.

Damnation or salvation: where exactly, Martineau teased the reader, would her Mississippi lead? She answered that question in two distinct ways. Her first publication on her American travels, *Society in America* (1837), synthesized her observations on the United States to compare the new nation—socially, economically, politically—"with the principles on which it is professedly founded." Her second work on America, *Retrospect of Western Travel,* was a conventional travel account—"more of my personal narrative, and of the lighter characteristics of men"—chronologically detailing Martineau's experiences to meet the demands of an expectant public. Both works were open to the symbolic meanings of the Mississippi.[27]

The Mississippi of *Society in America* was subsumed within a discussion of the American economy. Martineau approached her subject with caution: "the traveller from the Old World to the New," she warned, "is apt to lose himself in reflection when he should be observing" because the "old experience is all reversed." America was a land where it was possible "to watch the process of world-making" in both its "natural" and "conventional" manifestations. For Martineau, the Mississippi was a resonant symbol of both. To express its power as a "natural" world-maker, she was able to transform the traditionally lamented muddiness of the Mississippi into proof of its creative essence. It was "a sort of scum on the waters [which] betokened the birth-place of new land." In a holistic vision, she traced the passage of water, mud, and seeds, and charted the growth of both the river's deposits and the roots which bound them together into ever-increasing islands: "this was seeing world-making." What may have been unpicturesque and unsublime could nonetheless represent something far more astonishing than either: this was the New World, and everything, including aesthetics, was "all reversed."

This was equally apparent in Martineau's description of the "progress of conventional life." On board the steamboat *Henry Clay,* witnessing the river's constant flux and growth, she could turn to observe "every stage of [societal] advancement" on its banks: "from the clearing in the woods" to ever-progressing human settlements. Martineau went beyond Kemble's image of "energy and growing strength" to a direct opposition of Trollope's dismal, degenerative river.

The Mississippi, she felt, had to be seen with regard to the timetable of world-making. The freshly formed islands "may reveal no beauty to the painter"; the inhabitants on the river's banks were not a pleasing sight. Yet "to the eye of one who loves to watch the process of world-making, it is full of delight." For Martineau, therefore, the Mississippi was the newest and most fertile of the New World, still in flux, and still cause for optimism.[28]

Her reactions in *Retrospect of Western Travel*—like the narrative itself—at first appear less dramatic and more akin to the conventions of the American travel genre. She made reference to the food, her fellow passengers, the Kentuckians on deck, the dangers of steamboat travel—the remarkable and unremarkable details that comprised any traveler's steamboating experience. But halfway through the journey, "lost among islands in a waste of waters," Martineau described the way that the Mississippi "began to bear upon our imaginations." It was no Trollopian "heavy horror"; nor, perhaps surprisingly, was it a growing identification of the river with slavery. Rather, it was an awareness of the river and the powers of world-making described in *Society in America*—a new version of the picturesque communion with the landscape. Investing the gaze of the steamboat traveler with almost godlike powers, she felt "it was like being sent back to the days of creation." But it was also something more personal. Martineau looked down on the river to see what she described—playing with a familiar vocabulary—as the "picturesque" flatboats "at the mercy of the floods." Unexpectedly, she found the river not simply "mighty" and a symbol of "grandeur"; she was also able to discern its "beauty." The Mississippi provided her with a release from the social claustrophobia of the steamboat cabin. Alone on the gallery of the *Henry Clay*, pointedly shunning the female company of the cabin (those "working collars, netting purses, or doing nothing [. . .] dancing or talking"), she communed with the "very wild" river.[29]

What Martineau found in her solitude was a striking vision of womanhood, and of America, that affected her sufficiently to include it in both works. It was the image of "a woman in a canoe, paddling up against the stream." The two solitary figures—Martineau on her gallery, the nameless pioneer "going on a visit" in her canoe—faced each other across the Mississippi. Martineau was mesmerized by this resonant symbol—of struggle, of freedom, of transformation. Though she "could hardly have conceived of a solitude so intense as this appeared," something in her thrilled at the thought of "being alone on that rushing sea of waters." Survival in such a world, she concluded, would be dependent on "the spirit growing into harmony with the scene,—wild and solemn as the objects around it." Martineau's Mississippi, then, led to neither a purgatory nor a traditional picturesque paradise. Rather, it was a liberating, "wild and solemn" frontier—a perfect symbol of her American experience—that still offered the promise of the new.[30]

The adventures of Mrs. Hall, Mrs. Trollope, and Miss Martineau were para-digmatic, but the female travelers who came to the river in the post-Jacksonian years still reacted to the Mississippi in manifold interesting ways. Jenny Lind, for example, was "full of admiration with regard to the river," according to a fel-low traveler during her Barnum-sponsored tour in 1851, who "heartily enjoyed the wonder she exhibited over its striking peculiarities." Frederika Bremer, the popular novelist and fellow Swede traveling independently in the New World at the same time, became a firm friend of the songstress when their paths crossed in Cuba. Bremer was dogged by illness and depression, but her arrival at the river was a striking turning point: "And now I stood serene and vigorous by the Mis-sissippi, with the Great West open before me, with a rich future, and the whole world bright!" This millennial brightness—"the inner light in my soul conversed with the outward light"—illuminated Bremer's Mississippi.[31]

Bremer's representation of the cultural landscape through which she traveled introduced a new register of mythic symbols. Christianity featured prominently (her steamboat was a Noah's Ark); so did ancient Greek imagery—the Missis-sippi was a landscape for "the Titans of primeval nature." But she also brought to the river a range of Scandinavian resonances: "the achievements of Thor and Starkodder are renewed in those of the giants of the giant-river and the states of the Mississippi." The Mississippi Valley became a "new Jothunhem," the tradi-tional homeland of the frost and rock giants. This was a very different image of regeneration, one which figured the Mississippi as the river Iving—the border between the land of the giants and Asgard, the home of the warrior gods. For Bremer, "the joys of Valhalla" itself could be achieved in "the vine-crowned is-lands of the Mississippi."[32]

The issue that most animated female European travelers on the Mississippi, however, was slavery. Both abolitionists and those travelers supportive of the slave-holding South reacted to the artery of slavery in no consistent fashion. Reaching New Orleans, confronted by the realities of southern life, Bremer was forced to exclaim: "Mississippi, thou great Noah's flood, now do I know thy history to the end!" For Bremer, slavery was an unhappy reversal of the radiant promise of her Upper Mississippi, a dark rainbow that augured ill. But she found "con-solation and [. . .] hope" in the "conscience of the South." Barbara Bodichon—the model for George Eliot's *Romola*—found less to be positive about on her honeymoon. Engaging her fellow passengers in conversation about issues of race and slavery, she was forced to conclude that "amongst these people [. . .] every standard of right and wrong is lost." But rather than reading slavery into the river, the Mississippi, as it had for Martineau before her, provided a diverting escape from such company. Half of Bodichon's conception of the river was clearly connected to its social and political life—the half that she found "ugly and queer." The other half, the river divorced from its immediate realities, elicited a "strange [. . .] new phase of beauty" that left her, like Martineau, quite "bewitched." Ida Pfeiffer, on the other hand, was none too susceptible to such beauties. She echoed Mrs. Hall's earlier judgment. Her time on the river would have been "far pleasanter" if "one did not remember that the greater part of its population [. . .] are in bondage."[33]

Not all women travelers were sympathetic to the abolitionist cause. Mother and daughter travelers Lady Emmeline and Victoria Stuart Wortley were gratified with both the polite comfort that they found in the slaveholding world, and the sentimentalized landscape of the plantation that Ida Pfeiffer had described: "the neat houses of the planters, the sugar-mills with their lofty chimneys, the pretty-looking cottages of the slaves." Both Stuart Wortleys, unburdened by worries surrounding the slavery question, were "quite delighted" with the Mississippi. The banks of the river, Emmeline felt, were "busy" with the "hum of life"; "rising" settlements were "the germs [. . .] of future mighty cities." Amelia Murray, on the other hand, devoted little space to the river in her travels. She was keen to point out that the Mississippi was "ugly and muddy." This, though, was "the fault of the Missouri." That river, Murray argued, tacitly revealing her own prejudices, "darkens and spoils the complexion of the Mississippi after their union." Though Murray was deeply attached to the proslavery cause, for her the Mississippi was too close to miscegenation.[34]

In spite of the positive associations that so many women travelers had felt on the river, and regardless of the telling symbolic meanings they had found during their journeys on its waters, the image of the Mississippi at the end of the antebellum period could still seem predominantly unchanged from the hearsay of Kemble or the invective of Trollope. The well-traveled Isabella Lucy Bird, as late as 1859, wrote dismissively: "All intelligent readers are familiar with the [. . .] lawlessness of the Mississippi river, and the recklessness of human life displayed on the numerous steamers which traverse its mighty waters; it is not necessary to enlarge on such things as these." Train travel, too, meant that the river could be avoided or simply penciled into an itinerary. The railroad carried Isabella Trotter from Cincinnati to St Louis. A brief visit to the river assured her it was "dingy, muddy, and melancholy [. . .] tame and monotonous." That was enough for her. The river, an experience rather than an attraction, was not amenable to day-trippers. But one last female traveler remained, encountering the river in the final weeks before its closure for war, to give expression to a feeling discernible, but not explicit, in previous accounts. Emilie Marguerite Cowell was the last European woman to record her antebellum experiences on the Mississippi. Accompanying her husband—popular music-hall entertainer Sam Cowell—she set out for America in 1860. Her personal journal was most concerned with pressing financial worries and concerns for her husband's health. Nevertheless, the rivers of the West (which her husband had known as a child) captured her imagination. The last of the female commentators to embark on the antebellum river finally did away with the patriarch and rechristened the Mississippi as "the muddy Mother of rivers."[35]

"SCHOOLBOY DREAMS"

As it did for Priscilla Wakefield's fictional hero Arthur Middleton, boyish enthusiasm for adventure seems to have propelled many unwitting European men toward the Mississippi in the antebellum years. The river was the setting for a great deal of well-publicized exploration in the early nineteenth century, which may well have contributed to this feeling. A host of source hunters, following in the footsteps of Jonathan Carver and Zebulon Pike, headed for the Upper Mississippi. Pike was trailed by Lewis Cass in 1820, Giacomo Beltrami in 1823, Henry Rowe Schoolcraft in 1832, and, finally, cartographer Jean Nicolas Nicollet in 1836. Though Schoolcraft claimed the glory of the discovery of the source at Lake Itasca, and thereafter published voluminously, contradictory claims to the location of the "true" source continued almost to the twentieth century.

The aura of adventure was only compounded by a definitive early travel account which—despite professions of honesty—was as involved with the Mississippi of the imagination as Wakefield's had been. Then again, Thomas Ashe never quite claimed to tell the whole truth: "I write from the heart, from the impulse of the impressions made by real events." Since its publication, Ashe's *Travels in America* (1808) has resisted either absolute verification or complete debunking. This controversy compounded the mixture of romantic sensibility and excitement in his narrative. A sentimental traveler, he apparently sought out picturesque views and mortal danger in equal proportion. When confronted with "an object of inexpressible sublimity [. . .] tears gushed from my eyes." For Ashe, the Ohio was the "most beautiful river in the universe." The Mississippi, as ever, was a different matter—especially since it is debatable that he ever reached it. Ashe pictured the river as a threatening environment "where death attacked man in a variety of new and alarming shapes [. . .] where fate uniformly demands nine out of ten of every visitant." His guide, Cuff, "a mestee, of the Bandan nation," increased the drama by relating stories. He told Ashe "of accidents happening on the waters; of murders committed; robberies perpetrated; of whirlpools, cataracts, and rapid falls, &c. &c." The river took on a "dismal" quality. The waters seemed as "black as Erebus"—the classical embodiment of primeval darkness, and supposedly the father of Charon, the ferry-man on the river Styx. It was "pregnant with sufferings and dangers." It lacked the "profusion of local beauties" that made the Ohio so delightful; it was, for Ashe, "unmixed sublimity" that became "adverse to satisfaction and enjoyment."[36]

Ashe—actually or fictionally—reached the infamous Cave-in-Rock. Situated on the lower Ohio, the cavern was reputed to have served as "the headquarters of the criminals who [. . .] preyed upon primitive commerce between Pittsburgh and the Lower Mississippi" in the latter half of the eighteenth century. In the presteamboat era of the nineteenth century, the cave—largely deserted by its notorious inhabitants—was a popular destination for curious tourists. Ashe was no exception. He used the cave to transform his travel narrative into the adventure story that he (and his readers) so obviously craved: "I resolved to explore it, though it bore the reputation of being the residence of a band of robbers who for many years have infested the river." At the far end of the cave, his party discovered "putrid bodies" where, according to Ashe "they are frequently disturbed to gratify the curiosity of the river navigator." The tension was further increased by his resolve to explore the infamous upper cave. In reality, the upper cave was—and remains—"four feet wide and ten feet high." Ashe transformed it into a palatial vault, a mysterious, fabulous cavern which guarded its secrets well. The only thing missing from his narrative was an encounter with the river pirates themselves.[37]

Accusations of fictionality were leveled at Ashe's *Travels* soon after publication. In 1810, Christian Schultz labelled the work "a *compilation*" full of "*mistakes, misrepresentations* and *fictions.*" He cited Ashe's "talents, in giving a highly coloured picture, and magnifying the dangers and horrors of his situation." But as Otto Rothert noted, the "general condemnation gave the [. . .] book a wide circulation." If the spirit of exploration and adventure did color male tourists' expectations of the river, and a number of their accounts would suggest that it did, they would have been obliged to quickly reassess those preconceptions upon arrival. In the golden age of steamboating, the river still offered danger, but no longer the danger of the frontier. Instead, there was the danger of high-pressure engines, the discomforts of steamboat society, the threat of riverboat gamblers and confidence men.[38]

The *Edinburgh Review* noted in 1843, "It is the nature of an Englishman to think every thing ridiculous which contrasts with what he has been used to." They judged the Mississippi accordingly. Captain Marry-it, the parodic Frederick Marryat, described the manner in which European literary celebrities were lauded in the New World: "As all my yarns have been shipped to that "*New World*," the nations in course consider me as they do all foreigners that spin a single line, a great creatur—they'll hail me [. . .] I'll be promoted to their best society." Many of the European men who published accounts of the antebellum Mississippi were celebrities. As such, their accounts of the river were highly influential. They were also, some felt, compromised. Though not famous herself, Barbara Bodichon and her husband—in true, transformative Mississippi style—were continually mistaken for the ex-president of Mexico and his wife on their honeymoon. She found the lesson salutary: "Now we began [. . .] to pity from our very souls all the [. . .] Dickens [. . .] and Thackerays. It seems to me it is impossible to see anything in America if you are a distinguished person—all the ways of seeing are blocked up with eyes looking at you." The *Edinburgh Review* echoed this. Such men, it believed, could only see "their own importance reflected in the faces of the gaping crowd."[39]

Basil Hall, Frederick Marryat, Charles Dickens, and William Makepeace Thackeray were indeed literary celebrities. Dickens and Thackeray were hugely popular and traveled around America on lecture tours. Hall and Marryat had a cachet of their own. As the biographical preface to an 1895 collection of Hall's work described, "By those who were boys in the second quarter of the present century, [he] is remembered as one of the most popular writers of his time." Marryat also secured popularity as an adventure novelist (usually writing sea stories). All four writers disliked the Mississippi—often intensely. Save for Dickens, slavery played apparently little role in their disgust. As Marry-it summarized: "I'd rather weather Cape Horn in a grog can, than sail up one of these Yankee creeks in their leaky steam skows."[40]

Hall and Marryat were both captains in the Royal Navy, which might suggest some kind of affinity with the watery environment of the Mississippi. In Hall's case, this was not entirely false. Basil's eager rush "to catch a sight of the Mississippi" was, perhaps, the most vivid description of the childish excitement that many felt at their first vision of the river. The river was "the object I had so long wished to behold": "[I] felt myself amply repaid [. . .] for all the trouble I had experienced in coming so far." Reality soon intruded. He "was disappointed at its width." The "colour of the water," too, "was a dirty, muddy, reddish sort of white." Before leaving the rigging he had scrambled into to get a better view, Basil began to feel that he "had done injustice to the river."[41]

On entering the Ohio, Hall was happy, just like his wife, to note that it was "beyond all comparison more beautiful than that of the Mississippi," which was "generally low, marshy [. . .] swampy." Put plainly, "it was very uninteresting." Only in comparison with the Missouri—"dirty" and "contaminating"—did the Mississippi become "beautiful." Steam travel itself was an "association of head-rending annoyances." What Hall did find of particular interest—"finely contrasted with all this wretchedness"—was the "foliage" and "enormous stems of the trees in the forests." Though the landscape brought some interest to his Mississippi voyage, Hall had reservations about this aspect of the river, too. It was a product of the variable climate, and a pervasive "air of rankness" brought with it associations of pestilence, corruption, and degeneration. Generous to the end, Hall found this "striking and curious"—if "not so agreeable."[42]

Marryat was not inclined to be generous. The captain "could only regret that life was so short, and the Mississippi so long." Utterly disdainful of America and its institutions (save, perhaps, slavery) during his travels in the late 1830s, Marryat found the river to be a powerfully affecting symbol for his disgust. Fittingly, a traveler seeking to discredit Harriet Martineau's observations had an absolutely contrary reaction to the river. Not that Marryat was entirely blind to its appeal. The Upper Mississippi, he felt, was a "beautiful clear blue stream, intersected with verdant islands [. . .] very different in appearance from the Lower Mississippi." Indeed, as the landscape became "more level and flat," so did Marryat. Log houses looked like "dog-kennels." Hall's diverting flora became "creeping plants [. . .] with the apparent force of the boa-constrictor." Marryat feared that "most of them are poisonous," and understood that they carried "sudden death" in their "juices." The reasons for his revulsion on these "wild and filthy waters" were expressed as a conflation of morbid emotions. As he looked down on the river, Marryat reflected: "how uncertain is travelling in this region of high-pressure, and disregard of social rights [. . .] I cannot help feeling a disgust at the idea of perishing in such a vile sewer, to be buried in mud, and perhaps to be rooted out again by some pig-nosed alligator." He was "Right glad" to reach the "purer waters" of the Ohio. To put it simply: "I hate the Mississippi."[43]

Neither Dickens nor Thackeray found much to disagree with in Marryat's dismissal, though they reached that conclusion for different reasons, personal and political. Charles Dickens was intimately concerned with the mythical, imaginative role that the Thames, itself often picturesquely unappealing, had to play in the life of his characters. But faced with the Mississippi, he could not (at least in situ) tap into its imaginative power. For Dickens (using Marryat's words), the Mississippi was an arena where "no one can be very imaginative [. . .] you are teazed and phlebotomized out of all poetry." Traveling from Cincinnati to St. Louis in 1842, Dickens spent relatively little time on the Mississippi itself. It was enough for him to conclude that the Mississippi was a "foul stream." Unlike Trollope, whose Mississippi experiences swiftly destroyed her fragile dreams of America, Dickens reached the river having already suffered many disappointments in the New World. As such, the Mississippi became the focus and the prime example of his frustrations with both democracy and slavery. His fellow passengers seemed "oppressed by [. . .] tremendous concealments." Memories of the "funeral feasts"—the sullen steamboat mealtimes—"will be a waking nightmare to me all my life." The "magnetism of dulness" was compounded by his arrival at Cairo, where the river rolled along "wearily and slowly as the time itself." What aggrieved Dickens most about this "breeding-place of fever, ague and death" was its false promise. The Cairo City and Canal Company, established in 1837 by Darius B. Holbrook, was one of many Mississippi investment "bubbles" that burst "to many people's ruin." Though writing of financial devastation, it was the bankruptcy of his own dreams that Dickens railed against. Disappointment was a dominant trope in *American Notes,* and the Mississippi was its grossest symbol.[44]

His description of the "slimy monster" outstripped even Marryat's. Dickens compounded horror upon horror in an effort to re-create the river experience: "liquid mud [. . .] frothy current choked and obstructed [. . .] lazy foam [. . .] mud and slime on everything." Images of dismemberment—unidentifiable "monstrous bodies" and "matted hair"—accompanied hellish creatures of the night: "giant leeches [. . .] wounded snakes [. . .] frogs." Of these four literary Englishmen, Dickens's sense of disgust was the most extreme. Though not explicitly addressing slavery during his time on the Mississippi, in his final dismissal of the river Dickens alluded to the "ugly freight" that he could see it "dragging off towards New Orleans." At last, the implicit reason behind Dickens's hatred for the river became clear. He was the only one of these literary compatriots to react negatively to the Mississippi as the artery of slavery.[45]

Writing from New Orleans in 1856, with a hand still trembling from the vibrations of the rickety steamboat *Thomas Small,* Thackeray concluded that Marryat was a "vulgar dog." Nevertheless, his novels kept Thackeray "in amusement through Alabama & Mississippi too." Little else did. As he lamented, the "dreariness [. . .] *everywhere,* almost consumes me." Thackeray's experience of the

"Mrs. Sippy," as he re-Christened "the great dreary melancholy stream" to his daughters, encapsulated the weariness that was palpable in his letters. An abiding sense of a "grey-headed twilighty kind of life" pervaded his correspondence. Even to "sit down and describe scenery to [. . .] friends" seemed, to Thackeray, "trifling and hypocritical." He conceded that traveling in America would be different for "a man desirous for information"—"I ain't." What he was concerned with, however, was "ignoble dollar-hunting"—an overriding concern to provide for his daughters before his death. Little wonder that the Mississippi seemed "dreary & funereal."

Not that Thackeray was without an appreciation of landscapes—or, indeed, rivers. The Nile gave him the "keenest pleasure" with its "lonely beauty"; the Rhone was "generous" and "charmed me"; the Gunga of his childhood was "friendly & beautiful." The Mississippi, however, "gives me pain." It exuded a "great fierce strong impetuous ugliness." As for the steamboat passengers, he pictured a mannerless, Trollopian crowd in vivid detail: "I lay down my book in the boat a man walks up takes the book spits reads lays down the book spits again *at* me and rises. And to see the pocket handkerchiefs! I mean these 🔺 🔺 and the knives down the throats." Though this "rabble [. . .] turns my 🔺 gorge," it also worked to "warm up my sluggish old blood." The passenger list of the *Thomas Small*—a true Vanity Fair that resembled the passenger list of Herman Melville's imaginary steamboat *Fidèle*—was diverse even for the Mississippi: "a poor Giantess [. . .] the whiskered lady [. . .] a choctaw chief a mad woman screaming & calling to people from her stateroom a gentleman from the deck with delirium tremens." Thackeray admitted, "once [. . .] I could have made some fun out of these people." Now, however, "there are very few laughs left in me." Though miserable on the river, Thackeray believed that the settlements he passed, Cairo included, would inevitably grow and develop; but he did not want to "live in a country at this stage in its political existence." Rather, he succinctly and passionately expressed the lament of many Englishmen on the antebellum Mississippi: "O Lord, how I wish I was in the Gray's Inn Coffee House!"[46]

To truly appreciate the Mississippi, male European travelers needed to see with different eyes. A professional or trained gaze was more likely to view the Mississippi sympathetically—it could make the river come alive in unexpected ways. Richard Burton, who knew a thing or two about the world's rivers, found the Mississippi "glorious." Rather than a moment of revelatory self-actualization (like Martineau or Bremer), or morbid, disappointed introspection (à la Marryat, Thackeray, or Dickens), the Mississippi provided the sympathetic male traveler with an arena for his passions, a world still ripe for exploration and discovery. Two such travelers were Maximilian, Prinz von Wied-Neuwied, amateur naturalist and pioneer anthropologist, who traveled up the Mississippi and the Missouri to study and record Native tribes; and Charles Lyell, president of the Geological Society of London, who visited the river throughout the 1840s. Alexander Mackay, on the other hand, viewed the river in a distinctly non-European fashion. Though he had often traveled to the river in his "schoolboy dreams," it was not the Mississippi itself, but what it promised, that captured his imagination.[47]

Lyell and Maximilian both witnessed the Mississippi through the filter of a passion. Journeying in the early 1830s, the enthusiastic royal naturalist scrutinized the same banks from which Dickens and Marryat recoiled—and found a world of beauty. In an imposing imperial folio, Maximilian narrated his journey upriver from Cairo to St. Louis through reference to the flora and fauna that he passed. Every plant, flower, bush, shrub, and tree was a crucial part of the "romantic forest scenes" that met his gaze as he descended the river. There was nothing malignant in the "wilderness of fallen trees"—just untold natural riches. While the river itself was described respectfully—"wide and beautiful [. . .] noble"—it was the fecundity along both banks that he treated with reverence. The mass of vegetation that others found oppressive was opened up into a prose-poem of diversity, a mélange of sensations. The "highly aromatic [. . .] spicewood (Laurus Benzoin)" bordered "a delicate yellow flowering plant." The "narrow-leaved willow" thrived by "calcareous rocks." So too did "cotton trees [. . .] high old elms [. . .] the buds of the red oak [. . .] large red cedars [. . .] laden with their black berries"—in the hands of an observer like Maximilian, the Mississippi was allowed to display its beauties and find its meaning in what it created, rather than what it destroyed.[48]

Charles Lyell was largely responsible for the dissemination of the concept, crucial to the work of Charles Darwin, that the creation of the earth had taken place over a geological timescale, not a biblical one. Lyell did not view the river with a romantic eye, and "was disappointed that the 'Father of Waters' did not present a more imposing aspect." But his appreciation of the river was not much concerned with the picturesque. For the geologist, it was study that inspired aesthetic enjoyment: "when I had [. . .] contemplated the Mississippi for many weeks, it left on my mind an impression of grandeur and vastness far greater than I had conceived before seeing it." Confronted with one of the supposed mysteries of the river, Lyell instinctively "wished to know what foundation there could be for so marvellous a tale," and by maintaining this investigative attitude, he developed a distinctive relationship with the Mississippi. Looking down upon the waters over which he was steaming, for example, Lyell did not (*pace* Dickens) see "liquid mud." Instead, he saw a problem that needed solving (a variation, perhaps, of Martineau's world-making): how to "ascertain the proportion of sediment contained in the waters of the Mississippi." After some research, a little observation, and a few calculations, he concluded that "the quantity of solid matter annually brought down by the river [is] 3,702,758,400 cubic feet." Such numbers had a unique poetry—a sublimity—of their own.[49]

Alexander Mackay also happily traveled in what Christopher Mulvey has defined as the "statistical Landscape"—the world of oversized numbers that America could often become in travel narratives. Statistics, evidence of an over-reliance on navigation aids and guidebooks to pad out a text, often played a pedestrian role in travel accounts. To Mackay, such figures were truly poetic. His account of the river and its valley was "a hymn of praise to Commerce." Mackay saw the Mississippi like an optimistic American, and his adulation of commerce was reminiscent of both James Hall and the moving panoramas and bird's-eye views that were contemporaneously displaying the river to the world. Upon first viewing "the tumultuous current" of which he had long dreamed, his "indescribable emotions" were channeled into a consideration of the river's sublimity. For Mackay, this stemmed from an awareness of the Mississippi's totality. He wrote in rapturous terms, reaching a numerical climax: the river "passes through so many climes, and traverses so many latitudes, rising amid perpetual snows, and debouching under an almost tropical sun [. . .] draining into itself the surplus waters of about two millions of square miles!"[50]

For Mackay, the Mississippi had a "destiny" to "fulfil," and his rhetoric took on tones of adopted nationalism. Grand though the unpopulated wilderness of prehistoric times may have been, he felt that the transformation enacted by "industry" and "busy populations" would be "far grander." Anyone, according to Mackay, who could view the river as "nothing more than a 'muddy ditch'" (*pace* Dickens once again) was obviously "badly constituted." Indeed, Mackay specifically upbraided the legion of European river-haters: the Mississippi must become, he felt, "equally an object of interest to the Englishman as the American." And why? Mackay's answer might have given Marryat et al. a moment's unhappy pause (or wry amusement): the Mississippi is "destined to be the principal medium of communication between the great world and the region which [. . .] will yet witness the greatest triumphs of Anglo-Saxon energy and skill." To think anything less was "vulgar."[51]

* * *

By the time that the last antebellum Europeans were writing their accounts of the Mississippi, the nature of tourism on the Mississippi had changed once again. The paraphernalia of tourism built up around the river attempted to make it more conventionally and more generally amenable to the demands of pleasure seekers; the Upper Mississippi, at least, slowly gained a reputation for the picturesque. *Conclin's New River Guide* (first published in 1850) was a significant development in this process, since it was devoted to the Western Rivers and designed for steamboat tourists: "the travelling community has long demanded a book that would point out to them, as they passed up or down our Western Waters, the different localities, and give some accurate account of their history, population, commerce, pursuits, &c., and the character of the country of the interior." Rather less concerned with the needs of commercial travelers, Daniel Curtiss's *Western Portraiture and Emigrant's Guide* (1852) attempted to cater to those who traveled for pleasure in the steamboat cabin. Though differing little in detail from many other emigrant guides, Curtiss's work featured some important developments for tourists: numerous allusions to the works of other published travelers, including "several letters written by Rev. J. P. Thompson [. . .] who made a tour through some of the Western States during the past summer," and the occasional sentimental verse, such as Grace Greenwood's "admirable poem on horseback-riding."[52]

More unique was *Lloyd's Steamboat Directory and Disasters on the Western Waters* (1856). Alongside a brief history of steam navigation, steamboat lists, and charts of the river, *Lloyd's* was devoted to "a copious detail of those awful and distressing accidents which have been of too frequent occurrence in that region"— steamboat explosions. This was not "to gratify a morbid taste for the horrific" but to highlight the "gross and criminal mismanagement of steam power." Frequently, these disaster accounts were accompanied by an illustration of the calamity. The reader could learn of seemingly countless wrecks, like the "Explosion of the Moselle, Near Cincinnati, Ohio, April 25, 1838." The *Moselle* was "regarded as the very paragon of western steamboats." Soon after its departure from Cincinnati, the "whole of the vessel forward of the wheels was blown to splinters," the explosion like that "of a mine of gunpowder." Witnesses found "fragments of the boiler and of human bodies" and "twenty or thirty mangled and still bleeding corpses." "Death," Lloyd reported, "had torn asunder the most tender ties."[53]

More vital to the growth of tourism on the Upper Mississippi was the arrival of the railroad. In 1854, the Chicago & Rock Island's Locomotive No. 10 rolled into Rock Island. The Mississippi was now laterally joined to the East. Accompanying it was the high-profile, celebratory "Grand Excursion" party—composed of prominent public figures and eastern writers. A writer for the *New York Times*, one of the many journalists present, asserted that "the Upper Mississippi," always felt to be more picturesque than the Lower River, "must now become a route for fashionable Summer travel." The *New York Tribune* recommended its readers to follow "in the wake of the just completed Railroad Excursion" and "ascend the Upper Mississippi, the grandest river of the world." William Petersen concluded that "no single factor was so important in popularising the fashionable tour [of the Upper Mississippi] with Easterners" as these 1854 celebrations. Ironically, the railroad, the cause of the river's commercial downfall, was implicit in its late antebellum touristic blooming.[54]

No true tourist guide to the river was published in the antebellum years. John Disturnell's *Tourist's Guide to the Upper Mississippi* (1866) was the first of its kind. Its immediate postwar publication was evidence of its desire to point out, as Disturnell expressed it, that "the war has not destroyed the commerce of the western rivers, as has been erroneously supposed." It was already fading, though, as the frequency of railroad advertisements testified. Alongside its advice to invalids, advertisements for hotels, and tables of steamboat routes, Disturnell's guide provided information on the great number of towns and cities that it was now possible for a tourist in the Mississippi Valley to visit. One suggested excursion from Dubuque to St. Paul took in six notable towns on only its first leg to Prairie du Chien.[55]

The guide was also at pains to provide some of the picturesque associations and details that tourists had been seeking for decades, in a vocabulary that had changed little since the late eighteenth century. Disturnell's readers were directed to "Objects of Interest" like "Running the Mississippi River by Moonlight": it "presents varied beauties of the most romantic and picturesque character." The growing interest in (an often spurious) Native tradition was reflected in the description of "*Maiden's Rock,* or Lover's Leap [. . .] interesting in its romantic associations." By a picture of "the celebrated *Minne-ha-ha Falls,*" Disturnell quoted Longfellow to make an explicit association for his readers: "Here the Falls of Minne-ha-ha / Flash and gleam among the oak trees, / Laugh and leap into the valley." Indeed, two of Henry Wadsworth Longfellow's hugely popular works—*Evangeline* (1847) and *The Song of Hiawatha* (1854)—finally provided river travelers at the close of the antebellum period with powerful sentimental associations with the river. The Mississippi's appearance in Longfellow's treatment of the tragic story of Evangeline and the exile of the Acadians was particularly important, not least because Longfellow's New England imaginings were far more romantic than anything a real traveler was likely to encounter. In many ways, little had changed. Literary tourists were back on Priscilla Wakefield's genteel river:

Into the golden stream of the broad and swift Mississippi,
Floated a cumbrous boat, that was rowed by Acadian boatmen
[. . .] Day after day they glided down the turbulent river;
Night after night, by their blazing fires, encamped on its borders
[. . .] Lovely the moonlight was as it glanced and gleamed on the water,
Gleamed on the columns of cypress and cedar sustaining the arches,
Down through whose broken vaults it fell as through chinks in a ruin
[. . .] Then Evangeline slept; but the boatmen rowed through the midnight.[56]

"THERE IS POETRY IN WILDNESS"

You, therefore, who delight in the belles-lettres, shun, I conjure you, the banks of the Mississippi! The very air of that region is mortal to the muses.

It was through the medium of European travel accounts that most antebellum readers encountered the river textually.[57] Each armchair traveler must have created an imaginary Mississippi that was part Martineau, part Marryat; every tourist who arrived at the river carried their own unique Mississippi of the mind. And, of course, that traveler was rare who did not require some readjustment when faced with the reality of the river itself: as Mrs. Steele concluded, "I am glad I have looked upon the Mississippi. To read of it and to see it are two different things."[58]

Travel accounts were not the final word on the river; fictional accounts of the Mississippi also emerged. Europeans could certainly be disdainful of belles-lettres grown on the banks of the Mississippi. Dickens invented the character of Putnam Smif to do just that—one "raised in those interminable solitudes where our mighty Mississippi [. . .] rolls his turbid flood" and eager for literary patronage in England: "I am young, and ardent. For there is poetry in wildness, and every alligator basking in the slime is himself an Epic, self-contained. I aspirate for fame. It is my yearning and my thirst." Nonetheless, some Europeans, Dickens included, attempted to resuscitate the muse of the Mississippi and transform their personal experiences into literature—highly influential to antebellum audiences.[59]

Chateaubriand (who, like Ashe, may never have actually reached the Mississippi) was the first. Assessing the veracity of Chateaubriand's American itinerary and its attendant details, Richard Switzer has noted that "Paddling a canoe down the Ohio and Mississippi with a broken arm scarcely mended seems a highly un-likely activity for our author." Nonetheless, he used the Mississippi as the setting for *Les Natchez*—a startling concoction of history, ethnography, and mysticism that Margaret Hall had enjoyed. (Chateaubriand's English editor, in 1827, ex-cised the passages of "supernatural agency and allegorical personages" as the "exu-berance of youthful fancy.") Loosely based around the massacre at Fort Rosalie in 1729, Chateaubriand's popular novel made scant mention of the Mississippi itself—perhaps further proof that his travel claims were unfounded. Rather less fantastically, Thackeray seems to have been struck with amnesia when fictionaliz-ing the river. "A Mississippi Bubble," written in the persona of Mr. Roundabout, was urbane and debonair in tone. His "funereal" river became "the life-stream in America"—which was, perhaps, less complimentary than his readers may have realized.[60]

Dickens and Fanny Trollope, on the other hand, imaginatively returned to the aspects of the "foul stream" that had most disturbed them: Trollope, in the novel-length *Jonathan Jefferson Whitlaw* (1836), to slavery and the settlers who haunted the banks of the river; Dickens, in *Martin Chuzzlewit* (1844), to Cairo and all that it symbolized. Both writers found ambiguities in the river that had eluded them on its waters—but both agreed that the Mississippi would be a much better place without Americans. Frances Trollope's *Jonathan Jefferson Whit-law* (1836), subtitled *Scenes on the Mississippi,* follows the resolutely downward spiral of its eponymous antihero. A true son of the river, and a pointedly repre-sentative type, Whitlaw is born on the Mississippi's "slimy banks" near Natchez. Vicious, ignorant, and arrogant, Jonathan Jefferson grows up by the river under the supervision of his father, described as "a first-rate capital backwoodsman" and reminiscent of a semidomesticated Mike Fink. The focus of Trollope's novel was not, however, backwoods life. Materialistically and socially aspirational, the Whitlaws decamp to a holding nearer Natchez. There, the adolescent Jonathan Jefferson Whitlaw finds employment as an overseer at "Paradise Plantation," the home of Colonel Dart, "the largest slave-holder in the neighbourhood of Nat-chez." Ironically, away from the dispiriting environs of the river, Trollope was able to rediscover her abolitionism. Inspired by her disgust for the Mississippi, she wrote what might be considered the first antislavery novel.[61]

But in Trollope's imaginative revision of the river, the Mississippi was not just responsible for slavery and the creation and corruption of Jonathan Jefferson Whitlaw. Once transferred to their new home near Natchez, the Whitlaws live next to an immigrant family. The Steinmarks, in all their Old World perfection, also make their home by the Mississippi. German émigré Frederick Steinmark,

Trollope enthused, had "a character [. . .] essentially exalted" and was an abolitionist; his English wife, Mary Smith, was blessed with "unaffected natural graces." The Whitlaws represented one mode of Mississippi life, all too familiar to Trollope; the Steinmarks, on the other hand, represented an ideal possibility in which the river did not necessitate degeneration. Rather, ennobled by the wilderness, the Steinmarks strive to carve a new Europe from the forest.[62]

The narrative that follows is a confusion of conflicts and compacts that incorporates murder, lynching, and slave rebellion: Jonathan Jefferson Whitlaw is vengefully—and, Trollope suggests, righteously—murdered by the slaves he has tortured; abolitionist Edward Bligh is lynched by an angry mob. And as the Mississippi first ushered in the Whitlaws, so it concludes the novel. Finding no place for their humanity or finer sensibility along the river, the novel's sympathetic characters steam down the river, an escape route back to the safety and delights of Europe: "the paddles began to play, and in another five minutes they had lost sight of Natchez and its green bluff for ever [. . .] swift and prosperous was the voyage that carried them to the port of Hamburgh." Perhaps unsurprisingly, the novel was not a transatlantic success.[63]

Though equally interested in the potential exaltation of the river, at first Dickens seemed apparently no more ambivalent about the fictional river town of "Eden" in *Martin Chuzzlewit* than he had been about the Cairo that inspired it. (Both Thackeray and Anthony Trollope recognized the setting for the fictional town when they reached the junction of the Ohio and the Mississippi.) His anger was undiminished. As speculator General Choke ironically assures Chuzzlewit, attempting to persuade him to invest in the "Eden Land Corporation": "What are the Great United States for, sir [. . .] if not for the regeneration of man?" Dickens's anger at the disparity between the ideal advertised by land agents and the reality of river settlements—if not the ideal and the reality of the New World as a whole—drove the American section of his novel.[64]

The ambivalence in Dickens's imaginative account of the Mississippi centered around the character of Mark Tapley, Martin's irrepressible traveling companion. Faced with the miserable reality of Eden, Martin "lay down upon the ground, and wept aloud." Mark, undaunted, sets to work. Waking on their first morning in Eden, he "refreshed himself by washing in the river." Thus imbued with the animating Jacksonian spirit, Mark becomes the model of a Mississippi backwoodsman. Unlike some of their American neighbors, Tapley is under no illusion as to the nature of their location. He is openly critical of the American love of unfounded boasts: "they can't help crowing. They was born to do it." And so without "hope, or steady purpose in so doing," Mark works the land, helps his neighbors, cares for Martin, and even defends the merits of the Old World against the criticisms of the New. Peopled by a nation of honest Mark Tapleys, Dickens suggests, what might the Mississippi become? Inspired by Mark's example, Martin recognizes the error of his ways and finally achieves his own moment of Mississippi realization: "there were teachers in the swamp and thicket, and the pestilential air, who had a searching method of their own [. . .] So low had Eden brought him down. So high had Eden raised him up."[65]

In the antebellum period, particularly during the Jacksonian years of their greatest impact and importance, European travel accounts were rarely absent from the presses, or from the lips of Europeans and Americans who enthusiastically dissected their individual merits and offences. Many travelers were left disappointed and bemused by their experiences; many rejected the muddy river; some managed to find more in its waters than they might have imagined—but very few left the river unmoved. The importance of these accounts was felt beyond the antebellum years. When Mark Twain set out to reacquaint himself with the river that he had known so intimately in his youth, he turned primarily to the travel accounts left by Trollope, Martineau, Marryat, and their contemporaries. In *Life on the Mississippi* (1883), he made frequent reference to a wide range of antebellum travel accounts. He judged their accounts fondly: "All those tourists aimed at the truth; did their honest best to tell it, and always succeeded except when deceived by smarty natives of the practical-joker type of vermin. And with hardly an exception they told their harsh truths in the kindliest language." Not too surprisingly, Twain liked "Dame Trollope" and her "plain and unsugared truths" the best—but it was their communal existence as an unrivaled corpus of antebellum readings of the river that was most significant to him. Somehow appropriately, these contrasting and contradictory Europeans' attempts to answer the questions that the antebellum Mississippi so insistently posed proved integral to Twain's definitive postwar readings of the American river.[66]

4

Moving Panoramas
The "Useful Illusion" of the Visual Mississippi

I long for the return of the dioramas whose enormous, crude magic subjects me to the spell of a useful illusion [. . .] Those things, so completely false, are for that reason much closer to the truth, whereas the majority of our landscape painters are liars, precisely because they fail to lie.
CHARLES BAUDELAIRE, 1859

"Well who'd a thought it,—if they haven't got my very house right down here on this picture, yes,—that's the place—barn—the big walnut tree,—the old gate [. . .] well it *is* suprising how the mischief he come to get it so natural I don't know, *stop the boat and let me get out.*"
Unidentified moving panorama audience member, 1849

William Makepeace Thackeray expressed his most pressing problem with the Mississippi in simple but damning terms: "there is nothing to draw." As the antebellum years progressed, many artists disagreed. Visual representations of the river became increasingly defining. Through their depictions, the Mississippi was introduced to arguably its largest antebellum audience. Of course, an increasingly visual Mississippi brought with it its own set of problems. As travelers on the river had realized earlier in the century, the Mississippi was not amenable to traditional aesthetic and artistic dictates. The problem of the picturesque again presented itself to those attempting to contain the river in traditional landscape forms. The Mississippi's pioneering artists first brought attention to life along the river, rather than the river itself: John James Audubon focused on the Mississippi's ornithological delights; George Caleb Bingham created iconic, sentimental poses for its alligator-horses and focused on man's interaction with the river; numerous artists produced urban views of the increasingly industrialized river towns that were emblems of civic pride. For a solution to the problem of actually representing the river itself, antebellum America turned to a potent mixture of art, technology, commerce, and expansionist rhetoric: the moving panorama. As Dickens described them in 1848—for though they weren't, they certainly seemed it—the moving panoramas of the Mississippi were "a truly American idea."[1]

The 1840s were years of rapid urbanization along the Mississippi. After the slump of 1837, in John Rep's words, a renewed "speculative orgy of town platting occurred" up until the war, particularly on the Upper Mississippi. The river's position in national life was also changing. From Texas to Mexico to California, America looked west in the Tyler and Polk years. The Mississippi acted as a gateway in this process, but, increasingly associated with slavery and the plantation South, the river would no longer be a prominent symbol of America's westering spirit. At the river's economic and cultural peak, the seeds of its demise were sown; in the Golden Age of steamboating, the railroads began to threaten. Nonetheless, in the medium of the moving Mississippi panorama, representations of the river were again center stage in the national, and international, consciousness. The moving panoramas—emblems of the American belief in progress and expansion—defined the late antebellum years.[2]

"THE SIMPLEST, MOST FREQUENT AND COMMON OCCURRENCES ON OUR RIVER"

John James Audubon and George Caleb Bingham both spent vital years on and around the Mississippi, creating iconic images of antebellum America. Though separated by important decades, and though they engaged with very different aspects of life on the river, the imaginative vision of both artists was profoundly attached to the waters of the Western Rivers. As Perry Rathbone concluded, Audubon was a true pioneer, for Bingham and for others: the "pattern of his experience was [. . .] in every way characteristic [. . .] of the artist-explorer of the river in the first half of the nineteenth century." Audubon was born in Santo Domingo, the son of a French naval officer. When he reached the Western Waters in 1807, he opened a general store in Louisville, hoping to capitalize on the growth of the Ohio trade. "We prospered at a round rate for a while," Audubon wrote in later years, "but, unfortunately for me, he [Thomas Bakewell, his brother-in-law] persuaded me to erect a steam-mill [. . .] at an enormous expense, in a country then as unfit for such a thing as it would be now for me to attempt to settle in the moon [. . .] We also took it into our heads to have a steamboat [. . .] This also proved an entire failure."[3]

In 1819, Audubon was jailed for unpaid debts. Upon release, he turned from commerce to other skills that he had been refining throughout the period of entrepreneurial failure. Daniel Drake, that influential Cincinnatian, employed Audubon as a taxidermist at the Cincinnati College and gave him the opportunity of displaying his ornithological portraits. When Audubon's taxidermy contract ended, his obsession with ornithology grew: "I would even give up doing a head, the profits of which would have supplied our wants for a week or more, to represent a little citizen of the feathered tribe." At the age of thirty-five, without clear prospects, Audubon's ambitions finally coalesced—into a desire "to portray in the color and action of life and in their natural haunts, all the birds of America." And so he embarked on the Mississippi, into his "Aeneid." From October 1820 until the end of 1821, Audubon kept a journal of his travels on the Western Waters, seeking subjects for the work that would become *The Birds of America* (1827–38). Audubon's journal was a remarkable record of the day-to-day hardships of Mississippi flatboating on the cusp of the era of steam. As he recorded on November 17, entering the Mississippi for the first time: "here the traveller enters a New World, the Current of the stream [. . .] puts the Steersman on the alert and Awakes him to troubles and Difficulties unknown on the Ohio, the Passenger feels a different atmosphere, a very different prospect."[4]

In Audubon's visual work, the Mississippi never played a significant role. It did provide appropriate backdrops for some of his studies—as in a depiction of a Louisiana heron. But, like the journal, Audubon's most significant representations of the river were textual. His plans for a written companion to his bird portraits—the *Ornithological Biography* (1835)—were conceived early, perhaps as early as 1826. Given the amount of time Audubon spent on the Western Waters, it is unsurprising that the Mississippi filtered into these and other writings. They remain the most important testament to the influence of the Mississippi on his creative vision. For example, his powerful and emblematic portrait of the bald eagle, posed with a Mississippi catfish, showed no other sign of the river in its composition. Yet describing the white-headed eagle in his *Ornithological Biography*, Audubon explicitly transported his readers to its waters: "permit me to place you on the Mississippi, on which you may float gently along [. . .] The Eagle is seen perched, in an erect attitude, on the highest summit of the tallest tree by the margin of the broad stream. His glistening but stern eye looks over the vast expanse [. . .] Now is the moment to witness the display of the Eagle's powers."[5]

In numerous essays on American scenery and character beyond the ornithological, Audubon addressed culturally resonant aspects of life on the rivers. He engaged in a little frontier exaggeration, claiming, for example, to have met Daniel Boone: he "happened to spend a night with me under the same roof [. . .] this wanderer of the western forests approached the gigantic." He also defended the "squatters of the Mississippi" against their critics, particularly the "European" ones: "the Mississippi is the great road to and from all the markets of the world; and [. . .] affords to settlers some chance of selling their commodities, or of exchanging them for others [. . .] How many thousands of individuals in all parts of the globe would gladly try their fortune with such prospects, I leave you, reader, to determine." As for the river itself, Audubon could rarely resist rhapsodizing on its power: "the Mississippi, with its ever-shifting sand banks, its crumbling shores, its enormous masses of drift timber [. . .] and its mighty mass of waters rolling sullenly along, like the flood of eternity!" Representing that flood visually was another matter.[6]

George Caleb Bingham was the first artist to produce significant images of the river. He realized the potential of the Western Waters as a transcendent symbol of the antebellum nation, evoking, in Michael Shapiro's words, "with striking clarity the values and aspirations" of his America. Bingham was a Virginian by birth, and moved to Franklin, Missouri in 1818, at the age of seven. Apprenticed to a cabinetmaker at sixteen, Bingham soon dropped that profession and became a portrait painter. In 1836, his copy of a portrait of Fanny Kemble was warmly praised by the *Missouri Republican,* which predicted that the young artist would be "an ornament to his profession and an honor to Missouri." Simultaneously, the other consuming passion of his life crystallized. In 1834, the Whig party came together as a coalition of disaffected groups. For Bingham's work, including the river paintings, always showed a "prevalence of both explicit and veiled political imagery." The artist who would create elegiac, iconic portraits of the alligator-horses of the Western Waters was an ardent Whig—in essence, an "anti-Jacksonian."[7]

Like Audubon before him, Bingham spent time as an itinerant portrait painter on the Mississippi, working in St. Louis and Natchez. Then he turned east, traveling to Philadelphia and New York, where he was exposed to the proliferating "contemporary genre scenes" by the likes of William Sidney Mount. He was immediately moved to turn to the Western Rivers for inspiration, producing the now-lost *Western Boatmen Ashore* (1838). His emblematic trinity of boatmen, boat, and river was coalescing. Just such a composition appeared at this time in a political banner: "a western river, with a canoe on the water and the sun breaking forth from the clouds in the distance." His first trip to the East also taught him lessons about Jacksonian democracy and what he disapprovingly described as "the patriot mob." The next time he left Missouri, he spent an extended period immersed in the political hotbed of Washington. Marked by family tragedy and professional prevarication, these three years were unhappy. Inspired by another visit to the Pennsylvania Academy of Fine Arts, Bingham returned to Missouri in 1844. Just as Mark Twain would write *Life on the Mississippi* (1883) and find the impetus to complete *Huckleberry Finn* (1884) after he returned to the great river of his youth, so the genesis of Bingham's river paintings finally came with this return to Missouri.[8]

In the seven-year period from 1844 to 1851—while deeply involved in Missouri state politics—Bingham produced the majority of his river paintings. He ran twice, in 1846 and 1848, as a Whig candidate for the Missouri legislature, and successfully gained a seat (his only elected office) at the second attempt. Appropriately—for an artist torn between both East and West, and Jacksonian icons and Whig politics—a host of contradictory elements and influences were apparent in the conception and execution of Bingham's river works. The patronage of the American Art-Union was crucial. From 1845 to 1852, the Art-Union purchased nineteen of Bingham's paintings, making the organization his most significant patron. The Art-Union's predilection for western scenes—reflecting the nation's growing fascination with the West as, in Elizabeth Johns's phrase, "*the* arena for the development of the nation," compounded by contemporary events like the Mexican War and the California gold rush—was vital in Bingham's choice of subject matter. To some extent he was feeding eastern audiences the West that they wished to see. He had submitted *Western Boatmen Ashore* to the Apollo Association—the Art-Union's precursor—in 1838, to little acclaim. In 1845, Bingham sent four more paintings to the Art-Union, one of which was the fully formed river masterpiece *Fur Traders Descending the Missouri* (1845). The Art-Union paid seventy-five dollars for *Fur Traders,* a significant amount. Bingham's *Boatmen on the Missouri* (1846) earned him one hundred dollars; and when *The Jolly Flatboatmen* (1846) was purchased for 290 dollars, it reached a wide audience. The Art-Union used a print of the image "as a frontispiece to its *Transactions* of 1846 and then, the following year, as a black-and-white engraving [. . .] ten thousand were distributed to the Union's membership." Its reputation spread. John Banvard, trying to encourage interest in his moving panorama before its arrival in England, sent to *Howitt's Journal,* "an engraving of one of these peculiar boats, with its 'jolly flat-boat men.'"[9]

In contrast to the accounts of Mike Fink and other alligator-horses, Bingham's iconic boatmen were paragons. His *Jolly Flatboatmen* portrayed none of the boatmen's characteristic vices. (Nancy Rash has even argued that "the caged turkey," upon which a boatman dances, may refer to temperance: "having a turkey on" was a slang term in the 1840s for intoxication.) This image of joyous liberation and vitality was an uninterrupted and harmonious synthesis of key images: flatboat, boatmen, and river. The viewer is drawn into the group through the eye contact of the boatmen and, in terms of perspective, is situated on the river as if in a flatboat. The very presence of the boat and crew, the suggestion of items in the hold, and the raccoon skin (a Whig symbol) attest to the "the commerce that Whigs felt brought civilization in its wake." But in *The Jolly*

Flatboatmen at least, Bingham's rivermen inhabited an unspoiled wilderness, a river paradise in which the viewer could share.[10]

This was an extreme idealization of the frontier. Bingham figured the boatmen as happy harbingers of civilization. Whether or not eastern audiences were aware of it, however, this was at best a sentimentalization of the river's history; really, it was an illusion. For Johns, *The Jolly Flatboatmen* showed "incident and characters [. . .] associated with the Missouri of the late 1840s," and she was not entirely wrong. Flatboats still worked on the Western Waters in the 1840s, but Bingham's jolly flatboat seems to float on a pristine, preindustrial river without intimation of violence or danger. *The Jolly Flatboatmen* was part of the cultural process that celebrated frontier types, like Mike Fink, while simultaneously mourning their passing. For David Lubin, Bingham's river paintings purveyed "a dream of leisure, communal togetherness, and amiable accord with nature [. . .] a pleasingly nostalgic, even therapeutic, recourse from the daily grind." These representations of the river were both of their time and of the past; but given Bingham's Whiggery, their nostalgia was in no way simplistic.[11]

If *The Jolly Flatboatmen* appeared to be an image from the preindustrial river, other works like *Boatmen on the Missouri* or *Lighter Relieving a Steamboat Aground* (1846–47) seemed to portray a more modern, if not contemporary, Missouri or Mississippi. There was a difference, subtle but discernible, between the jolly flatboatmen and these apparently more modern counterparts. The jolly boatmen were vice-free, veritable frontier-dandies, sharply outfitted and fully clothed (a freshly washed shirt hangs over the edge of their boat). The later boatmen are an increasingly rag-tag bunch, miscellaneously and partially clothed in torn and grubby cast-offs. The boatmen *Relieving a Steamboat* displayed two of the boatmen's famous vices: a man facing the viewer in the foreground smokes a pipe; at the front of the boat, a man drinks from a jug of whiskey. Unlike the commodious jolly flatboat, there is little room on either craft for the viewer. For Michael Edward Shapiro, the Missouri boatmen were "beacons of the future." Though such an interpretation fits with Bingham's politics, it is difficult to agree with this assessment. These contemporary portraits of boatmen betray a greater degree of authentic detail and less elegiac haze. Perhaps what is discernible, therefore, is a simultaneous tension between a celebration of the common frontiersman and uncertainty about the populist Jacksonian style of democracy (the very issue to which Bingham would turn after his river paintings).[12]

Tellingly, in these river paintings the resonance of Bingham's composition was unsettled by an ambiguous component: the steamboat. The symbol of the steamboat most frequently represented progress, industry, and commerce. In

Bingham's works, its power was uncertain. *Boatmen on the Missouri* may seem to attest to the passing of the frontier type it portrayed: a steamboat and its ominous smoke appear in the distance as a threatening portent of the future, suggesting disruption, even destruction, of a little flatboat in the foreground: "As though cognizant of their own near extinction as a breed," Barbara Groseclose has argued, "the boatmen wait to surrender their portion of the West." But the men in the boat appear to be engaged in selling wood to the steamer. Rather than displacing them, the steamboat is the very reason for their continued presence on the river. Equally, his depiction of a *Lighter Relieving a Steamboat Aground* may seem to draw a contrast between fallible technology and resolute frontiersmen: while an insignificant steamboat languishes in the river, the boatman's arm propels its cargo, slowly but surely, to safety. Originally entitled *Mississippi Boatmen Listening to a Yarn,* the painting appears to be another frontier idyll. Nancy Rash has argued for a different interpretation: "Bingham the artist was here painting a work that spoke to issues of grave importance for Bingham the Whig politician." Bingham and the Whigs were, at the time of this composition, keen to endorse federal funding for internal improvements (what Crockett had argued for), specifically the clearing of the Western Waters. The issue was hotly contested; in *De Bow's Southern and Western Review,* in January 1852, an impassioned plea appeared under the title "The Great Importance of Improving the Mississippi River." *Lighter Relieving a Steamboat Aground* could therefore be read as an expression of Bingham's "convictions about the importance of clearing the rivers" expressly to facilitate commerce and the industrialization of the river.[13]

Contemporary reaction to Bingham's river paintings, especially in the Missouri press, was unequivocally positive. For the *Missourian Republican:* "Mr. Bingham has struck out for himself an entire new field of historic painting, if we may so term it. He has taken our western rivers, our boats and boatmen, and the banks of the streams, for his subjects. The field is as interesting as it is novel [. . .] To look at any of his pictures, is but to place yourself on board of one of the many crafts which float upon our streams [. . .] he has taken the simplest, most frequent and common occurrences on our river—such as every boatman will encounter in a season [. . .] but which are precisely those in which the full and undisguised character of the boatman is displayed." Shapiro has concluded that in "the rivers, rafts and people of the 1840s, Bingham found a Western American ideal. Cleansing these stevedores of their flaws, he displayed them as poised, hearty men in tune with themselves and their pace in creating the nation's future." Bingham did not find them, he created them; neither did the cleansing process remove all ambiguities. He did, however, provide the alligator-horses with iconic poses that would dominate representations of the presteamboat-men in the remaining antebellum years and beyond, even after Bingham's fame waned. At his most elegiac, Bingham provided an illusion of life on the Western Waters that proliferated throughout America and the world. The key to this was his blend of cultural and political influences: remarkably, Bingham created Whig alligator- horses.[14]

PANORAMANIA

Traveling along the Hudson in 1831, enamored with the scenery, Frances Trollope thoughts of her friends back in England and expressed the river's beauty with a telling comparison: "Not even a moving panoramic view, gliding before their eyes for an hour together, in all the scenic splendour of Drury Lane or Covent Garden, could give them an idea of it." What was this medium that would display the Mississippi River to worldwide audiences in the late antebellum years? At its most basic, it was an enormous canvas fastened between two rollers, wound at a steady pace from one roller to the other in front of an audience; it simulated physical movement and presented the viewer with a succession of landscapes and views—in the case of Mississippi panoramas, the course of the river from the viewpoint of a traveler on a steamboat. The American panoramists of the Mississippi were a compelling mixture of artist and entrepreneur. John Banvard—the creator of the first Mississippi panorama to appear before the public, and the defining panoramist—encapsulated these contrasting elements. Self-taught artist and businessman, poet and promoter, philanthropist and fraud, Banvard was lauded as an artist, an educator, and a showman. He made his fortune touring Europe and America with his Mississippi panorama. He died poverty-stricken in his son's spare room in the Dakota Territory.[15]

In 1847, the year that John Banvard first toured America with a moving panorama of the Mississippi, the panorama was not a new medium. The first wave of "panoramania" followed Robert Barker's invention of the panoramic rotunda in 1787. In this, its earliest and most enduring manifestation, the panorama was a 360-degree painted prospect that surrounded a central point of observation. This was Barker's innovation: a painting that encapsulated and immersed the viewer in a representation of nature, simultaneously removing any means of comparison with reality. Typically, the viewer entered along a darkened corridor that led upward to the central observation platform. As well as disorientating the viewer, it made their emergence into the daylight of the panorama more spectacular. The umbrellalike roof of the viewing platform—the "vellum"—and the foreground that bordered the platform obscured the top and bottom edges

of the painting. As the medium developed, the foreground was frequently deco-
rated with paraphernalia suitable to the scene. As Barker's application for a patent in 1787 suggested, the panorama was from its inception a fusion of art and
technology. It was none other than Robert Fulton who obtained the rights to
show panoramas in France. He mounted a rotunda on the Rue des Panoramas
in 1799. Barker's panorama constantly underwent technical modification: cyclo-
ramas, cosmoramas, neoramas, myrioramas, georamas, pleoramas all came and
went. Difference was as much a marketing ploy as it was a true extension of the
medium. Showmanship was crucial to the success of any new exhibition.

The panorama was twice transformed in ways that were significant. The diorama of Daguerre and Bouton opened in 1822. Where the 360-degree panoramas
had been static, the diorama introduced a new and exciting element of movement—temporal rather than spatial. Its canvas was transparent and painted on
both sides, and it was lit by a window of ground glass. Standing between the
light source and the canvas was a series of colored screens suspended by cords.
Through careful manipulation of lighting and screens, the picture presented to
the audience slowly changed. As Walter Benjamin described, "People sought to
copy the changing time of day in the countryside, the rising of the moon, or
the rushing of the waterfall." Unlike the static panorama, the length of its shows
allowed for a regular turnaround of paying customers. Daguerre provided the
moving panoramists with a successful business plan.[16]

The moving panorama was the other significant transformation of Barker's
invention. Despite Dickens's assertion—and a general assumption that the panoramists did little to dispel—the moving panorama was not an American invention. As Frances Trollope knew, it originated on the London stage, primarily as a
backdrop for pantomime. In 1820, two years before the appearance of Daguerre's
diorama, a critic described an interlude in Covent Garden's *Harlequin and Friar
Bacon; or, the Brazen Head:* "twilight darkens and still the packet sweeps along,
and still remote vessels pass her; the steam-boat is seen smoking on its way
[. . .] morning shews the mountains round the bay of Dublin." The "whole
scene received great applause." Thomas Grieve was responsible for this and many
other early examples of the moving panorama. He also realized the suitability
of the medium for the depiction of river journeys. A substantial portion of his
panorama commemorating George IV's visit to Scotland in 1822 consisted of
the river procession from Greenwich to the Nore. Rolling the canvas vertically,
Grimaldi was even able to take a balloon trip from London to Paris in *Harlequin
and Poor Robin,* at Covent Garden in 1824. But it was not until the late 1840s,
long after the first wave of enthusiasm for the moving panorama had dissipated,

that moving depictions of a steamboat journey on the Mississippi became sensations in America and Europe.[17]

The moving Mississippi panorama was a transatlantic medium: an American modification of a European art form, its creators were also inspired by the precedents set by earlier American artists and showmen in Europe. Large-scale historical paintings became fashionable in the latter half of the eighteenth century. Benjamin West was an American painter who trained in London and went on to become president of the Royal Academy. A painting like his *Death on the Pale Horse* (1817) was a paradigm of the genre. West's arrangements for the display of his picture (measuring 15 by 25 feet) were apposite to the Mississippi panoramas. He built a gallery solely for the display of the painting and charged an entrance fee. The painting was hung low, dramatically lit, and framed with a curtained proscenium arch. This increased the sublimity of the work, drawing the viewer into the events depicted on the canvas. It transformed the giant work into an exhibition in and of itself. Engravings were sold to visitors. West's method of display was copied by other artists, but it was predominantly fellow Americans (John Singleton Copley, Mather Brown, John Trumbull) who followed his lead.[18]

A growing interest in western imagery—inspired by travel accounts and James Fenimore Cooper's novels, best-sellers in pirated London editions—presented further visual commercial opportunities. George Catlin exhibited his Indian gallery and museum in Philadelphia and New York before traveling to London in 1840. He established a template of advertising and promotion that Banvard would follow almost to the letter upon his arrival in London. Catlin made much of the eight years he had spent among the tribes he sketched and exhibited (and thus helped to further the image of the hardy, itinerant artist promoted by the panoramists). During his travels up the Mississippi and the Missouri, Catlin had met the Honorable Charles Augustus Murray, one of the army of European travelers who commented on antebellum America. (In Murray's *Travels in North America* (1839), the Mississippi had played an archetypically gloomy role: "I cannot deny that my first feeling was disappointment [. . .] his stream is extremely muddy, and his banks low and tame." But Murray realized, "when you [. . .] use the eye of the imagination as well as that of nature [. . .] you begin to understand all his might and majesty.") Murray was also the master of the queen's household. He was able to secure Catlin the prestigious and popular Egyptian Hall in Piccadilly as a venue (which Banvard would use eight years later), a fashionable guest list for private viewings, and a crucial command performance. (Royal patronage was equally vital to Banvard's success. His promotional material relied heavily on his own appearance before the queen at Windsor Castle.)[19]

Catlin captured the attention of the paying public with showmanship. His Indian gallery traversed the boundaries between art, education, and entertainment. Commerce and culture were intertwined. Alongside his paintings, he displayed a twenty-five-foot-high wigwam and a "tableaux Vivants Indiennes." As Richard Altick relates, the Indians who comprised the lively tableaux "were in fact local talent—twenty men and boys (for squaws), probably with Cockney accents but chosen for the presumed Indian cast of their countenances, who, decked out in feathers and war paints, uttered war cries, performed war dances, demonstrated 'Indian file,' held a war council, and smoked the peace pipe." These illusory Indians served until Catlin was able to recruit nine Ojibbeways from Arthur Rankin, a showman passing through Manchester. But they caused problems for Catlin that the Londoners did not—problems that led to bankruptcy. Alcohol led to frequent disturbances, and Catlin failed to persuade either Londoners or Americans that "these poor unfortunate people" were deserving of attention or sympathy. Frederic Madden, keeper of printed books at the British Museum, visited the exhibition in January 1844, but was keen to leave as "soon as the ceremony of *shaking hands* commenced [. . .] as I had no ambition to grasp the palm of a dirty savage." The moving panoramists learned from such mistakes, as evinced by their choice and treatment of subject matter. The panoramas kept a comfortable distance between spectator and subject. And yet, decades later, in attempting to give the public reality instead of enjoyable fiction, Banvard would also ruin himself.[20]

Static panoramas, dioramas, giant history paintings, and Indian galleries all provided models of entrepreneurship for the moving panoramists. They were art forms in which Americans, at home and abroad, had prospered. Alternatively, John Vanderlyn, the man who introduced the panoramic rotunda to New York, also provided a telling lesson. He attempted to exhibit panoramas of Old World views to the burgeoning New World, and died in poverty (like so many in the exhibition business) in 1852. Thematically, other artists provided different forms of inspiration, particularly in their treatment of American subject matter.

Thomas Cole, a British immigrant to America, was a vital figure. He was familiar with a variety of panoramic forms and applied some of their techniques in his work. When visiting Red Mountain in New Hampshire, for example, he applied viewing techniques learned from visiting panoramic rotundas to increase his aesthetic appreciation of the view. Cole wrote to his patron, Daniel Wadsworth, in 1827: "[I] climbed without looking on either side: I denied myself that pleasure so that the full effect of the scene might be experienced," just as the spectator climbed in a panoramic rotunda to arrive at the viewing platform: "I looked abroad!—With what an ocean of beauty and magnificence, was I surrounded." A concomitant effect on Cole's work was apparent. His *View from Mount Holyoke, Northampton, Massachusetts, after a Thunderstorm* (1836), better known as *The Oxbow*, was a prospect that challenged picturesque landscape conventions (like Gilpin's prohibition against long views: "Extension alone, though amusing in nature, will never make a picture") while also engaging with them.[21]

The implicit "narrative" of *The Oxbow* was influential. As Angela Miller has noted, the painting could "be read from left to right." The tale it told was one of urbanization and progress. A typically picturesque gnarled tree and storm cloud worked as repoussoir objects in the image, drawing the viewer from desolate wilderness on the left to increasingly urbanized pastoral on the right: "Were the painting panoramically extended to the right [or rolled past in the style of a moving panorama], one can easily imagine that it would trace the successive stages of urbanisation." *The Oxbow* should be seen as a successful experiment in what Alan Wallach terms the "panoptic sublime"—an answer to the question, "How could a panoramic view be represented on a two-dimensional surface?" Here was a conceptual bridge between the static panorama and its moving counterpart.[22]

Cole himself served as a staffage figure in *The Oxbow*, ambiguously located in the middle of the canvas between the wilderness and the urban landscape. This was the position that much of Cole's work inhabited. His seminal "Essay on American Scenery" (1835), contemporary with *The Oxbow*, resonated with uncertainty about the nature of American progress: "there are those who regret that with the improvements of cultivation the sublimity of the wilderness should pass away [. . .] the ravages of the axe are daily increasing [. . .] oftentimes with a wantonness and barbarism scarcely credible in a civilised nation." On one level, Cole felt that this was "a regret rather than a complaint; such is the road society has to travel." On another, he was less circumspect about his distaste for the "meagre utilitarianism" of "go-ahead" Jacksonian democracy.[23]

Cole's allegorical sequence *The Course of Empire* (1836) was engaged in this debate. As a narrative sequence, the five paintings shared panoramic qualities with *The Oxbow*. In their unity of place, and movement through time, they were akin to Daguerre's dioramas. Cole predicted to patron Luman Reed, "Very few will understand the scheme [. . .] the philosophy that may be in them." The canvasses charted the course of an imagined civilization from "The Savage State" to "The Pastoral or Arcadian State," to "The Consummation of Empire," to its "Destruction" and eventual "Desolation." But was this empire imagined? Or was it, perhaps, Andrew Jackson's America? Beyond the imperial expansion of the post-Revolutionary years, as Barringer has highlighted, "the idea of America as an empire [. . .] was eminently applicable in the Jacksonian period, when the nation grew incrementally in size." For opponents of populist Jacksonian democracy, like Cole himself, the years leading up to the exhibition of this imperial sequence in 1836—the peak of the Jacksonian spirit of expansion and speculation, the year of Crockett's death and popular transcendence—"were full of ominous signs." They would culminate in the ruinous depression of 1837. *The Course of Empire* can be seen as an expression of Cole's fear that his adopted nation would not be set free from the cycles of imperial rise and fall so apparent in the Old World.[24]

But Cole was right to think that his "philosophy" would not be apprehended. The critic for the *New-York Mirror* spoke for many in his interpretation of Cole's sequence: "The climax in the course of man's progress, which Mr Cole has here represented, is *that* which *has been* and was founded on the usurpation of the strong over the weak; the perfection which man is hereafter to attain, will be based upon a more stable foundation: political equality; the rights of man; the democratick principle; the *sovereignty of the people*." Jacksonian America lauded Cole and absented itself from his critique of empire. Reading Cole's works as a hymn to American progress and American exceptionalism had profound effects for the moving panoramas and American art as a whole. As Stephen Mills has noted, Cole's "followers developed a more patriotic genre from such inauspicious beginnings." The most important (at least thematically) was Asher Durand's *Progress (The Advance of Civilisation)* (1853). It was painted for Charles Gould, treasurer of the Ohio and Mississippi Railroad. Depicting a similar transformation from rural to urban, and employing the same composition as Cole's *Oxbow,* Durand visualized the advance of American industry and transportation seemingly without Cole's uncertainties (and with minimum effect on the millennial landscape). As America developed from carriage, to steamboat, to railroad and telegraph, a bright future beckoned. In panoramic fashion, two Native Americans gazed at this brave new world from the far left of the picture, displaced in the forward rush.[25]

In its apparently unambiguous presentation of industrial advance, Durand's *Progress* was thematically identical to the moving panoramas of the Mississippi. Both were related to the nationalistic rhetoric that flourished in the first half of the nineteenth century. George Bancroft—who served as Polk's secretary of the navy—wrote in *The Progress of Mankind* (1854) that American "civilisation flows on like a mighty river through a boundless valley [. . .] wider, and deeper, and clearer, as it rolls along." In Anders Stephanson's words, a "great destinarian outburst occurred during the 1840s as a result of the need to understand and legitimate [. . .] aggressive annexation of territory." This was the moment that the moving panoramas—"movies for manifest destiny," to borrow Kevin Avery's apt phrase—appeared before the public.[26]

At the end of *Life on the Mississippi,* Mark Twain's comic panoramist appears as a figure from the history of the river. The narration with which he regales his fellow passengers is a fervent blend of (ironically overwrought) manifest destiny rhetoric: "progress [. . .] banner-bearer of the highest and newest civilisation, carving his beneficent way with the tomahawk of commercial enterprise, sounding the warwhoop of Christian culture [. . .] ever in his wake bloom the jail, the gallows, and the pulpit." Twain's caricature was fitting. Promotional material produced by Banvard and others showed a similar attention to the "larger mythic history of manifest destiny." Banvard, as he himself described, "commenced the undertaking" of his panorama not for personal "gain," but because of "a patriotic and honourable ambition." Risley and Smith provided the following description of a scene from their panorama: "the swart Indian on the borders of his native river stands in fine contrast with the white captain who rules the palace that is steaming by."[27]

The final thematic inspiration for the panoramists—many of whom lived on or near the river before commencing their panoramas—may well have been bird's-eye views of Mississippi river towns. These popular images were proudly displayed in private homes and public spaces like taverns, hotels, and banks. They appeared, in John Reps's words, "at a time when Americans hungered for information about the development of their country"—particularly those living on a frontier that was constantly changing around them. Through bird's-eye views, the people of the Western Waters were afforded a rare reflection of themselves, or how they wished to be. The prints employed a panoramic bird's-eye view to maximize profit and minimize effort. Sometimes they appeared to "stretch the rules of linear perspective to the vanishing point of disbelief" to ensure that as many of the buildings in a community as possible—and thus potential customers—were visible. But this also emphasized the regular blocks of town planning and the dead straight roads that shot into the horizon. These prints, with the river as a constant foreground presence, were a testament to the hope for an ordered, industrial, well-governed life on the frontier.[28]

James Kershaw's *Map and View of St. Louis, Mo.* (1848), for example, included a host of incitements to civic pride. A panoramic view of the town was accompanied by a street plan. Steamboats, both docked and on the river, symbolized prosperity and trade; chimney smoke—from river or factory—was a gratifying sight. Sketches of important public works served as a border. Illustrations such as the *Tobacco Warehouse,* the *Missouri Engine House,* and the *Gas Works* may not have provided picturesque gratification, but they represented a solid civic infrastructure and increasing industrialization and were therefore proudly displayed as evidence of a projected longevity. As J.D.B. de Bow's *Commercial Review of the South and West* proclaimed in 1846, "the growth of the various cities which scatter themselves throughout the valley of the Ohio and Mississippi rivers, has been so rapid and extraordinary, as scarcely to be credited by those whose minds have been educated in other sections of the world." The proscenium arch of the panorama worked to the same effect as the rigid lines of these bird's-eye prints. The moving panorama arranged the river and its component parts into a linear narrative. It corrected the wilderness. As many frustrated Mississippi tourists would have realized, it provided useful illusions. The river was straightened, its waters were purified, its boatmen scrubbed, and its river towns—even the likes of Natchez-under-the-hill—were sanitized. Its regular mechanical movement, without the chance of explosion or snag offered by a steamboat, suggested steady progress; the unfathomable river was neatly captured between two rollers. John Banvard was the first to capture it.[29]

"THE LARGEST PAINTING IN THE WORLD"

The moving panoramas of the Mississippi created by John Banvard and his competitors have disappeared. Chronologically, John Banvard (1846), Smith and Risley, Samuel Stockwell (1848), Henry Lewis, and Leon Pomarède (1849) all brought Mississippi panoramas before the public, and competed for their attention in terms of artistic ability, accuracy, and, most importantly, size. None of their extraordinarily popular portraits of the river survived into the twentieth century. Only one, created by Dickeson and Egan, remains, and since it ranges through time and space in its choice of subjects, it is not a true example of the genre. As McDermott lamented, "every aspect of life along this mighty stream had been recorded that posterity might be fully informed how the father of rivers looked and behaved in the fabulous forties." But they are all gone: misplaced, worn out by the years of travel, cut up into smaller sections. One of Banvard's grandsons dimly remembered playing on his panorama in the basement of the artist's home—after which, nothing. Henry Lewis sold his panorama in 1857, to a planter returning to Java. Befitting their cultural prominence, however ephemeral, they did leave significant traces. The medium generated a great deal of peripheral material. Promotional literature, sketchbooks, and lithographs of scenes from the panoramas all exist. In part, therefore, the style and content of this cultural phenomenon can be reconstructed.[30]

Whether or not John Banvard was responsible for the idea behind the moving Mississippi panoramas, he accrued the associated fame. As a child in New York, Banvard was surrounded by artistic spectacles—even the occasional moving panorama. At the age of fifteen, he ran "Banvard's Entertainments" (a Barnumesque mixture of camera obscura, diorama, and Punch and Judy) for his classmates. Banvard originally exhibited a moving panorama of Venice, but discovered (like Vanderlyn before him) that Old World views were not sufficiently interesting to the paying public. As such, he took to the Western Waters. As Banvard romantically described the genesis of his so-called "Three-Mile Painting," establishing the degree of self-promotion that accompanied these giant paintings: "A tiny skiff was floating upon the mirror'd surface of the [. . .] noble Mississippi [. . .] unguided by its solitary occupant, a boy, of scarce sixteen, who sat, with folded arms, contemplating with wonder and delight, the glowing scenes around him. That boy was JOHN BANVARD. He had heard, and now realized, that America could boast the most picturesque and magnificent scenery in the world [. . .] the boy resolved within himself to be an Artist, that he might paint the beauties and sublimities of his native land." Amplification of the river's picturesque qualities was of great importance in this patriotic enterprise: "His grand object [. . .] was to produce *the largest painting in the world*. He determined to paint a picture of the beautiful scenery of the Mississippi," even though the urban river, by necessity, formed much of the focus of the panorama, "which should be as superior to the streamlets of Europe—a gigantic idea! which seems truly kindred to the illimitable forests and vast extent of his native land." Following family hardships in New York, Banvard headed west at the age of fifteen; "being fond of adventure, he started down the river," and traveled extensively on the Ohio and the Mississippi. Exhibiting a diorama in a flatboat was fraught with disaster. Banvard even claimed that "the boat was attacked by a party of Murell robbers, a large organized banditti [. . .] and our hero came near losing his life." Surviving, he "engaged in painting at New Orleans, Natchez, and subsequently at Cincinnati and Louisville" and produced his panorama of Venice. Money came from river trading (commerce, as ever, the lifeblood of the river), and with "the capital thus accumulated, he commenced his grand project of painting the Panorama of the Mississippi."[31]

In 1840, he began his preliminary sketches of the river in a small skiff. "For this purpose," his audience was informed, "he had to travel thousands of miles alone in an open skiff, crossing and recrossing the rapid stream, in many places over two miles in breadth." The mammoth preparatory work over, Banvard began the panorama. In the autumn of 1846, it was finally ready for its premiere in Louisville. The first night, rain kept away his audience. Undaunted, Banvard knew the route to success along the river: "the next day he sallied out among the boatmen, by the river, and gave them tickets; telling them that they must see it; that it was their river he had painted. At night, the boatmen came [. . .] they were delighted, and their wild enthusiasm was raised as one well known object after another passed by them. The boatmen told the citizens it was a grand affair." Its success was assured.[32]

As the huge painting slowly unwound from one roller to the other, visitors to Banvard's exhibition saw the banks of the Mississippi, the Missouri, and the Ohio roll past as if they were on board a western steamer. They passed ancient settlements and pioneering towns, fellow steamers, flatboats and keelboats, swamps and snags. "Mississippi Waltzes" were played in the background (often by Banvard's wife), while Banvard, on a platform at the side of his canvas, provided a didactic narration filled with local color. A souvenir pamphlet was available providing a brief biography of the artist, an unaccredited reproduction of Timothy Flint's "The Rivers" and "Life on the Mississippi," and a rather bald description of the sights depicted in Banvard's work. Some editions contained a tale of Mike Fink—Morgan Neville's "The Last of the Boatmen." New Orleans followed Louisville, then Boston and New York; then, in 1848, Europe.[33]

Banvard's exhibition opened at the Egyptian Hall in London shortly before Christmas. During the twenty months of its residency, 604,524 paying customers were said to have attended. Ever the consummate publicist, Banvard arranged an advance showing for the press. The *Morning Advertiser* was suitably impressed: "It is impossible to convey an adequate idea of this magnificent exhibition." The *London Observer* agreed: "this is truly an extraordinary work." The London *Examiner*—like many of those who witnessed Banvard's performance—was almost more interested in the spectacle of the artist himself: "a mixture of shrewdness and simplicity [. . .] which is very prepossessing; a modesty and honesty, and an odd original humour." So too the *Illustrated London News:* "Mr Banvard [. . .] relieves his narrative with Jonathanisms and jokes, poetry and patter, which delight his audience mightily." Henry Crabb Robinson, a central figure of the London literary scene, was less enthusiastic: "It is an execrable daub of a picture. And the intense vulgarity of the Yankee explainer actually excited disgust." Nonetheless, *Scientific American* summed up Banvard's London season in glowing terms—and with a telling awareness of the way that the panorama took its place alongside other prominent representations of the river: "The Panorama of the Mississippi has had an astonishing effect upon all classes in London. The most of the English people think that our Western country is nothing but a wild-man-of-the-woods region, and no doubt but many places on the Mississippi are wild enough, but Banvard's panorama presents many scenes where the poet might indulge his fancy and the lover of the picturesque sigh to behold in reality."[34] Dickens was one of the few Londoners who had beheld the Mississippi firsthand. He joined the crowds at the Egyptian Hall to review the "American Panorama" for the *Examiner*—and was far more impressed with Banvard's reproduction of the river than he had been with the "foul stream" itself. Dickens recommended the exhibition "to the consideration of all holidaymakers and sightseers this Christmas." Though this was not "a refined work of art," it had considerable appeal—an illusion with a number of uses. First, it was "an easy means of travelling, night and day, without any inconvenience from climate, steamboat company, or fatigue." Second, it was a way to see "all the strange wild ways of life" that could be found upon the Mississippi. Crucially, it was a way to "acquire a new power of testing the descriptive accuracy of its best describers"— presumably including Dickens himself. Finally, after running through the details of Banvard's life as romantically presented in "Adventures of the Artist," Dickens ended on an admonitory note: "It would be hopeful, too, to see some things in England, part and parcel of a *moving* panorama: and not of one that stood still, or had a disposition to go backward."[35]

For the hundreds of thousands of viewers who went to see Banvard's moving panorama, what was the appeal? Education, exoticism, progress, and travel for the masses—"emphatically of the people," as Dickens's fictional Mr. Booley described the panorama. This was a far cry from Barker's vision of the medium. When he created the panoramic rotunda, Barker imagined that his invention would be patronized by an elite. Entrance for the first panorama was set at a prohibitive three shillings; his advertisements were addressed to "the nobility and the gentry." This figure was soon reduced to one shilling, "the standard for all exhibitions throughout the nineteenth century." His target audience became simply "the public." Barker also tried to make it clear that his work was "intended chiefly for the criticism of artists, and admirers of painting in general." The panorama—in all of its manifestations—never managed to achieve the artistic approval that it initially sought. Its appeal was resolutely populist. Charles Robert Leslie, in a lecture at the Royal Academy in 1849, expressed the uneasiness of many within the artistic community: "[I find] something unsatisfactory—to speak from my own feelings I should say unpleasant—in all Art of every kind of which deception is an object."[36]

The panoramic view was associated with ideas of power; the democratization of an imperial viewpoint perhaps added to the uneasiness of commentators like Leslie. In his essay "Panopticism," Foucault wondered whether Jeremy Bentham was "aware of the Panoramas that Barker was constructing at exactly the same period." The chronological relationship of both ideas was highly suggestive. Both the panorama and Bentham's "Panopticon"—a prison organized around a central viewing tower that provided a constant, invisible surveillance of all inmates—allowed the viewer to occupy "exactly the place of the sovereign gaze": central and elevated. As Alan Wallach has noted, both views "covered the entire lateral circuit of visibility" and "aspired to control every element within the visual field." (This caused unique problems for Anton von Werner, a German panoramist in the late nineteenth century. When faced with the prospect of a visit from the kaiser to his panorama of *The Battle of Sedan*, Werner slightly raised the viewing platform for the imperial visit. The perspective of the kaiser remained above that of his subjects.)[37]

A democratic cultural phenomenon, the panorama was dependent on and responsive to the growing middle classes, who formed the bulk of its audience. Bourgeois self-improvement legitimized the medium. In 1867, John Ruskin looked back at the height of moving panorama popularity and declared that they had been "a school both in physical geography and in art." For Stephan Oettermann, the panorama was swiftly established as "an instrument for glorifying the bourgeois view of the world." For the same shilling that could purchase entertainment in the "labyrinth of [. . .] not infrequently nasty exhibits in Savile House" at Leicester Square, the panorama offered art and education. There remained some for whom any public exhibition was tainted by association. Accordingly, miniature reproductions of popular panoramas were available for home study. Portable moving panoramas, annotated with useful information, were sold to tourists traveling abroad: "By the panoramic picture," they advertised, "you may identify every point of interest."[38]

The vogue for foreign travel was an important part of the panorama's appeal. Destinations as disparate as the Holy Land and the Antarctic were made panoramically available without the worries of time or money. In presenting its viewers with depictions of far-flung corners of the globe, the panorama led them to the realization that the world was much smaller and more available—especially in 1848, a year of European turmoil and American expansion—than they may once have thought. As James Kirke Paulding noted as early as 1828, just before his creation of the *Lion of the West*, "the wonderful facilities for locomotion furnished by modern ingenuity have increased the number of travellers to such a degree, that [. . .] all ages and sexes are to be found on the wing." The fashionable tour of the Mississippi was opened to all—without the unpleasant hardships faced by real travelers on the river.[39]

The new modes of industrial steam travel had also created a shift in the way that travelers experienced the landscape. In *The Railway Journey* (1980), Wolfgang Schivelbusch coined the idea of "panoramic travel." It was a term that encompassed first, the new method of traveling through the landscape that steam travel inaugurated; and second, the new modes of vision required to cope with such movement. Schivelbusch followed Erwin Straus's contention that these modes of industrial travel carved a distinction between the "landscape" experienced by eighteenth-century travelers, and the "geographical space" that nineteenth-century passengers came to understand. In a landscape, "each location is determined only by its relation to the neighboring place within the circle of visibility." Eighteenth-century travelers moved from one town to the next, in touch with the landscape around them, visually aware of the details that they passed. Geographical space, however, was "closed" and "systematised": "every place in such a space is determined by its position with respect to the whole." The sole focus of the journey in geographical space was the destination.[40]

For those who were accustomed to the slower pleasures of the stagecoach, this necessary adjustment in perception was often an uncomfortable one. John Ruskin lamented that "all travelling becomes dull in exact proportion to its rapidity"; if a traveler is forced to take in even as little as "two cottages at a time, it is already too much." But as Sternberger concluded, "the railroad [and the steamboat] elaborated the new world of experience [. . .] into a panorama." The view from a railroad carriage or a steamboat cabin could offer a panoramic world of delights. Sternberger continued: "the views from European windows had lost their depth, becoming part and parcel of the same panorama world surrounding them [. . .] constituting a painted surface everywhere." To fully appreciate these new modes of travel, the traveler had to settle into modes of vision that were often uncomfortable and disorientating. A large part of the moving panorama's appeal, therefore, lay in its ability to combine the simulation of industrial travel through geographical space, with the enjoyment of picturesque landscape. This process was particularly suited to the Mississippi. The river, as Mulvey has emphasized, "was horizon and foreground in one" to its travelers: it "went beyond the limits of vision." As Fanny Trollope experienced it, "At no point was there an inch of what painters call a second distance." The moving panorama provided a corrective to this and other visual problems.[41]

Each panorama also allowed its viewers to distill two thousand miles of the Mississippi experience into a two-hour spectacle. It provided a perfect antidote to Ida Pfeiffer's complaint about the river: "this is a grand thing to think of at first, but after a few days one gets tired of the perpetual monotony." As the promotional material for Risley and Smith's moving panorama of the Mississippi highlighted: "We may trace its crooked course upon the map, read animated descriptions of it, but these sink into nothingness in comparison with its faithful representation upon canvass, embodied in the glowing tints of nature. We see, as it were, the living reality spread before us." Since the panoramas were copies of the river, the public required reassurance that the canvas that rolled slowly past them was a real copy, an authentic simulation. Promotional material eagerly provided it. Upon their arrival in London soon after Banvard, Risley and Smith, for example, were quick to boast of the "completeness and fidelity" of their work. Distilled though this panoramic Mississippi experience may have been, it retained the power to move its audiences in startling ways. Henry Lewis's "Great National Work," as he described his panorama in advertisements, elicited a response that the *Kentucky Courier* reported in the summer of 1849: "A respectable old gentleman from the country [. . .] burst out, 'Well who'd a thought it,—if they haven't got my very house right down here on this picture, yes,—that's the place—barn—the big walnut tree,—the old gate [. . .] if there ain't old Bally and the white mare, well it *is* surprising how the mischief he come to get it so natural I don't know, *stop the boat and let me get out.*'"[42]

Commentators emphasized the authenticity of the experience. Dickens stated that this "easy means of travelling" gave the spectator "a thorough understanding of what the great American river is." Longfellow noted in his diary as early as December 17, 1846, during the composition of *Evangeline:* "I see a diorama of the Mississippi advertised. This comes very *á propos.* The river comes to me instead of my going to the river"—and afterward judged, "One seems to be sailing down the great stream [. . .] Three miles of canvas, and a great deal of merit." The effect of the condensed Mississippi experience on Henry David Thoreau was profound: "I went to see a panorama of the Mississippi, and as I worked my way up the river in the light of to-day, and saw the steamboats wooding up, counted the rising cities, gazed on the fresh ruins of Nauvoo, beheld the Indians moving west across the stream [. . .] I saw that this was a Rhine stream of a different kind; that the foundations of castles were yet to be laid, and the famous bridges were yet to be thrown over the river." As Dickens's panoramic world traveler

"Mr. Booley" concluded: "When I was a boy, such travelling would have been impossible [. . .] some of the best results of actual travel are by such means available to those whose lot it is to stay at home."[43]

Umberto Eco's "Travels in Hyperreality," his experiences in search of the "absolute fakes" of America, provide a vocabulary strikingly applicable to the moving panorama phenomenon. The philosophy informing attractions like the Palace of Living Arts Wax Museum in Los Angeles was the same as that which motivated the moving panoramas more than a century earlier: "We are giving you the reproduction so you will no longer feel any need for the original." Equally telling were Eco's experiences on modern-day, Disney-created Mississippi rides—the descendants of the moving panorama. Deliberately traveling in the space of twenty- four hours from "the wild river of Adventureland to a trip on the Mississippi, where the captain says it is possible to see alligators on the banks of the river and then you don't see any [. . .] you risk feeling homesick for Disneyland, where the wild animals don't have to be coaxed." Just like Disneyland's reconstructed Mississippi, the moving panorama was "more real than reality." Any incident that could happen to a traveler—and many that could not—happened on the moving canvas: fires, pirates, Indians, whirlpools, snags, crashes, or tornadoes, all in the safety of the exhibition hall. The simulation went further. Leon Pomarède, a French émigré who planned a panorama with Henry Lewis before the pair quarreled over the terms of their agreement, included steamboats that appeared to move against the current. Later, when observers complained about the mimetic omission, he devised a system to pipe steam through their funnels. As Rebecca Nichols, a western poet, described her experience with Samuel Stockwell's panorama: "the illusion was momentary, but it was complete."[44]

The "Panorama of the Monumental Grandeur of the Mississippi Valley," the only remaining Mississippi panorama, represented the last flush of the moving panorama boom. Dr. Montroville Wilson Dickeson, "late Professor in Philadelphia College of Medicine; Member of the Academy of Natural Science, and Fellow of the Royal Society of Copenhagen, &c., &c.," did not commission his panorama until 1850, when the novelty of Banvard's work had worn thin. It provided the main feature for his traveling museum of Indian artifacts, and worked as a backdrop to his "scientific lectures on American Ærchiology." The man who received the commission was either I. J. or John J. Egan. Little is known of the artist. In many ways, the Dickeson-Egan panorama was an unusual variant of the form. Unlike its counterparts, it did not provide an unbroken view of the riverbank. Simulation was not its intention. Rather, it "derived unity from [Dickeson's] lecture." It was predominantly concerned with "the ANTIQ-UITIES & CUSTOMS OF THE UNHISTORIED INDIAN TRIBES who dwelt on this continent 3,500 years ago." A passing interest in Indian mounds and native ritual and myth formed part of any panorama, providing useful associations with which to entertain the viewer. Banvard, for example, composed a poem titled "The White Fawn of the Mississippi River"—a spurious Indian myth; Twain's panoramist narrated a mangled version of Winona's fate at Maiden's Rock. Dickeson was unique in making such stories the focus of his moving panorama. Little mention can be found of the panorama in the contemporary press, even though Dickeson's Indian collection was shown at the Philadelphia Centennial Exposition of 1876. Nonetheless, this curious ambassador of the medium allows a glimpse of what nineteenth-century audiences flocked to and absorbed in the thousands.[45]

Visitors needed to arrive by eight. Entrance cost 25 cents for adults, 12½ for children under twelve. The panorama stood 7.5 feet tall. To cover the "15,000 feet of canvas" that Dickeson's advertising boasted, the panorama would needed to have been approximately 2,000 feet long. The real figure is more like 300 feet, but exaggeration was an established part of the genre: Dickeson and Egan only claimed the length of half a mile for their work; Banvard claimed three miles; Smith and Risley, four; Stockwell, that his painting was three times the length of Banvard's. To have displayed Banvard's three miles of canvas in the one-and-a-half hours that the Bristol *Gazette* stated as the exhibition's duration, the canvas would have passed in front of the spectators at three feet per second, far too fast for a leisurely Mississippi excursion. The panoramas were still monumental works, however, and would have seemed so to their audiences.[46]

Dickeson's performance was divided into three sections. Though there was little thematic unity within them, section one was wholly concerned with "the aboriginal monuments of a large extent of country once roamed by the RED MAN." Sections two and three introduced an element of history, taking the Mississippi as a backdrop. From Circleville—the panorama began on the Ohio—the viewer was taken on a journey past "the leading peculiarities in the construction of [. . .] Mounds, Tumuli, Fossas, &c." to which Dickeson had devoted the past twelve years. The rituals of Indian daily life featured prominently, from the "Cado chiefs in full costume" to their "piscatory exploits." The infamous "Cave in the Rock" appeared, not as the hideout of pirates and murderers, but as a significant archaeological site. Slaves were shown opening burial mounds. Dickeson's presentation of Native life and Native archaeology was in keeping with the expansionist spirit of the times, a legacy of Jacksonian removal policies.

Braves and "youths at their war practice" appeared as figures from a bucolic pre-history. The "terraced mound in a snow storm at sunset" seemed a scene from the dawn of creation. Then white men entered the panoramic history lesson. The massacre of the French at Fort Rosalie was the dramatic highlight of section two. Dickeson seems to have specifically chosen it as a climax, offering the "Mode of scalping" as a dramatic finish. By section three, the Native American had been fully consigned to the realms of "Ærchiology." Dr. Dickeson himself was pictured, sketching on the spot as promised in his advertisements, the American Egyptologist. Soon, it was sunset at the "temple of the Sun."[47]

Dickens, for one, was quick to realize that the moving Mississippi panorama was, in many ways, a hymn of praise to the settler—and conversely, in the words of the Bristol *Gazette,* an apparently inevitable ushering away of "savage [. . .] life." As Dickeson made clear in his promotional material, Indians were history: these were "TRIBES who dwelt on this continent 3,500 years ago." This country was "once roamed by the RED MAN." Banvard's panorama shared thematic affinities. As he described the course of the Missouri River: "Openings of the trees, and the sound of the axe echoing through the woods, betoken the appearance of civilisation [. . .] you have passed the wild regions of the savage, and are now among the abodes of white men." In Dickens's review of Banvard's panorama, he devoted significant space to a description of the portrayal of "dead Braves, with their pale faces turned up to the night sky [. . .] nearer and nearer to which the outposts of civilisation are approaching with gigantic strides to tread their people down." It was, he felt, "suggestive matter." He returned to it, ambivalently, semi-ironically, when he chronicled the fictional adventures of Mr. Booley. Booley related his panoramic travels to his brother "social Oysters":

> He was struck, too, by the reflection that savage nature was not by any means such a fine and noble spectacle as some delight to represent it. He found it a poor, greasy, paint-plastered, miserable thing enough [. . .] It occurred to him that the "Big Bird," or the "Blue Fish," or any of the other braves was [. . .] doing very little for science, not much more than the monkeys for art, scarcely anything worth mentioning for letters, and not often making the world greatly better than he found it. Civilisation, MR BOOLEY concluded, was on the whole, with all its blemishes, a more imposing sight, and a far better thing to stand by.[48]

Though Henry Lewis's panorama has long been lost to history, he left a fascinating record of his work that stands alongside Dickeson and Egan's panorama as a remaining glimpse into this lost world. When his touring days were over—the European Mississippi panorama market had been exhausted by 1853—Lewis settled in Düsseldorf, a popular destination for American painters (George Caleb Bingham studied there in the 1850s). Lewis's panorama had not been a great success. Bad luck had played its part: a cholera epidemic in Louisiana and Cincinnati, for example, had helped keep the crowds away. Eager for funds that would enable him to marry, Lewis set about publication of *Das illustrirte Mississippithal* (1854–57). (He borrowed his title—translated, *The Valley of the Mississippi Illustrated*—and perhaps the idea from John Casper Wild, who had produced a series of delicate lithographs of the Mississippi in the early 1840s.) Lewis's work was composed of seventy-eight colored plates, engravings of the scenes and views that he had included in his panorama, alongside text that described his exploits on the Mississippi. The publication of the book, in twenty parts, was begun by Arnz and Company in 1854. Lewis stated in a preface that it was his intention "To render each single number, as is practicable, complete in itself, with regard to the history and geography of that particular region"—almost like a pictorial guidebook. Financial difficulties meant that the remaining fourteen "Fascicles" were published in 1857 by Elkan and Company, and his marriage was continually postponed.[49]

Lewis lamented the "rascally delays" that bedeviled his project and blamed them for ruining sales of the work—which was, he felt, "got up in a very common way." Common or not, Lewis's series of prints remains extremely valuable. As John W. Reps has asserted, these prints stand as "[the] earliest complete look at the results of the rapid progress of urbanisation along the great river." By the time of its publication in 1853, *Das illustrirte Mississippithal* had already become a work of history. Urbanizing communities expanded rapidly, constantly altering the appearance of the waterfront that Lewis had captured.[50]

There was another important dimension to the history of Lewis's panorama and his illustrations of the Mississippi. Captain Seth Eastman of the First Infantry was stationed at Fort Snelling in 1841. Eastman had been trained in topographical drawing at West Point, and upon his arrival at the river he began to sketch the Mississippi and the local Indian tribes. His friend Charles Lanman—who had embarked upon his own journey up the Mississippi at the time—considered his "Indian Gallery" to be "the most valuable in the country, not even excepting that of George Catlin." Eastman accumulated numerous Mississippi sketches, seventy-nine of which Henry Lewis saw and purchased when the two artists met at Fort Snelling in 1847. Eastman was on one of his last tours in the army; Lewis was on the sketching trip that would develop into his panorama. It now seems likely that the offer which Eastman talked of in a letter to Lanman dated November 1, 1847, came from Lewis: "there have been several artists here this summer. It has been proposed for me to join one or two of them in Painting a panorama of the Mississippi." Eastman did not accept the offer. Rather, he and Lewis entered into an arrangement concerning the purchase of Eastman's river sketches. As Henry wrote to his brother George, these were "the very sketches we want"; their acquisition "may render our affair of much more ease and importance than we thought."[51]

Lewis used the sketches as templates for scenes in his panorama. John Francis McDermott has made an irrefutable case that seventeen of the fifty-nine plates which depict scenes above St. Louis in *Das illustrirte Mississippithal* "were copied by the lithographer from originals by Eastman." This is not, however, to "imply any impropriety on the part of Lewis" in putting his name to Eastman's work (or the work of his numerous assistants—most notably, Charles Rogers). It was all part of the showmanship that required every panoramist to be, like Banvard, the itinerant artist alone in the wilderness, the sole guiding force behind the epic work. Lewis worked hard in promoting Eastman's work, and Eastman was at liberty to reproduce identical sketches when illustrating Henry Rowe Schoolcraft's Indian books.[52]

The most interesting dimension of the use of Eastman's sketches in Lewis's prints is the direct comparison that can be made between both works, one public and one private. In McDermott's judgment, Eastman "was [not] painting [. . .] to thrill the stay-at-home white man with glimpses of savage ways, and raw adventures"; the panoramists, on the other hand, were doing precisely that. Eastman's sketches contained an immediacy and a freshness that can still transport the viewer back to the Mississippi that flowed in the 1840s. Most of his sketches, almost all in pencil, were taken in the field. Lewis's polished lithographs provided a perfect visual counterpart to the process of urbanization; Eastman's expressive, controlled sketches evoked the lonely wildness that the giant river was slowly losing (but would never lose completely). Viewing his drawing *Twenty Miles below the Mouth of the Ohio,* it is possible to appreciate the extraordinary vistas that were both a burden to homesick Europeans (Fanny Trollope's "heavy horror") and a magical, American wonderland, a birthplace of cultural heroes—the landscape which Emmeline Wortley found "so imposing—its bends and curves so glorious and beautiful—that I could not find it monotonous."[53]

Still, it is apparent that Lewis's panorama did not entirely romanticize the Mississippi into a European view. Trollope had wished for a picturesque "ruined abbey, or feudal castle" to complete the scene. Instead, Lewis provided gas works, engine houses, and smoking chimneys precisely like the ones that appeared in the bird's-eye prints. Still, there was also a degree of sentimentalization evident within Lewis's prints—the towns are almost uniformly clean, neat, well ordered, unpeopled, even a little fairy tale (perhaps an inspiration for the later river views of Currier and Ives). They stood in stark contrast to Seth Eastman's sketches, like his drawing *Cassville, Wisconsin.* Eastman depicted rugged pioneer houses which, though sturdy, were ramshackle—surrounded by an imposing natural world that seemed truly wild. Man could and would survive here, but not without effort, and not yet (truly, not ever) as part of a wholly urbanized environment. In that sense, Eastman's river was more prescient than any of its improving fictions.[54]

"FINE AND ROMANTIC SUBJECTS [. . .] FOR THE PENCIL OF THE ILLUSTRATOR"

American illustrated magazines, emerging in the 1850s, played host to the last flourishing of antebellum Mississippi views. Magazines like *Gleason's,* later *Ballou's, Pictorial Drawing-Room Companion, Frank Leslie's Illustrated Newspaper,* and *Harper's Weekly*—all modeled on the *Illustrated London News*—featured numerous wood engravings of river towns. Though a world away from the woodcuts that filled the *Crockett Almanacs,* they employed the same basic technique: wood engravings were the most practical method of illustration for periodicals combining text and pictures. *Leslie's* and *Harper's* enjoyed great popularity and "appeared in large editions for many decades." As America approached the Civil War, these were the images of the Mississippi that proliferated most widely. Though generally an engaging mixture of authentic observation and picturesque detail—the presence of iconic jolly flatboatmen was one of the sentimental necessities for a river view—these illustrations were not always so polite. In 1858, "Arrowsmith," in *Harper's New Monthly Magazine,* produced a burlesque panorama of the hackneyed elements found in representations of the river throughout the antebellum years—"Designed for Exhibition in England."[55]

The popularity of river views in illustrated magazines continued after the war. Indeed, it is argued that *Harper's Weekly* and its rivals "came of age during the Civil War," having responded to public demand for visual information about the conflict by creating "a unique and compelling pictorial record of each week's events." Alfred Rodolph Waud trained in London and worked for *Harper's* as a war correspondent. Immediately after the war, the magazine dispatched him to the South; he traveled down the Mississippi by steamboat and produced numerous views of river towns. In 1871, the short-lived *Every Saturday* sent Waud to cover the same territory, and his illustrations of the river also appeared in William

Cullen Bryant's renowned *Picturesque America* (1874). The river views that Waud produced were exemplary: delicate, detailed, and epic in scope. Notable, too, was the influence of the panoramic viewpoint on Waud's compositions. Many of his river-town views are long and sweeping, taking in an extensive vista. Of course, these postwar illustrations of the river also held a new interest for viewers: locations along the Mississippi, especially Vicksburg, had become famous because of their war history. Having illustrated the war, Waud produced the definitive first glimpses of the newly peaceful river.[56]

Years after he produced these important illustrations, the Mississippi still held a powerful appeal for Waud. Presumably inspired by the success of Twain's river writings, in 1885 Waud planned to produce an entire book on the river entitled *The Father of Waters: The Mississippi from Lake Itasca to the Gulf of Mexico.* As Waud wrote in an unpublished draft: "I have been convinced from the time that I made the first trip on the river [. . .] that it was *the subject* [. . .] I do not see why 100,000 of the Mississippi book should not be sold, and for many years continue to sell as a standard." Waud envisaged that the book would be filled with a wealth of material, ranging through topography, scenery, geology, resources, commerce, and history: "In all these, fine and romantic subjects exist for the pencil of the illustrator, in a field that has by no means been worked out." It seems, from Waud's draft of the title page, that he wanted Charles Dudley Warner to supply the text. He also thought that the work could be "abridged" and sold as a guidebook "on the R.R.s and steamboats, and at tourists' points of attraction." Waud's plans came to nothing; the Mississippi River was robbed of representations that would indeed have come to be "standard."[57]

Instead, the most significant postbellum visual representations of the river were the prints of the river produced by Currier and Ives. Throughout the second half of the nineteenth century, the company released a huge variety of romantic and sentimental images of the antebellum river, including "at least two hundred prints of some of the most luxurious steamboats of the period," and a visual counterpoint to *Lloyd's* accounts, "more than fifty steamboat disaster prints." The influence of George Bingham's popular images was evident, though further sentimentalized, and their cartoonish boatmen frequently struck the same poses as his *Jolly Flatboatmen.* Their portrayal of steamboats, as in Frances Palmer's *"Rounding a Bend" on the Mississippi* (1866), had a distinct and definitive charm: grand, imposing, powerful, ornate, and swift—commensurate to the giant river on which they sailed. But Currier and Ives also used the river to eulogize the antebellum South. Palmer's *Low Water in the Mississippi* (1868), for example, was an early example of postwar plantation sentimentalization. An idyllic plantation house is visible through the twilight and the trees; a southern belle promenades; happy slaves dance outside a picturesque cabin; the *Robert E. Lee* steams down the river. Such was the dominant visual Mississippi in the latter half of the nineteenth century.[58]

John Banvard knew the value of illusion. Self-promotion and a degree of hucksterism were crucial components of the moving panorama business. Still, critical plaudits were heaped on Banvard's head. As the *Times* (London) described, "Mister Banvard has done more to elevate the taste for fine arts, among those who little thought on these subjects, than any single artist since the discovery of painting and much praise is due him." Banvard returned to America in 1852, a wealthy man. Initially he spent his time and money building "Glenada," a replica of Windsor Castle, on a sixty-acre Long Island lot. In the short-term, he remained wealthy. Banvard wrote plays and poetry; he provided the Union with his charts of the Mississippi to assist their fight for the river in 1861; above all, he collected. In London, Banvard was fascinated by the Royal Museum and particularly its Egyptian artifacts. On a sketching trip up the Nile for a panorama of the Holy Land, Banvard began his own collection. Soon, Glenada was filled with a "large collection of curiosities" gathered from "all parts of the world." And then Banvard became aware of the remarkable success of one man: P. T. Barnum. The enterprise in which Banvard became so interested was Scudder's American Museum, purchased by Barnum in 1841: "By 1866, Barnum's total ticket sales were greater than the country's population of 35 million." Barnum's museum was a potent mixture of freak show, magic, and spectacle, supported by his consummate manipulation of advertising and the press. In Terence Whalen's words, "reality was but a minor impediment to Barnum's inventiveness."[59]

Banvard, forgetting the lessons of a lifetime, reasoned that if a museum of fakes could attract public interest, then a museum filled with the genuine artifacts that littered Glenada would guarantee big business. Perhaps believing his own press, Banvard saw himself, the Mississippi panoramist, as the defender of truth, authenticity, and education. With the help of an old sailing partner, William Lillienthal, "Banvard's Museum" was financed by the floatation of a stock of $300,000. Contractors and laborers were paid with the shares; others were purchased by prominent New York families. But Banvard had no experience of running a proper business venture. Neither the business nor the stock was registered with the State of New York. The shares were entirely worthless. When the museum finally opened its doors, it was unequivocally "the best museum in Manhattan." Barnum realized this. During the summer of 1867, the two entrepreneurs were locked in battle. Banvard had been at pains to ensure that his museum was well ventilated. Louvers and windows had been installed all the way around the auditorium. Barnum saved on the expense and simply placed an advertisement in the *New York Times* falsely claiming that his museum was "THOROUGHLY VENTILATED! COOL! Delightful!! Cool!!!" Banvard boasted the real "Cardiff Man" skeleton. Barnum had a fake. In pride of place, Banvard displayed the "*largest painting in the world*"—his Mississippi panorama. Barnum had a Nile panorama, probably copied from Banvard's. Barnum's intelligent advertising more than made up for the shaky provenance of his exhibits, and it would be his spirit that dominated the final antebellum years of the Mississippi. On September 1, the doors to Banvard's museum were locked for the last time. He had forgotten how useful illusion could be.[60]

5

Crime and Punishment

"Extraordinary metaphysical scamps" in the Mississippi Underworld

"And is not my friend politic? Is not my friend sagacious? By your own definition, is not my friend a Great Medicine?"
"No, he is an operator, a Mississippi operator; an equivocal character."
HERMAN MELVILLE, *The Confidence-Man*, 1857

I read romantic rose-coloured accounts of those old days [. . .] when the steamboats that plied between New Orleans and St. Louis were floating gambling dens. Strange odds and ends get into the press and come to me. It's very pretty to read about, but the real thing was not so nice.
OLD MR. MARTIN of St. Louis, 1896

"Some stories are told about steamboats," wrote Herman Melville in *The Confidence-Man* (1857), "fitted to make one a little apprehensive." Whatever else the Mississippi may have been in the antebellum years, its reputation as the scene of crimes, mysteries, and transgressions was profound. Drinking and gambling were the tip of a Mississippi iceberg that descended through extortion and prostitution to organized crime and cold-blooded murder; its murky waters showed a dark reflection and provided the ingredients for much myth making. The river, at least imaginatively, was the arena for high stakes, long shots, hope, and luck. Often, the ante was life and death. But there was little romance attached to the river's darker tributaries. The Mississippi resonated in late antebellum American culture as an illicit underworld inhabited by alligator-horse boatmen, devilish gamblers, murderous robbers, and criminal conspirators who planned the overthrow of the river's newly developed urban centers, if not the world. Above all, slavery loomed large. Indeed, the stories of crime and gambling that came to dominate popular discourse about the river were predominantly stories of the Lower Mississippi. Just as the divisions fracturing the nation slowly expanded, so the Mississippi took on a dual personality. As the Upper Mississippi became increasingly associated with the picturesque, tourism, and growing urbanization, so the Lower Mississippi, and its world of slavery, became the scene of degeneration. George Byron Merrick, pilot on the Upper Mississippi from 1854 to 1863, remembered that, "the play was not high on the upper river [. . .] The passengers were not great planters, with sacks of money [. . .] The operators, also, were not so greedy as their real or fictitious fellows on the lower river." (Though even Merrick's boat, the *Fanny Harris,* was "favoured with the presence, more or less intermittently" of a trio of gamblers.) If it was, at least in part, a fiction, as it often seems to have been, the invention of the Mississippi underworld in popular culture was symbolically wed to slavery and the South.[1]

"The valley watered by the Mississippi," wrote Alexis de Tocqueville, "seems to have been created for it alone; it dispenses good and evil at will, and it is like the valley's god." Melville's vision of the Mississippi chimed with this: "the dashing and all-fusing spirit of the West [. . .] which, uniting the streams of the most distant and opposite zones, pours them along, helter-skelter, in one cosmopolitan and confident tide." The journey of the steamboat *Fidèle* in *The Confidence-Man* was an April Fools' Day expedition from St. Louis to New Orleans (and, perhaps, the apocalypse), populated by a representative multitude—extraordinary, and yet typical for the antebellum Mississippi:

> Natives of all sorts, and foreigners; men of business and men of pleasure; parlor men and backwoodsmen; farm-hunters and fame-hunters; heiress-hunters, gold-hunters, buffalo hunters, bee-hunters, happiness-hunters, truth-hunters, and still keener hunters after all these hunters. Fine ladies in slippers, and moccasined squaws; Northern speculators and eastern philosophers; English, Irish, German, Scotch, Danes; Santa Fé traders in striped blankets, and Broadway bucks in cravats of cloth of gold; fine-looking Kentucky boatmen, and Japanese-looking Mississippi cotton-planters; Quakers in full drab, and United States soldiers in full regimentals; slaves, black, mulatto, quadroon; modish young Spanish Creoles, and old fashioned French Jews; Mormons and Papists; Dives and Lazarus; jesters and mourners, teetotallers and convivialists, deacons and blacklegs; hard-shell Baptists and clay-eaters; grinning negroes, and Sioux chiefs solemn as high-priests. In short, a piebald parliament, an Anacharsis Cloots congress of all kinds of that multiform pilgrim species, man.

As the nation drew close to Civil War, the Mississippi became a river of the underworld—leading this heterogeneous American crowd confidently into darkness and damnation.[2]

The river's reputation for double-dealing had been established early—because of a Scottish gambler. John Law was born in 1671, the scion of an ancient Fife family. A mathematical prodigy, Law neglected the duties of his father's countinghouse and was frequently seen in London gaming houses. A model for the gamblers who would later proliferate on the Mississippi, Law, as Charles Mackay described him to antebellum readers, was "vain of his person, [and] indulged in considerable extravagance of attire." To the women, he was "Beau Law"; to the men, "Jessamy John." For almost nine years he was successful; then, as his "love of play increased in violence, so it diminished in prudence." The family estate was mortgaged, and a dueling murder led Law to flee the country into a dissipated exile that saw him tour the gaming tables of Europe for almost two decades, studying the economies of the countries through which he traveled. During a sojourn in Paris, he made the acquaintance of the Duke of Orleans.[3]

When Louis XIV died in 1715, it was the Duke of Orleans who assumed control of France (in lieu of the seven-year-old heir). Law had a zeal for paper currency and proposed financial schemes in a variety of countries to little result; now he presented himself to the duke and offered paper currency as the solution to France's economic straits. The duke granted him the authorization to found the bank of Law and Company. Its paper currency was a success. Law, inveterate gambler that he was, then proposed to the regent that he should found a company "that should have the exclusive privilege of trading to the great river Mississippi and the province of Louisiana." The country was "supposed to abound in precious metals." The Mississippi Company, incorporated in 1717, was to reap all the riches for twenty-five years. It took as its emblem "an old river-god leaning upon a cornucopia from which poured golden coins."[4]

At the peak of speculation in Law's Mississippi ventures, those "of every age and sex, and condition of life, speculated in the rise and fall of the Mississippi bonds." In the Place Vendome, and later the grounds of the Hotel de Soissons, crowds thronged around Law's residence, conducting business with the stock-jobbers and gamblers who congregated there. Immense riches were made. "Seeing their fortunes double or triple in a single day," wrote an observer in the 1750s, "the Mississippians gambled with abandon. Gambling losses were not really considered as such, but only as deductions from the immense profits on the other side." But the collective Parisian vision of a river of wealth soon evaporated: the bubble burst, and bankruptcy abounded. In a popular print, the Mississippi was represented—"with his wooden leg"—as a figure in the vanguard of the procession of the "Goddess of Shares," driven in her triumphal car by the "Goddess of Folly." Law himself was cursed in popular song as "le fils aine de Satan." And the memory of Law's disastrous system was persistent: over a century later, Alexandre Dumas compared the "speculation" of the evil banker Danglars with "the chimerical Mississippi, which Law formerly supplied for the good Parisians, those Cockneys in speculation." (The damage to the river's reputation was only amplified when, years later, new "Mississippi Bonds" from the

Planters' Bank proved to be an unwise investment for many Europeans, including William Wordsworth's sister-in-law.)[5]

In Louisiana itself, the effect of Law's scheme was profound. Just before the demise of the Mississippi Company, in an effort to restore public confidence and produce some of the promised wealth of the Mississippi, Law's Company endeavored to provide Governor Bienville with colonists. Albert Phelps described the result: "the government went boldly to the task of ransacking the jails and hospitals. Disorderly soldiers, black sheep of distinguished families, paupers, prostitutes, political suspects, friendless strangers, unsophisticated peasants [. . .] all were kidnapped, herded, and shipped under guard to fill the emptiness of Louisiana." In Mackay's words, the "very refuse of the population" flowed up the Mississippi. Two-thirds disappeared and never reached their official destination. These immigrants were fundamental to the social development of the river: at a stroke, the Mississippi demimonde had been created.[6]

So who was it that populated the Mississippi underworld? River pirates, slave stealers and illegal slave traders, counterfeiters, horse thieves, and prostitutes all thrived—but it has always been the gambler that defined the river's nefarious associations. Popular mythology would suggest that the antebellum river was home to a race of dashing gamblers: handsome, roguish, morally ambiguous—but essentially honest. In the twentieth century, Tyrone Power was one of the many Hollywood actors to incarnate this Mississippi gambler-hero (in a 1953 film). But almost exactly 120 years before Power took on that role, his great-grandfather, the Irish actor William Grattan Tyrone Power, toured America. His itinerary took him along the Mississippi. When he arrived at Natchez-under-the-Hill, the most notorious river haunt of gamblers, prostitutes, and worse, he was shocked at what he found: "The impunity with which these professed gamblers carry on their trade, and the course of crime contingent upon it [. . .] is one of the most crying evils existing in this society. The Legs are associated in gangs, have a system perfectly organized, and possess a large capital invested in this pursuit; they are seldom alone, always armed to the teeth, bound to sustain each other, and hold life at a pin's fee [. . .] not a steamboat stirs from any quarter, but one or more of the gang proceed on board, in some guise or other."[7]

In the antebellum years, there was little conception of the honest gambler-hero. No differentiation was made between gamblers and other members of the criminal fraternity, and the gambler was often seen as the worst of the breed. Condemnation in the press developed into vigilantism along the river. Gamblers and robbers were seen as river devils, kin to the old tempter himself. As an inhabitant of Vicksburg wrote in 1835, under the name of gambler "are classed a host of desperadoes who belong to the newly settled parts of the country, who are not only cheats at games of chance, but robbers, murderers, and felons in all crimes." Occasionally, an antebellum description afforded the gambler some recognizable charm, as *Emerson's Magazine and Putnam's Monthly* did in October 1857: "the 'Father of Waters' bears upon his bosom a crowd of men (often gentlemanly, jovial fellows) who have erected gambling into a profession; they are a 'breed' particular to the river [. . .] they dress well, smoke well, drink well, and with a dash of swagger and a spice of blackleg, they [. . .] are not thought so ill of."[8]

The Mississippi itself was a popular symbol of capricious luck. George Wharton, in one of the sketches he produced for the *New Orleans Delta* in 1852, described the "difference between a better and abettor at Monte." Wharton outlined the typical progress of a game for those innocents caught in the grip of a professional gambler: "the tide of good fortune, which had so long wafted the [victims] buoyantly along its silver current,—like the Mississippi river, made a sudden *detour,* and disembogued itself into the lake at the elbow of the 'professor.'" The dupes were left in "shoaly water." By struggling to get back "into the current again," they ended up in "deep water."[9]

Given the particulars of gambling psychology that Gerda Reith has highlighted, it is little surprise that the Mississippi proved a fertile environment for gaming. Games of chance, and their area of play, are "characterised essentially by their *separateness,* both temporally and spatially, from everyday life." They "involve both a physical and a mental crossing of a threshold out of the ordinary world and into the world of play [. . .] players within it are animated by a different set of motivations from those of everyday routines in which they are free to experiment with new roles and to temporarily adopt new identities." In this "realm of activity, set against the world of utilitarian goals," the "fluid 'gambling identity' [. . .] is released from the strictures which usually govern" its actions. Both the "world of play" and the liminal world of the Mississippi conferred a potent sense of mutability on the individual: the "fluid" sense of self experienced by a traveler on the river; the communal anonymity of the steamboat cabin; the instability of identity stretched to an extreme by the gamblers who disguised and playacted their way up and downstream. It proved a potent combination.[10]

"I NEVER GAMBLE, STRANGER," SAYS I, "PRINCIPLED AGAINST IT"

The boatmen and backwoodsmen who lived and worked along the Mississippi played an equivocal role in the river's underworld. On the one hand, they made up the majority of the customers for infamous river-town areas like Natchez-under-the-Hill—in Memphis it was "Pinch-Gut"; Vicksburg had "The Kanga-roos"; in New Orleans, "The Swamp." Alligator-horses on a spree, with a pocket-ful of money, were willing targets for gamblers and prostitutes. This had been the case since the late eighteenth century, when river piracy briefly dominated the Mississippi underworld. The Cave-in-Rock was notoriously employed as a con-fidence trick on those descending the Ohio on their way to the Mississippi. As the Cave-*Inn*-Rock, operated in 1797 by Samuel Mason (a Revolutionary soldier turned outlaw), it was advertised as "Wilson's Liquor Vault and House for En-tertainment." Weary boatmen pulled in at the cave expecting a comfortable res-pite from the hardships of flatboat work. Thus, as Otto Rothert described, they were "simply and easily delivered into the hands of the banditti" lurking inside.[11]

As Michael Allen has highlighted, "rivermen loved to gamble." They were "the best known and most zealous of the Mississippi Valley's early gamblers." It was one of the iconic poses that George Caleb Bingham chose as a subject—for *Raftsmen Playing Cards* (1847). In response to Bingham's painting, Jackson Lears has commented that "there must have been times when the raft floated with the current, and a late afternoon glow descended, and someone suggested a friendly game." Such tranquility was hardly in keeping with the known character of the boatmen. Perhaps more telling were the experiences of J. G. Flugel, traveling down the Mississippi in 1817. The boatmen "John and Strauss" were gambling for jewelry and pelts. One called the other "a cheat, liar, etc." so that "sharp words passed between them." This process of gambling and fighting continued throughout the journey. Christian Schultz, too, noted that the boatmen with whom he traveled commonly lost "in one hour [. . .] the hard earned wages of a two month voyage." As Ned Buntline expressed it, "Many of them come down on *flats* to see *sharps* as soon as they reach the city."[12]

For Davy Crockett, or at least one of his popular incarnations, gambling was a "gentlemanly and rational amusement," a test of skill, but not a means of pecuniary gain. Such a contest, between Crockett and Mike Fink, was described in the *Crockett Almanac for 1840*. After testing their shooting prowess on a cat's ears and a pig's tail, Mike took the honors by shooting the comb from his wife Sal's hair. The contestants retired for a glass of "flem-cutter." Professional gam-blers were another matter. One of the most influential portraits of an antebellum Mississippi gambler appeared in Richard Penn Smith's *Col. Crockett's Exploits and Adventures in Texas* (1836), released after Crockett's death at the Alamo.[13]

On his way to Texas, Smith wrote, Crockett steamed down the Mississippi with a "pretty particularly miscellaneous [. . .] crowd." Moving through the busy steamboat crowd of "merchants and emigrants and gamblers," Crockett found a crowd surrounding a "thimblerig" operator (a game, like monte, with three cups and a pea). He was "a tall lank sea sarpent looking blackleg, who had crawled over from Natchez under the hill [. . .] picking up their shillings just about as expeditiously as a hungry gobbler would a pint of corn." The metamorphic gambler invited Crockett himself to test his luck; the frontiersman was not tempted: "I told him [. . .] that I would never bet any thing beyond a quart of whisky upon a rifle shot, which I considered a legal bet, and gentlemanly and rational amusement [. . .] 'I never gamble, stranger,' says I, 'principled against it; think it a slippery way of getting through the world at best.'" Crockett finally consented to gamble for "drinks for the present company." The pea moved from one thimble to the next. When it came to rest, Crockett insisted on lifting the middle thimble himself: "and sure enough, the pea was there; but it mought have been otherwise if he had had the uncovering of it." Crockett's disapproval of Thimblerig's prestidigitations was typical in popular accounts. (Thimblerig, however, resolved to put aside his cheating ways and followed Crockett to Texas; he fought and died valiantly at the Alamo, a prototype of the gambler-hero.)[14]

Jim Bowie, on the other hand, was a keen gambler and, whether concocting fraudulent land claims or trading slaves with Jean Lafitte, often lived outside the law. J. E. Jefferson, a Texan general, remembered that "almost everyone in that section in those days played poker and other games," but felt it necessary to point out that Bowie "was not a professional gambler." Ironically, in later years, Bowie was often popularly portrayed as one of the "knights-errant" who were "a menace to the river gamblers for several years." This popular reputation stemmed from a legendary altercation, with perhaps some basis in truth, between Bowie and "one of the foremost desperadoes and gamblers of Natchez": John Sturdivant. Sturdivant made the mistake of choosing Young Lattimore as a victim. Lattimore, having sold his family's cotton crop in Natchez, soon found himself Under-the-Hill without a cent. His father turned to Jim Bowie, a family friend, for help. Bowie confronted Sturdivant: "one of your blacklegs brought this boy in here about an hour ago, and some of your professional thieves robbed him of his father's money." A knife fight ensued, and Bowie was the victor.[15]

Moral distinctions about gambling were often obscure—even in these popular accounts. Captain Charles Ross recorded a story, grimly realistic in detail, which pitted gamblers and boatmen against one another. Supposedly he "had often heard" it from Jim Girty himself. In June 1815 (presumably fresh from the Battle of New Orleans), Girty's crew arrived at Natchez-under-the-Hill, where it "was the custom of that day to give the hands a holiday." The crew "scampered away for the dance houses." Late at night, leaving his men "dancing and [. . .]

betting on the roulettes with the gamblers," Girty retired to his boat. When the next day came, "all hands were on board, but some had their heads badly bruised." After the "gamblers had won all their money [. . .] a fight ensued—the gamblers came off victorious." The crew refused to carry on downriver until they had been revenged. They insisted that Girty should help them: "I repaired with my whole crew to the dance houses, armed with knives, axes, and setting poles. The gamblers expected us, and were armed with pistols, knives, and guns. The fight immediately commenced. They at first gave us a hard fight, but their ammunition was soon spent, and they gave ground leaving three dead on the spot. One of our men was mortally wounded." Girty was arrested while burying the dead member of his crew. He escaped prosecution: a woman "that kept a dance house" poisoned the only witness. (In one version of Girty's life, the boatman was ultimately "cut to pieces by a gang of gamblers in a saloon and brothel owned by his mistress.")[16]

In one of the most significant antebellum novels to deal with the river's underworld, *Marie; or the Gambler of the Mississippi*, Justin Jones featured these two stock characters, alligator-horse and villainous gambler, in a conflict that epitomized their antebellum cultural roles. Dick Denton is described as a Kentuckian, a "sinewy and honest-looking old boatman." Like many of his colleagues, he likes to gamble when on a spree in New Orleans. He is one "whom it has cost many a watchful night and toilsome day to scrape together the amount he stakes here this evening, and yet though he may lose all, the utmost gains he could hope are small." Soon enough, Denton's "last red cent" is gone—because he falls into the company of the gambler, con man, kidnapper, and murderer Rainsford. The boatman puts his gambling days behind him, and in the novel's violent climax, Denton effects his revenge on the murderous "gambler": "he lay crushed, bleeding and senseless beneath the feet of the brave boatman."[17]

In Greek mythology, water deities were able to shift and change their shape at will—an ability, as Percy Gardner highlighted in 1878, that became particularly evident when a water deity battled with a hero: "Nereus when seized by Herakles, Proteus in the grasp of Menelaüs, Thetis beneath the rough wooing of Peleus, all change their forms rapidly [. . .] So too Acheloüs, when a suitor for the hand of Deianeira [Heracles' wife] [. . .] They become 'a bristling boar, a fierce tigress, a scaly serpent, a tawny lioness,' or even assume the more intangible form of fire or water." The struggle between protean water deity and classical hero was replayed in the contest between gambler and boatman—one, like Thimblerig, shifting, elusive, and connected to the nature of the river on which they battled; the other, like Crockett, strong, straightforward (at least in comparison to the gambler), and opposed to the manipulation of reality. Here, the alligator-horse represented "sturdy integrity and [. . .] patient mastery" in opposition to a growing spirit of "tackiness and posturing" in "a whirligig, exploitative social world."[18]

Melville's alligator-horse, Pitch, played just such a role in *The Confidence-Man*. William Lenz has described Pitch, dressed in a "bear and raccoon costume," as "a parody of the Davy Crockett [. . .] backwoodsman." He displays some of the backwoodsman's linguistic qualities, including his own catchphrase: "My name is Pitch; I stick to what I say." Pitch's stolid cynicism allows him to see through much of the unfounded confidence that he encounters: "Now the high-constable catch and confound all knaves in towns and rats in grain-bins, and [. . .] in this boat, which is a human grain-bin for the time." When Pitch is eventually conned by the man with the brass plate, he is able to realize his mistake. He cannot, however, "comprehend, the operation, still less the operator. Was the man a trickster, it must be more for the love than the lucre. Two or three dirty dollars the motive to so many nice wiles?" Melville realized "that the heroic frontiersman mediating between nature and civilization [was] in 1857 no longer an adequate symbol of American experience."[19]

"THE FIEND!"

At the beginning of *The Confidence-Man*, a peddler jumps aboard the *Fidèle* to hawk "in the thick of the throng, the lives of Measan, the bandit of the Ohio, Murrel, the pirate of the Mississippi, and the brothers Harpe, the Thugs of the Green River country, in Kentucky—creatures, with others of the sort, one and all exterminated at the time, and for the most part, like the hunted generations of wolves in the same regions, leaving comparatively few successors." In Germany, they had Schinderhannes—"the robber of the Rhine"—who was, in Charles Mackay's words, "a great favourite on the banks of the river which he so long kept in awe [. . .] they are proud of him." In early eighteenth-century London they had the criminal mastermind of Jonathan Wild. American river robbers never achieved much popularity in life; in print, they proliferated. James Hall, for example, in *Letters from the West* (1828) and *The Harpe's Head: A Legend of Kentucky* (1833), disseminated the bloody life and death of Wiley and Micajah Harpe to a wide antebellum audience. But it was John Murrell, man and myth, that attracted the most significant antebellum attention.[20]

Murrell's myth was far more powerful than Murrell the man. As far as the *Lynchburg Virginian* was concerned, he was "an incarnate fiend." According to

Mark Twain, he was a "wholesale [. . .] rascal." For Herbert Asbury, he was "probably the most extraordinary criminal America has yet produced [. . .] his exploits have never been equalled." Murrell's reputation for robbery, slaughter, and conspiracy was elaborated until it dominated popular associations with the river's underworld. But as James Penick has described, the real John Murrell was at best an "indifferent thief [. . .] probably never a highwayman or a murderer." In the popular imagination, he was transformed into "a master criminal." The creation of the pirate of the Mississippi was largely due to a document which (though attributed to one Augustus Q. Walton) was probably written by Virgil Stewart, the man who claimed the glory of Murrell's capture: the *History of the Detection, Conviction, Life and Designs of John A. Murel* (1835).[21]

According to this account, Stewart's relationship with Murrell began in Madison County, Tennessee (where the real Murrell made his home in the early 1830s). In 1834, Murrell was suspected by the locals of stealing slaves. When Murrell set out on a journey to Randolph—a town on the Mississippi—Stewart volunteered to follow him and discover what he could. Though at first simply following, Stewart decided "that he would venture a trick on him." Gradually sidling up to Murrell, Stewart greeted the robber and identified himself as "a traveler from the Choctaw Purchase in search of a lost horse." Steadily Stewart gained Murrell's trust; they traveled on together. According to the *History*, Murrell was a garrulous companion. He happily spoke at length about past crimes and plots imminent. As he talked, Stewart claimed that he recorded evidence against him on "small pieces of paper not larger than a dollar"; he scratched "proper names and places" on his "boot legs, fingernails, saddle skirts, and portmanteau with a needle, as he would be riding, and listening to Murel's horrid account of himself." When the real John Murrell was eventually arrested, he was, largely thanks to Stewart's testimony, incarcerated and sentenced to ten years hard labor for slave stealing in July 1834. Stewart's pseudonymous *History* was published in March 1835. Not one of its claims about a widespread conspiracy and imminent slave uprising had appeared in Stewart's court testimony. In the *History*, Stewart created the John Murrell of myth. He was the true con man of the piece: he scammed Murrell, and he hoodwinked the public.[22]

In Stewart's account, John Murrell was a resonant combination of mannerly gentleman, charismatic con man, braggart, counterfeiter, slave stealer and habitual murderer. His far-reaching organization, the Mystic Clan, spread along the river—in Murrell's words, it was "a noble band of valiant and lordly bandits." Its Grand Council named "men of high standing; and many of them in honorable and lucrative offices." Clearly the inspiration for many fictional gamblers who followed, Murrell described his life as a young criminal dandy in New Orleans, dressing "with so much rigging and glittering jewelery," and forging connections with "all the speculators that visited New Orleans; and [. . .] every fellow who would speculate that lived on the Mississippi river." But it was slave stealing that characterized his criminality. This was not abolitionism. The slaves that Murrell lured away with the promise of financial gain and freedom ended up dead in the Mississippi—eviscerated, not liberated. And he had bigger plans. All of Murrell's efforts were directed toward exciting "a rebellion among the negroes throughout the slaveholding states," allowing Murrell and his clan to pillage and murder at will: "My heart began to beat high with the hope of being able, one day, to visit the pomp of the southern and western people in my vengeance, and of seeing their cities and towns one common scene of devastation [. . .] I intend to head the company that attack [New Orleans] myself. I feel an ambition to demolish the city which was defended from the ravages of the British Army by the great General Jackson." "I will have the pleasure and honor," he gloated, "of seeing and knowing, that my management has glutted the earth with more human gore, and destroyed more property, than any robber who has ever lived in America." The date of uprising was to be Christmas Day 1835. So said Murrell the myth, Stewart's bitter mouthpiece.[23]

In the audacious character roles ascribed to him, Murrell approached the apotheosis of metaphysical trickery. Whether acting as lawyer (he had "dived into the quirks of the law") or doctor (in South America he "passed as a doctor, and commenced practising medicine"), Murrell gained admittance into respectable society. His favorite role was more impudent. Dressed as a man of the cloth, Murrell claimed to have "preached some d——d fine sermons, and scattered some counterfeit United States' paper among my brethren." The *Lynchburg Virginian* reacted with horror: "the fiend! Covered with crime, and yet daring to ascend the pulpit, as the messenger of the Most High! Did he not fear that he might be blasted by the lightning of heaven?" Murrell was a carefully constructed bogeyman. He played on innate antebellum fears. He appeared at a time—the mid-1830s—when the Mississippi's centers of population, and polite society within them, were established but not secure. The apparition of his secret criminal brotherhood paralleled the development of the nascent organizations that were beginning to flourish in river towns, dedicated to the public good. Christopher Morris has elucidated the case of Vicksburg: in 1831, the town formed its "first voluntary militia" and a "temperance Association," followed by "the Clerks' Debating Society [. . .] the Vicksburg and Warren County Colonization Society [. . .] the Carpenters' Society [. . .] the Anti-Duelling Society [. . .] the Mechanics'

Mutual Benefit Society." Yet urbanization and industrialization had not taken hold; the river was still partially a frontier, and Murrell threatened anarchy.[24]

On the Lower Mississippi, fears were heightened by the *History*. The excitement of a slave uprising was to be Murrell's crowning glory, and Nat Turner's rebellion, in 1831, had made such a prospect seem plausible. Murrell, the king of an imaginary Mississippi underworld, was publicized throughout antebellum America—but initially, many were skeptical about the veracity of the claims made in the *History*. The *Lynchburg Virginian* confessed that when "we first read the pamphlet giving the details of Murrel's infamous career, we were disposed to look upon it as we do the biographies of villains generally, with 'many grains of allowance.'" Nonetheless, as Christopher Morris has noted, "the pamphlet widely circulated." In the long term, Stewart did far more than fashion a mythic villain; he almost created a self-fulfilling prophecy.[25]

According to Henry S. Foote, writing in 1870s, the *History* "awakened the most wide-spread excitement and alarm [. . .] The people were apprehending that all the unnameable horrors of a servile revolt would soon blaze forth among them." At the very least, its appearance was a timely coincidence. In late June, rumors concerning the existence of precisely the sort of plot outlined in the *History* began to circulate in Madison County, Mississippi. One slave owner claimed that "several slaves had shown her disobedience and insolence" and asserted that she had overheard them in secret discussions that involved talk of "killing." Investigations commenced, suspicions spread, dubious confessions began to percolate. It was soon believed that Murrell's insurrection, even though he was imprisoned, was under way: brought forward to the "4th July; on which night the whites were to be indiscriminately butchered (with the exception of a few chosen females)." Mob violence erupted. In towns throughout Mississippi, slaves were summarily hanged alongside white men who were implicated as leaders in the conspiracy (generally those of itinerant professions like gamblers, steam doctors, and even boatmen already mistrusted by the communities through which they traveled). Violence engulfed the river.[26]

In the antebellum years, Murrell's was not the only nefarious organization to threaten river towns. In 1847, over a decade later, Jonathan Green (the prolific reformed gambler turned writer) attempted to disseminate a very similar rumor. Writing with a "trembling hand," Green admitted that "it may require a stretch of credulity" to believe in the "deeds of darkness" committed by the Secret Band of Brothers (who also based themselves in New Orleans—for Green, a "city of Sodom"). The persistent reader would, however, be rewarded with "the naked truth" about this "blackhearted, treacherous band of men." The *Philadelphia*

Courier agreed that it was "a most fearful and startling exposition of crime." However, Green's Secret Band failed to provoke any vigilantism. Missing from Green's covert conspiracy was the element of racial tension that had sent the Mississippi into a state of emergency in the 1830s. As Penick has highlighted, "most people believed the robbers involved in the Murrell conspiracy and [. . .] abolitionists were birds of a feather." The southern press described both groups in the same language. What the *Columbus (Miss.) Democratic Press* wrote about the *"white men"* who were alleged to have attempted an insurrection among the "generally contented" slave population might have been said of Murrell's men or the gambling fraternity: "fiends, for men they can hardly be called: they must be devoid of all the common attributes of human nature."[27]

Away from the chimeras of Murrell, the connection between blacks and black-legs along the Mississippi would seem to have been more powerful and more intrinsic. As Botkin noted, "the most widespread of the gambling yarns tells how a sharper is found out and makes his getaway from his vengeful pursuers by disguising himself as a Negro deckhand or cook." In the southern world in which he thrived, such a transgression was the gambler's most accomplished—and, for the society that he threatened, most unacceptable—confidence trick. It spoke of a kinship between two marginalized groups, both only thriving on the margins of respectable white society. The epithets of "Murrell," "gambler," "abolitionist" and "slave" were all equally effective in shutting down debate and dissent.[28]

Though hardly ardent abolitionists, it is clear that there was often a mutually beneficial relationship between the gambler and the free black and slave workforce employed along the river. In his autobiography, Henry Watson, himself a gambler (so that he could "gain money from those who had the chance of making more than I made"), complained that white professionals would often "fasten upon the poor, degraded slave, who has received some little trifle for an extra piece of labor to gull from him that which he has paid so dearly for." But other examples testified to a more sympathetic relationship. A story repeated with a variety of sharpers in the lead role—here told by George Devol—told of the way that gamblers paid the black workers at the steamboat landing to establish their character: "While the passengers were all out on the guards and I was bidding the 'coons' good-bye, my 'nig' would cry out: 'Good-Bye, Massa George; I's goin' to take good care of the old plantation till you comes back.'" In such a scenario, black and white worked together to manipulate society's assumptions for their mutual gain. Such a relationship crossed social boundaries. Stewart reported that John Murrell, when in conversation with a slave, offered him his flask and insisted that the other man drink first—"O! no, Clitto, after you. (Clitto drinks, and then Murel after him)." A more profound example—almost unbelievable without external corroboration—could be found within George Devol's biography. In the years before the Civil War, in a steamboat barbershop, Devol met Pinkney Benton Stewart Pinchback. Pinch, as Devol and colleagues knew him, was the son of a Mississippi planter who had freed his slave mother. Growing up in a degree of affluence, Pinch "spent his time shooting craps with his fellow truant schoolmates." When his father died, the family found itself in uncomfortable straits. In 1854, Pinch "signed on the first riverboat that needed a cabin boy."[29]

Pinch became the personal servant of Devol and his partners of the time—Tom Brown and Holly Chappell. They "instructed him in the mysteries of card-playing, and he was an apt pupil." Together, Devol remembered, they made "a strong team": the sharpers worked the cabin passengers, and they "staked [Pinch] to open a game of chuck-a-luck with the niggers on deck." Pinch continued to work himself up the ratings of the steamboat crew. Just before the war he was made a steward, the highest rank that a black man could reach. So he was frustrated in both his occupations: no further progression was possible on the riverboats, and even "the sharpest colored gambler could only fleece his own kind." Pinch joined the Union army in August 1862, having petitioned Benjamin Butler himself. Pinch opened a recruiting office: in the black regiment that was formed, only he passed the qualification examination. After the war, as Devol proudly related, "he got into the Legislature, became Lieutenant-Governor, and by the death of the Governor he slipped into the gubernatorial chair." For six weeks, Pinkney Benton Stewart Pinchback, George Devol's erstwhile monte partner, was the first black governor in the United States.[30]

Henry Bibb also had an extraordinary story to tell. The slave of a brutal owner, Deacon Whitfield, Bibb tried unsuccessfully to escape with his family. Recaptured, Bibb was to be sold down the river, apart from his wife and children. When he was sold to "a company of men, fifteen or twenty in number, who were Southern sportsmen," his situation looked inauspicious. And yet, as Bibb himself marveled: "Although they were wicked black legs of the basest character, it is but due to them to say, that they used me far better than ever the Deacon did. They gave me plenty to eat and put nothing hard on me to do. They expressed much sympathy for me in my bereavement; and almost every day they gave me money more or less." Bibb's relationship with the gamblers soon became such that they returned to the deacon in an attempt to purchase his wife and children. He refused, and Bibb "could see the sympathetic tear-drop, stealing its way down the cheek of the profligate and black-leg." The gamblers "were disgusted at the conduct of Whitfield and cried out shame, even in his presence. They told him that they would give a thousand dollars for my wife and child, or any thing in reason." To no avail. Though they could not reunite Bibb with his family, the gamblers resolved to help him further. With his agreement, they determined to sell Bibb to an owner from whose clutches the chance of escape seemed good, giving Bibb a portion of the profit and advising him on his escape. Soon after, he was free. Thus, though not freeing Bibb themselves, all the time keeping a keen eye for their own profit (and almost losing him in a bad bet before their plan could take shape), the gamblers were sympathetic to his plight and were happy to help him in his struggle against respectable southern society.[31]

Thomas Buchanan has shown that the black blackleg himself was no uncommon figure in the Mississippi underworld. As a runaway Kentucky slave remembered: "I got me a job and worked as a roustabout on a boat where I learned to gamble wid dice. I fought and gambled all up and down de Mississippi River." In 1841, confessions were taken from four black men—three free, one slave—for more serious crimes. They were hanged for robbing a St. Louis countinghouse, killing two clerks, and burning the building. The *Louisville Journal* described them as "desperate rascals, thieves, robbers, cut-throats, and blacklegs." Madison Henderson, Amos Warrick, James Seward, and Charles Brown were not above "occasionally swindling other working-class people." Primarily, however, they preyed upon the richer elements of the citizenry—"bankers, shopkeepers, plantation owners, and merchants." Henderson thought himself "sufficiently smart to make my way through the world, and get what money I needed [. . .] on the river." His colleague, Charles Brown, attempted to use the wealth he conned to "liberate runaway slaves." Their rascality, to quote Buchanan, was an act of "resistance [. . .] a challenge to antebellum society"—and, perhaps, the most powerful example of the way that the river's underworld intersected with slavery in ways that were powerfully threatening to the South.[32]

John Murrell, the mythical inaugurator of this connection, constantly appealed against his sentence; nothing came of it. In jail, he contracted tuberculosis and was granted an early release in April 1844. The recommendation described his behavior as "exemplary and unexceptional." He died on the first of November. As legend has it, his body was disinterred, the head removed and displayed at county fairs—"ten cents a peep."[33]

"THE MORALS OF VICKSBURG"

When William Grattan Tyrone Power witnessed the river's underworld in 1834, he prophesied that "the people themselves, will, no doubt, one day interfere to abate this terrible scourge [. . .] the retribution will be awful." A year later, that prophecy came to pass. The Vicksburg timeline has often been confused with the simultaneous bloody events of the Murrell conspiracy in nearby Madison County; despite the proximity of time and geography, they were unconnected. Events in Vicksburg began at the Fourth of July picnic hosted by the recently formed Vicksburg Volunteers militia. The usual round of speeches, drills, and food and drink was derailed by an altercation between members of the militia and Francis Cabler (or Cobler), a professional gambler (or blacksmith turned boxer who mixed with the blacklegs), who rowdily interrupted proceedings. Not long after his ejection, Cabler returned—armed "with a brace of pistols [. . .] declaring his intention to shoot the man who had offended him." The gambler was apprehended by the militia, and whipped, tarred, and feathered. An Anti-Gambling Committee was immediately formed: "its citizens issued an ordinance," reported *Niles' Weekly Register,* "that all gamblers and other suspicious persons of ill-fame should forthwith quit the precincts of the town, or Slick's law should be administered to whomsoever refused."[34]

Early on the morning of July 5, "a military company" was mustered to descend upon the Kangaroos. Most of the swamp fraternity had taken the opportunity to depart. Many congregated on Palmyra Island, along the Mississippi to the south of Vicksburg. The armed band made its way to all suspected houses of ill repute. Roulette wheels and faro sets were piled high in a bonfire of gambling vanities. Five gamblers remained. Holed up in the Vicksburg Coffee House, "North, Adams, McCall, Dutch Bill, and another [name not recollected]" were surrounded by the makeshift force. After an exchange of shots, Dr. Hugh Bodley rushed a door. He was gunned down. The hideout was stormed and the gamblers apprehended—one, allegedly, in a "mangled and helpless condition." Having been marched the mile back to town, the gamblers were summarily hanged—from an oak tree, or in a poplar grove, or, most likely, from gallows in the square outside the courthouse. A roulette wheel was placed around the neck of one of the sharpers, since he ran a crooked game. A group of black musicians were ordered to strike up "Yankee Doodle." Bodley's brother cut the rope.[35]

The Vicksburgers erected a monument to Bodley. Its inscription reads: "Murdered by the Gamblers July 5, 1835 while defending the morals of Vicksburg." Justification for the lynchings soon appeared in the press. One Vicksburger talked in terms of a "revolution [. . .] conducted by the most respectable citizens." The hanged men had been "obnoxious in a manner which the law cannot reach." They had been "unconnected with society by any of its ordinary ties." H. R. Howard, who produced a compilation of documents concerned with the Murrell conspiracy, concluded that "it will ever reflect honour on the insulted citizens of Vicksburg, among those who best know how to appreciate the motives by which they were actuated [. . .] Their city now stands redeemed and ventilated." Howard concluded that "the difficulty with the gamblers at that place was unconnected with the [Murrell] insurrection"—except in "the high state of excitement that pervaded the whole southern country."[36]

Nonetheless, in the weeks following Vicksburg, connections were made. The *Mississippian* explicitly called on the army to clear out (from the Arkansas morass, the alleged home of Murrell's headquarters) the "gamblers and abolitionists from the lower country." Other accounts insinuated the same links: an apologia appeared in *Niles' Weekly Register* that insinuated a connection between the two events: the Vicksburg "desperadoes," it claimed, formed "squads at all the principle [*sic*] points on the western rivers," and challenged "any one who dared to call them to account." Their crimes, like Murrell's, were organized "by system." The *Lynchburg Virginian* moved closer to an explicit connection: it hoped to "excite a salutary caution in the public mind [. . .] particularly in reference to that vagrant crew, which infests all towns especially, having neither 'a local habitation nor a name;' who, being evidently without means of livelihood; subsist by roguery, and who are always ready to embark in any scheme of villainy which promises to supply their craving appetite for plunder." Mississippians knew, in Penick's words, that "Vicksburg gamblers and [Madison County] robbers were cut from the same cloth." The Madison County lynchers sent a letter of commendation to their river-town colleagues, for meting out justice to "the inhuman monsters who have been engaged in plotting and maturing such diabolical measures for the destruction of the lives of the innocent and virtuous."[37]

"The proceedings at Vicksburg," reported the *Louisville Advertiser,* "have kindled a spirit throughout the lower country which is breaking forth at every point, and obliging the blackleg fraternity to make their escape with all haste." Purges took place along the river. The *Louisville Journal* warned that "'judge Lynch' has recently been holding court in our city." A public meeting in Natchez sent its condolences to Vicksburg "in the loss of their beloved citizen" and resolved "to adopt the most rigorous measures for the extirpation of gambling"—but only through the use of "every legal expedient." The Honourable Charles Augustus Murray, in Natchez in 1836, reported that "Judge Lynch [. . .] compelled some hundreds of the most notorious characters to leave the place at a few hours' notice." Another public meeting was called in New Orleans, this time "to adopt proper measures relative to the individuals lately expelled from Natchez." The meeting resolved that it was "unconstitutional, illegal, tyrannical, cruel and inexpedient to adopt or resort to any violent measures." Mobile followed, with the proviso that "the citizens [. . .] disapprove of gaming, and gamesters," and with the warning that "gamesters and vagrants" could expect to be expelled "whenever they may be identified."[38]

Henry Watson, the slave who had complained of the predatory nature of professional gamblers, suffered as a result of the actions in Vicksburg. Judged, along with "a free coloured man," of being the principal black gambler in their river town, he was sentenced to sixty lashes at the public whipping post. "After I had got over my flogging," Watson claimed, "I resolved never to gamble again." Other gamblers and prostitutes sought sanctuary on the river. On July 13, steamboat *Mogul* reported that "she saw at Natchez, as she passed down, several boats crowded with persons who had been ordered from that place, in consequence of their abandoned character [. . .] and also saw [. . .] one or two flatboats crowded with the same description of persons, but principally females." On July 15, "we learn that the citizens of Vicksburg were about to charter a steamboat to remove the gamblers, who had taken up their residence on Palmyra island."[39]

Many commentators were critical of events in Vicksburg. *Niles' Weekly Register* condemned "the professed gambler" as "a moral upas that blasts and withers"; but it concluded that the manner of justice was "disgraceful to all the parties concerned": the "barbarism of the punishment" was not "less heinous in our eyes than the reckless disregard of the laws." Duke W. Hullum agreed: "I am the aged and distressed father of John Hullum, who with four others, fell a victim to the fury of a relentless mob at Vicksburgh, on the 5th day of July last." Hullum's deeper grievance was with the hypocrisy of the mob. He saw gambling as "a great and growing evil," but he took issue with the distinction "drawn between the professional and the occasional gamester [. . .] One act of gaming is as much an evidence of evil propensity, as one theft distinctly marks the rogue." Hullum asserted that in river towns "the despicable vice is [. . .] generally practised, among the officers of the law from the supreme judge to the constable." Vicksburg's actions, he concluded, were the product of "wicked hearts, bad passions, personal revenge and a reckless spirit." Hullum even asserted that "one of the principal actors [in the Vicksburg lynch mob] was in the constant habit of visiting gaming houses, and who had previously, by his seductive arts, contributed perhaps more than any other man, to lead the unfortunate victim of his personal vengeance into those sinks of iniquity."[40]

The Vicksburg lynchings were one of the most important antebellum events on the Mississippi. (Twain, traveling past the river town fifty years later, "drifted into talk [. . .] about the lynching of the gamblers in Vicksburg.") In the antebellum years, Jonathan Green interpreted the bloody events as a result of the "deeply demoralizing influences" that "gambling and its attendant evils" had on the community. For Ann Fabian, the gambling fraternity was seen to be "undermining the symbolic presentation of authority that supported a threatened world run by slaveholders." John Findlay has concluded that middle-class mob affirmation "heralded the closing of the frontier [. . .] that ultimately asserted eastern culture over western ways." For Christopher Morris, such actions belied "a nagging sense among Vicksburg residents that they were losing control of their city to strangers." The equivocal role of gambling, and gamblers, in antebellum river society was clearly central to events.[41]

Despite the lasting fame of the Murrell conspiracy and the Vicksburg hangings, and their importance for the popular portrayal of crime along the river, gambling and gamblers apparently continued to proliferate in river towns and steamboat cabins—particularly in the South. Frederick Law Olmsted, traveling by steamboat in Alabama in 1856, recorded that "Sunday was observed by the discontinuance of public gambling in the cabin, and in no other way. At midnight gambling was resumed, and during the whole passage was never at any other time discontinued." The apocryphal corruption of the Lower Mississippi was ascribed to its very waters. Melville described its course in "The River," a short sketch connected with the composition of *The Confidence-Man:* the muddy Missouri intrudes on the Mississippi at St. Louis "like a Pawnee from ambush [. . .] The peace of the Upper River seems broken in the Lower, nor is it ever renewed. The Missouri sends rather a hostile element than a filial flow."[42]

Gambling was clearly an important part of antebellum southern culture. Kenneth Greenberg noted that the "honourable men of the antebellum South [. . .] wagered with a frequency and an intensity widely noted by visitors to the region." W. J. Cash concluded that the ability "to lose the whole of one's capital on the turn of a card without the quiver of a muscle" was one of the essential attributes of the southern man. Aged fifteen, Andrew Jackson wagered all he owned "on the throw of the dice." A few years later, Robert Remini concluded, "he would surely have gone bankrupt had he not regularly engaged his landlord in bets that kept him solvent. Sometimes it was horseraces, sometimes cards." Seargeant Smith Prentiss was described by Joseph Baldwin in admiring terms: "He bet thousands on the turn of a card and witnessed the success or failure of the wager with the *nonchalance* of a Mexican monte-player [. . .] Starting to fight a duel, he laid down his hand at poker, to resume it with a smile when he returned."[43]

One antebellum writer concluded that the "man of the West and South" had "to bet his life every day to make a great profit." He was "a born gambler" who could either risk a fortune "on a single throw in cotton or grain specula-tion" or stand "at a faro-table with a stoic manner declaring *I don't give a damn.*" "Of course," remembered a gambler in the 1890s, "everyone gambled; if they had not done so the professional's occupation would have been gone." Henry Adams remembered that antebellum cotton planters were the type "from whom one could learn nothing but bad temper, bad manners, poker, and treason." Jonathan Green even asserted, "I have no doubt [. . .] that as many as three fourths of all the citizens of Vicksburg were more or less addicted to gambling." If the North censored the professional gambler because of the way he won his money—as Karen Halttunen described, gambling "undermined all desire to practice industry"—then the South hated him because he refused to lose it. For the professional gambler, "the best bet was a sure bet—which was no bet at all for a Southern man of honour."[44]

These issues were connected to the more general antebellum American fear of the confidence man. Karen Halttunen, in her study of the confidence man who appeared in "advice manuals" addressed to young men, concluded that he rep-resented "a symbolic expression of two social problems." First, "the problem of establishing and recognizing social identity in a republic based theoretically on the boundless potential of each individual"; second, that of "securing success in the anonymous 'world of strangers' that was the antebellum city." For Halttunen, the advice-manual confidence man—"whether rake or pimp, gambler of thief"—was a seducer of youth. Young American men entering the city were in "a condition of liminality" (personally, geographically, and socially), which made them partic-ularly susceptible to the threat of corruption. The confidence man "was a mod-ern industrial version of the trickster"; his "power to pollute young men resided in the threat he presented to the legitimate leaders of the American republic."[45]

Along the Mississippi, the same essential models served as cautionary coun-sel. As a correspondent from Vicksburg described the gamblers who thrived in their town, "they would decoy the youthful and unsuspecting, and, after strip-ping them of their possessions, send them forth into the world the ready and desperate instruments of vice." Henry Ward Beecher warned of men "often met on steamboats, travelling solely to gamble [. . .] He deals falsely; heats his dupe to madness by drink, drinking none himself [. . .] at a stray look, he will slip your money off and steal it." Jonathan Green's antigambling works abounded with examples of young men brought to ruin through the machinations of a gambler, and typically they were set on and around the Mississippi. The case of "A Young Man Brought to Ruin and an Untimely Death by Gambling" was an archetypal warning. The victim's degradation was charted by his journey down-river, ever nearer to New Orleans and his doom—poverty and suicide. In Green's account, professional gamblers were men who had "acted badly, and disobeyed their parents."[46]

The steamboat presented as many social difficulties as the antebellum city. It had always been dominated by "a system of horizontal social relations," in which outward appearance provided little indication of social status. An orderly taxonomy was impossible. For every blackleg who dressed and affected the manners of planter aristocracy, there was a gambler who adopted the appearance of a green cowboy returning from market. The game of social expectation was played at both ends of the scale, and, as Melville understood, the vanity fair of steamboat life provided an unrivaled panorama of American society within which to play. Only the gambler had a panoptic vantage point.[47]

"SCHEMES OF DEEPER VILLAINY"

The three components essential to the emergence of the Mississippi underworld in popular fiction were established in 1835: the Murrell conspiracy and its connection to slavery; the Vicksburg lynchings; the equivocal Mississippi gambler. Their influence was immediately apparent. Crockett's acquaintance Thimblerig, for example, was described as having "luckily made his escape a short time before the recent clearing out of the sleight-of-hand gentry" in Natchez. Published as much as twelve years later, *The Female Land Pirate; or Awful, Mysterious, and Horrible Disclosures of Amanda Bannorris* (1847) was the story of a Murrell moll, based in Vicksburg, that revisited familiar ground: her husband "followed gambling for a living"; she took up "a career of voluptuousness"; the Murrell gang involved them in "schemes of deeper villainy." James Copeland, a late antebellum river robber, was captured and hanged in 1857. He narrated his story to a local doctor. Alongside tales of arson, robbery, and bloodshed along the Mississippi, Copeland outlined his initiation into a robber "Clan": "I was [. . .] invested with all the signs, words and tokens, and fully instructed in the mysteries of the Clan, I was taught their mode of secret correspondence, by means of an alphabet or key, invented by the notorious Murrell, of Tennessee."[48]

William Gilmore Simms was swift to realize Murrell's fictional potential. In *Richard Hurdis* (1838) and *The Border Beagles* (1840), Simms used some of the elements found in Walton's narrative to construct popular adventure novels that were, however, ambivalent in their presentation of Murrell. Simm's outlaw was a romantic figure. In *Richard Hurdis,* the titular hero plays Stewart and infiltrates Clement Foster's "Mystic Brotherhood" by masquerading as a riverboat gambler. The uniform that he adopts makes it apparent that the iconic look of the Mississippi gambler was well established by 1838: "Having a proper regard to the usual decoration of the professed gamblers of our country, I entered a jeweller's establishment and bought sundry bunches of seals, a tawdry watch, a huge chain of doubtful, but sold as virgin, gold [. . .] my beard was suffered to grow goat-like, after the most approved models of dandyism." Aided by Hurdis, the officers of the law attack and disperse the Mystic Brotherhood. Foster/Murrell escapes, however, floating downriver on a cotton bale: the "clever scoundrel [. . .] laughed good-naturedly [. . .] pulled his hat with a polite gesture."[49]

Foster returned for more nefarious activity in *Border Beagles,* but the gentleman-outlaw was less fortunate in his fate. Captured by officers of the law, Foster and his associates are dragged off by a mob and "hurried into eternity without a moment's grace—their prayers drowned—their convulsions mocked in the frantic joy and the exulting shouts of the populace." "Foster," Simms continued ambiguously, "died as he had lived, a brave fearless man." Edgar Allan Poe noted that both books "excited very general attention and curiosity [. . .] although disfigured by some instances of bad taste." Simms was certainly susceptible to some penny-dreadful tactics. He wrote a new preface to an 1855 edition of *Richard Hurdis,* and he claimed: "I knew Stuart, the captor of Murrell, personally; and had several conferences with him, prior to the publication of his narrative."[50]

Sometimes, the influence of these defining events was more implicit. In *Marie, or, The Gambler of the Mississippi,* the character of Rainsford was symbolically important in the development of the cultural gambler (and, in his exploitation of honest boatman Denton, actually echoed Murrell's description of an event from his early years). Though hardly the charming trickster who would develop in the postwar years, Rainsford helped point the way forward. He was a penny-ante con man, an inadequate seducer, an incompetent gambler: "everything that was base and black-hearted." But he looked the part: "a man of stout build and an unprepossessing sensual but rather handsome countenance, on which the marks of deep dissipation were apparent"; he "dressed showily, wearing an inordinate quantity of flashy jewellery." The author clearly intended him to be a representative type: "He was that character of a man often found in the world and particularly in the south-western portion of the United States, who would lie, swindle and cheat to procure money, which he squandered on every passing whim, and yet with whom the love of gold was subservient to his hatred and revenge." In Rainsford, the seeds for popular development were sown. Covered with the sympathetic patina of age, he would lose his "sneaking, cur-dog expression," gain a handsome face, a willing heroine, a run of luck: the gambler-hero would emerge from Rainsford's insalubrious cocoon.[51]

The issues surrounding Vicksburg's mob violence were explored further in the work of Friedrich Gerstäcker. A popular German novelist, Gerstäcker was familiar with life on the Mississippi. After his arrival in New York in 1837, he soon "spent every dime." He spent the next six years working his way "all over the United States." He became a "stoker on board a steamboat" and "a sailor in the American river boats." In "Up the Mississippi," Gerstäcker used his experience to produce an account of seven days on an American steamboat. A series of criminal events punctuates the journey of the *Oceanic;* the steamboat becomes both courthouse and gallows. A professional gambler is discovered to have cheated, attempts murder, is accosted but absconds. A steamboat explodes, and a man is spotted stealing plunder while the "white arm" of a drowning woman is "raised in entreaty"; an Arkansas lynch mob hangs him. The black cook of the *Oceania* is accused of abusing "a poor deaf and dumb girl, an orphan" and a German immigrant. After a foiled escape attempt, the bound cook is thrown into the river. Gerstäcker wrote that "all, passengers and sailors, regarded the negro's death as just and in order." Yet the mood on board the *Oceania* is irrevocably altered: "most of the men sat silent, busily engaged with their own thoughts." When the boat arrives in St. Louis, crowds applaud their actions; but the black population of St Louis "retired timidly to their houses, and did not appear in the streets." (Steamboat justice was not just a figment of Gerstäcker's imagination. Henry Hugunin recorded that the passengers of the *Eclipse* apprehended a dishonest gambler, called a jury, tried him, and sentenced him be tied for an hour, by the neck, to the steamboat's piston rod.)[52]

The same ambiguous issues were center stage in Gerstäcker's adventure novel *The Pirates of the Mississippi* (an updating of Murrell's conspiracy). Back in the flatboat days, Gerstäcker wrote, the Mississippi was inhabited by "a well-organised band of robbers"—the Stack Island gang. The law had been ineffective to stop the murder and plunder; "the backwoodsmen were compelled to act in their own defence." But "the watchfulness of the river population had somewhat abated." The Stack Island gang "reassembled" and—working in conjunction with the gang of one "Morell"—"perpetuated numberless cruelties" along the river. The gang was far-reaching: "there is hardly a town in the whole West, where either constable, or gaoler, or lawyer, or magistrate, or postmaster" was not allied with them. To combat the modern Stack Island robbers, the citizenry are driven to vigilantism. Indeed, the Vicksburgers are their role models: "Yes; we saw that at Vicksburg [. . .] What did the magistrates do there? Nothing! The townsfolk were obliged to act for themselves; and if they had not hanged the criminals without ceremony, they would have been at liberty, to the scandal of human nature and the injury of the State." Just like the inherent meaning of the Murrell conspiracy and the Vicksburg hangings, Gerstäcker's novels appealed to the burgeoning middle class and implicitly supported mob violence.[53]

Taking up the trope of conspiracy, the translation of the urban mystery novel to the Mississippi represented a dramatic development in the popular conception of the river's underworld. The model for the genre was Eugène Sue's enormously popular *Mysteries of Paris.* Released serially between 1842 and 1844 in France, swiftly translated and distributed around Europe and America, Sue's novel claimed to take James Fenimore Cooper's descriptions of "the ferocious habits of the savages" as its inspiration for placing "beneath the eyes of the reader, some episodes of the life of other barbarians [. . .] in the midst of us." Soon, most major, and many minor, conurbations had their own mystery to enjoy—often, like the Murrell conspiracy, implicating recognizable, high-ranking local figures in the narrative. As the author of the ironic *Mysteries of Fitchburg* asserted, there were "mysteries enough, forsooth, everywhere in abundance; and all over the world, even."[54]

The genre was formulaic, composed of overarching plots (often Jesuitical or Masonic) that threatened the order of society; mysterious Gothic settings; mystifying tunnels and hidden passageways; convoluted plots; a pervasive air of mystery and obfuscation—secrets that needed to be unmasked. The city was disorientating; the urban mystery amplified the confusion but also claimed to provide answers. Richard Maxwell has distilled the European urban mystery into its most defining and interconnected "figures": labyrinths, crowds, and panoramic vistas. For Werner Sollors, the genre acted as "a tour guide to slummers who were ready for the descent, for initiation into the underworld, in the age of nascent tourism." Such tropes resonated along the panoramic, mazy, sinister Mississippi. River towns produced the most extraordinary antebellum American variations on these established themes. Melville was aware of the genre, and in *The Confidence-Man,* a novel that shared thematic and tonal qualities with mystery novels, he transformed the *Fidèle* from a Mississippi steamboat into its own urban mystery. The boat is mazelike, dreamy, shifting—a city or world in miniature: "from quarters unseen, comes a murmur as of bees in the comb. Fine promenades, domed saloons, long galleries, sunny balconies, confidential passages, bridal chambers, state-rooms plenty as pigeon-holes, and out-of-the-way retreats like secret drawers in an escritoire, present like facilities for publicity or privacy [. . .] one would little divine what other quarters of the boat might reveal."[55]

Ned Buntline's *The Mysteries and Miseries of New Orleans* was the first true urban mystery based in a river city. Buntline's novel was stranger even than most urban mysteries. A portmanteau novel, it begins as an urban mystery; then, halfway through, it transforms unexpectedly into a propagandist, anti-Spanish piece ("there *is* a word in the lexicon of life *more* infamous than *coward;* that word is Spaniard!") and decamps to Cuba. (Presumably, Buntline introduced Narciso López's doomed filibustering expedition as a contemporary reference point for readers eager for representations of the Cuban insurgents filling newspapers. Departing from New Orleans, such expeditions were readily associated with the Mississippi.) It was telling in its presentation of the dissipated mores of the inhabitants of New Orleans.[56]

In Buntline's novel, everybody gambles. The colonel is a textbook gambler-villain. Buntline described him in the uniform that had become standard by the 1850s: "a large, showy man, wore a heavy pair of whiskers [. . .] dressed fashionably, and wore jewelry enough to stock a show case." Buntline condemned this "*professional*" as "one of those genteel sharks, who [. . . .] pass for gentlemen, living on a *supposed* fortune, when, in fact, they are nothing but *gamblers,* and have no income except it be gained by the chances or the trickeries of the gaming table." Other characters, amateurs, gamble in different ways: one successfully, winning "three thousand [. . .] within a month"; one recklessly, "nerving himself with repeated doses of brandy [. . .] until he had lost during the evening near one thousand dollars"; one, never for money. But games of chance are not just played for profit: the inhabitants of New Orleans, as Buntline portrayed them, play for hearts too. A convoluted series of wagers are established on the grounds of seduction. Revenge and murder follow.[57]

The Mississippi mystery novel reached its apotheosis at the hands of German American authors whose work was not always translated into English. Tens of thousands of German emigrants arrived in the West following periods of German civil unrest of the 1830s and '40s. For the immigrant, as Barbara Lang has argued, the urban mystery had a strong resonance. Translated to the New World, the medium reflected the newcomer's sense of America as "an enigmatic, mysterious underworld where dark forces and rules different from the immigrants' old home-country dominated." It provided answers to the insistent questions posed by a confusing social world where the sources of power seemed obscure. The genre allowed "for the dramatization of the impact of [. . .] new experiences" in "a new environment." The prolific Friedrich Gerstäcker was the first to produce a German American mystery with his translation of George Lippard's *The Quaker City, or Monks of Monk Hall* (*Die Quakerstadt und ihre Geheimnisse*) in 1846. Three German mysteries actually set on the Mississippi were written in the antebellum years. Heinrich Börnstein's *Geheimnisse von St Louis* (*The Mysteries of St. Louis*) was released in 1851. Translated into English almost immediately, Börnstein's novel employed a standard mystery novel formula, and took as its premise "that the Jesuit Order was plotting to subvert the United States of America and establish a new despotic Middle Ages under papal leadership." Emil Klauprecht, also the author of *Mississippi Wasser und Ohio Wein*, released *Cincinnati; oder, die Geheimnisse des Westens* (*Cincinnati; or, the Mysteries of the West*) in book form in 1854; the Baron Ludwig von Reizenstein's *Die Geheimnisse von New Orleans* (*Mysteries of New Orleans*) shocked the German reading public from 1854–55. Their visions of the Mississippi underworld were rather more startling.[58]

Encompassing the history of the river from de Soto onward, taking in the secret history of plots and imagined rebellions along the way, evoking lush gambling dens and secret hideouts, dealing not only with a Jesuit conspiracy but with a combined Irish and Yankee plot—Emil Klauprecht's novel has been rightly described by George Schoolfield as "the most important piece of creative literature produced by a German-American during the nineteenth century." Klauprecht imagined a criminal organization called the "Tunnel Rats." The most mysterious and pervasive of all imagined antebellum criminal conspiracies, the Rats convened in mysterious tunnels in secret locations. When they congregated to "hear the semiannual accounting," the "most colourful company which could be raised in the United States" gathered together—"from all the classes of society." There, "bums without coats or vests" sat alongside "gentlemen with earnest faces and the respectable manner of the *bourgeoisie*." A special wing of the organization, the Water-Rats, composed of "seventy stewards, waiters and chambermaids," was devoted to crime on the river itself.[59]

The most notable of Klauprecht's many Grand Guignol characters was steamboat captain George Butler. (For immigrants, subjected to deck passage and the arbitrary power of river crews, the steamboat captain was far less vaunted than cabin passengers found him.) As Butler and his partner are described, "A better pair of Goddamn *blacklegs* is not to be found on the Western Waters." He is "full of the most poisonous rancor." Before becoming "a river character," Butler had been a Jacksonian politician. Despite the excesses of his character—steamboat racing, willful destruction, torture, murder—Butler has a charm and a "raw sensuality" that make him an interesting prototype of the rakish gambler-hero. In Klauprecht's vision, murder was an innate feature of life along the river. The "old divinities of the valleys of the Ohio and Mississippi" demanded this "harvest of corpses from the culture to revenge it for the vanished sacrifice of their red worshippers." For Klauprecht, there was a controlling "evil spirit of the Mississippi."[60]

Reizenstein agreed. He also felt that Ned Buntline was a "disreputable novelist" who "launched the literature of mysteries on American soil and thereby utterly killed all their enchantment as well as any interest in them." The baron's own *Mysteries of New Orleans* (*Die Geheimnisse von New Orleans*, 1854–55) bore little resemblance to Buntline's—or, for that matter, any other antebellum treatment of urban life. Reizenstein exploited the fantastic potential of the mystery novel, and wedded it fully to a powerful political concern. In many ways the darkest antebellum vision of the Mississippi, the baron's river ran red with the blood of slavery. Reizenstein felt that the urban mystery was the correct medium for his astonishing vision, since "extraordinary events often give us the key to the unbelievable, and what is most improbable becomes true." His target was the entire antebellum South; his attack on the system of slavery took no prisoners. As Steven Rowan judged, "Reizenstein's peculiar vision of New Orleans [. . .] crossed the boundaries of acceptable taste [. . .] and squatted firmly on the other side."[61]

The plot—convoluted even by mystery standards—was remarkable for the themes that it addressed: Reizenstein gleefully ignited flammable issues like the occult, child murder, prostitution, pervasive disease, anticlericalism, transvestism, and lesbianism. The novel is enigmatically concerned with the schemes of Hiram the Freemason—an ancient, supernatural being—and his efforts to bring about the birth of "the messiah who is to liberate the niggers." Reizeinstein's vision of the creation of a new "Toussaint L'Ouverture" for the Mississippi—the child of a German count and a black prostitute—is apocalyptic. Hiram's expectations for the future are expressed in vibrant millennial terms: "beauty will raise itself to eternal glory, no more compelled to rub and waste its wild, untamed sensuality within the chains of slavery." With New Orleans as his base and the Mississippi as his artery, this new Toussaint will "redeem beauty from the filthiness, torment and misery of the world." Taking the phrase as its motto, coda, and trope, the reader of Reizenstein's astonishing mystery was warned in no uncertain terms: "*Ruin awaits him who does not take heed!*" Clearly, these urban mysteries were intrinsically subversive. They gleefully spread chaos and confusion with their interpretation of the Mississippi's underworld and their fervent representations of the evils of slavery. As America slid toward war, they unflinchingly sought to uncover the Mississippi's dark and secret heart, elided or hidden in the rhetoric of progress and success that frequently dominated antebellum discussion of the river. Melville's *Confidence-Man* shared their apocalyptic resonances.[62]

THE CONFIDENCE-MAN

According to Timothy Flint, the boatmen called the Mississippi the "wicked river." In the antebellum years, there was little divide in the popular imagination between the Mississippi's professional gamblers and the devil. Surrounding every blackleg was a suspicious cloud of brimstone. The model for devilish gamblers was Satan himself—or at least Milton's Satan. The Garden of Eden saw the first con trick; Eve was the first sucker. The "guileful Tempter," as Milton described him, disguised himself as a serpent—"the subtlest beast," the "fittest imp of fraud"—to hide his "dark suggestions." John Law was called the eldest son of Satan; John Murrell was an "incarnate fiend"; the ranks of lesser criminals and gamblers who prospered along the Mississippi were no less diabolic.[63]

The gambling parlor was known as a "hell"; playing cards, as Robert Burns described them, were "the devils pictur'd beuks"; they carried the smell of "sulphur and Satan." When Davy Crockett first saw Thimblerig, he thought that the sharper "had adopted the example set by the old tempter himself, to get the weathergage of us poor weak mortals." Natchez, in the words of Thimblerig himself, was "an unholy spot [. . .] Satan looks on it with glee, and chuckles as he beholds the orgies of his votaries." After the expulsion of the Vicksburg gamblers, the *Louisville Journal* reported that "the river towns are alarmed at the fearful introduction of a 'legion of devils' amongst them." One disapproving commentator warned parents who continued to play games of chance that they were "the fatal source of the entire evil," helping their children into the clutches of "satanical" blacklegs. In 1861, the Baron von Reizenstein, not content with having created the apocalyptic Hiram, began the abortive *Wie der Teufel in New Orleans ist und die Dächer von Häusern abdeckt* (The Devil in New Orleans, and How He Lifts the Roofs of Houses). His allusion was to Alain René le Sage's eighteenth-century satire *Le diable boîteaux* (1707). For Reizenstein, the devil had moved from Paris to New Orleans, and in his new home he found plenty of his "beloved" as he "raised both roofs and petticoats."[64]

P. T. Barnum—the man who helped to foster a culture of humbug that perfectly complemented the gambler's rise to prominence—realized the infernal, transformative possibilities of the Mississippi. While managing Jenny Lind's tour along the Mississippi, Barnum entertained his fellow passengers on the steamboat *Magnolia* with "a number of legerdemain tricks." The next day, the "mulatto barber declined taking my money." Having witnessed Barnum's sleight of hand, the barber thought he had "the powers of a league with the devil." Never one to refuse a moment of suggestibility, Barnum assured him that such was the case. He had sold himself for nine years' worth of earthly power. The power that most impressed the barber was Barnum's ability to magic money from even the most secure hiding place. With the help of a co-conspirator (placed by the stove), Barnum requested a cent from the barber that he would send "to his Infernal Highness, and bring it back forthwith." Throwing the coin in the air, it disappeared, only to return under a shaving-cup: "It was scorching hot! 'The devil has had it. It is hot yet,' said the barber."[65]

Apocalyptic visions spread along the antebellum river. The threat of the devil coming to the Mississippi was the subject of John S. Robb's "The Second Advent!" Throughout the early 1840s, Parson William Miller gained national prominence by predicting that the world would end in April 1843. Despite the earnest sincerity of many Millerites, he became fair game for the likes of Robb. His sketch told of Tom Bangall, a steamboat engineer who doubted the truth of Miller's predictions: "I'd like to see old Miller set fire to the Massissipi!" Tom's colleagues slowly assured him that the apocalypse was indeed coming; when a steam-pipe happened to scald him as Miller's allotted time drew close, Tom was certain that the end was nigh: "Jest as I thought—the d—l's got me, *s-l-I-c-k* enough, and I'm burnt already to a cinder!" Matt Field, writing for the *New Orleans Picayune,* was actually traveling on a steamboat to St. Louis at the predicted time of Miller's apocalypse. On that fateful day, he expected "to see the Mississippi turned into a roaring cataract of lurid flame"; but "the performance was not to come off." For those who took apocalyptic predictions in earnest, events along the river could often assume a more ominous cast: "steamboat accidents [. . .] could assume a portentous significance." According to Ernest Sandeen: "Many millenarian newspapers [. . .] carried a column entitled 'Signs of the Times,' which contained news of ominous events and portents of the end of the world. One of the most common items in these columns was the notice of the explosion of a steamboat."[66]

If the devil seemed to have the upper hand on the antebellum Mississippi, the river was a spiritual battleground nonetheless. Timothy Flint witnessed "the wretched remains of that singular class of enthusiasts, known in this country by the name of the "Pilgrims" [. . .] They were sick and poor; and the rags with which they were originally habited to excise attention [. . .] were now retained from necessity." More significant was Nauvoo, a river town in Illinois that was home to Joseph Smith and the Mormons from 1839 to 1845. Hounded out of

Missouri, Smith found the site of Nauvoo an "unhealthful [. . .] wilderness": but "believing it might become a healthful place by the blessing of heaven to the Saints, and no more eligible place presenting itself, I considered it wisdom to make an attempt to build up a city." This New Jerusalem "was a prime attraction to the Mississippi River tourist traffic." Not all were sympathetic to the settlement. In familiar terms, one critic asserted that the Mormons had "a vast and deep-laid scheme" of conquering their neighboring river states and "erecting upon the ruin of their present governments a despotic military and religious empire, the head of which, as emperor and pope [would be] Joseph Smith." Joseph Jackson was one of many to write scandalous exposés about "the damnable practices carried on in the name of religion." As in Vicksburg, mob violence erupted: Joseph Smith was lynched by an Illinois mob in 1844; the Mormons were hounded west in 1845–46. Their Nauvoo temple was razed.[67]

The persistent antebellum themes of apocalypse and devilry suffused *The Confidence-Man.* Melville had in fact experienced the evocative world of the Mississippi steamboat firsthand. The only evidence of the voyage is one brief assertion: "visited my now venerable kinsman [uncle Thomas Melvill] in his western home" in Galena, Illinois. This bald statement sheltered a wealth of experience; it provided Melville with "a massive store of detail and imagery." Melville also knew the literature of the West. The work of James Hall was the most obvious source of material for his Mississippi novel; Timothy Flint has been put forward as an inspiration; the widespread accounts of river robbers must have informed his conception of the novel; his heterogeneous steamboat crowd resembled Thorpe's "Big Bear"; in tone, *The Confidence-Man* resembled the cynical southwestern humor of Joseph Baldwin's "Ovid Bolus" or Johnson Hooper's "Simon Suggs," whose "whole ethical system lies snugly in his favourite aphorism: IT IS GOOD TO BE SHIFTY IN A NEW COUNTRY." In short, the book abounded with details and characters that echoed other narratives of the river and river country. As Hershel Parker outlined, Melville conjured up a cast of "confidence men, Western Robbers, P. T. Barnum's freaks, Jeremy Diddlers, land frauds, water cures, prowling Jesuits, Indian-haters and counterfeit bill detectors." And in the wide cast of characters populating the *Fidèle,* commentators have identified the shadows of Emerson, Thoreau, Poe, and even Fanny Kemble.[68]

John Seelye has argued that the "ironic, closely-worked fabric [of the novel] is the wrong canvas upon which to depict the great, sweeping panorama of the Mississippi"; but it would be wrong to imagine that there was no sense of panorama within the novel. The Mississippi, Melville knew, had a resonant symbolic power; the epic vista of the river provided a crucial backdrop to the events of the novel. Melville created an environment in which dark forces operated, a setting that threatened and confused as much as Reizenstein's New Orleans. Melville's favorite symbol was that of "boat-as-world." Making that boat a representative steamboat meant that, more powerfully than any other antebellum novel, Melville's obfuscatory text evoked the Mississippi's, and America's, undercurrents.[69]

Perhaps it did so too well. Contemporary reviews were quick to point out its complications. The *London Illustrated Times* assented that it "appeared an excellent idea to lay the opening of a fiction [. . .] on the deck of a Mississippi steamer"; the "philosophical abstractions" left the reviewer with the feeling that events were more fitted to "the atmosphere of the planet Sirius, than on the deck and in the cabin [. . .] drinking, smoking, gambling, and talking about 'confidence.'" The *Leader* enjoyed the "vivid, natural Mississippi landscape" and the "bright American touches." The *New York Dispatch* found the "variety of disguises" implausible, and felt the subterfuge of the confidence man tended "to show that the passengers of a Mississippi steamboat are the most gullible people in the world, and the most ready to part with their money." Similarly, the *Boston Daily Advertiser* thought that the confidence man succeeded in getting the passengers' money with "rather more facility than is quite natural," and felt that the message of the novel was "that the world is full of knaves and fools, and that a man who ventures to believe what he is told him, necessarily belongs to the latter class." As the *Burlington Free Press* concluded: "the world is not made up of cheats and their victims." Melville—like Murrell, Barnum, Devol, and any number of Mississippi gamblers—knew otherwise. In the figure of the devilish confidence man in any and all of his guises, Melville located the defining spirit of the age. No simple gamblers' tricks or sharpers' scams would fool this operator; no "*Counterfeit Detector*" could provide protection.[70]

Pitch, the cynical alligator-horse, is not the only western type to fall foul of his tricks. Even the *Fidèle*'s resident gambler is duped. Charles Arnold Noble, an Alabamian, "a Mississippi operator [. . .] an equivocal character," approaches Melville's metamorphic con man as an easy mark. Wherever Melville's knowledge of a Mississippi gambler's modus operandi originated (perhaps a gambler had sidled up to him on his steamboat journey; perhaps he had read Henry Ward Beecher), his description of Charlie's behavior is textbook. Though all things to all men, Charlie picks the wrong sucker on this April Fools' Day. Accosting the cosmopolitan with "the bluff abord of the West," Charlie employs the same genial tactics of insinuation used by the confidence man himself. He implores the cosmopolitan to drink—"let me fill your glass again." But Charlie

is led a merry dance in an attempt to keep up with his victim's tortuous phi-
losophizing and requests for money. What could be more unsettling (or unexpected) for a riverboat operator than a plea from an apparently ripe victim not
to "turn the cold shoulder to a friend [. . .] whose pennilessness should suddenly
be revealed to you?" Deeply unsettled by the whole affair, Charlie rises from his
conference with the confidence man "somewhat disconcerted."[71]

Pitch and Charlie, the defining types of the antebellum river, fare better than
most of their fellow passengers. The confidence man adopts a variety of roles,
apparently peddling delusive optimism and unscrupulous stock throughout the
boat. "Along the Mississippi," as the man with the weed warns, "business is not
so ceremonious as at the east." The agent for the Seminole Widow and Orphan
Asylum solicits funds for his "recently formed" charity; he is also the inventor of
a "Protean easy-chair" and has plans for a "World's Charity." The representative
of the Black Rapids Coal Company attempts to deal not only in the stock of
his own company but in lots in the river town of "New Jerusalem," referencing
Nauvoo, "originally founded by certain fugitive Mormons." The herb doctor
convinces a miser of the efficacy of his product and prizes "a dollar-and-half"
from his grip. The cosmopolitan, with nothing for sale, begs charity from Charlie Noble, enchants him, receives a free shave from the barber, and concludes the
novel by recommending a toilet as a "life-preserver [. . .] and a very good one."
The *Fidèle* does not reach New Orleans; the sense of conclusion in the last pages
is ambivalent and bleak. Were these operators really Satanic? Where did Melville
put his confidence? At the conclusion of the novel, he was "ill, tired, and close
to a breakdown." In his vision of this most representative American steamboat's
passage down America's river, no aspect of antebellum culture was spared the
lash of his bitter satirical vision: everyone was a sucker, and everyone was a confidence man. Where should the reader look for confidence? Like any passenger
on an antebellum Mississippi steamboat, the readers of *The Confidence-Man* are
beset by threats and promises—and finally left to shift for themselves. They must
find their counterfeit detectors and life preservers wherever they can.[72]

When the "waning light" of the solar lamp is finally extinguished in the
Fidèle's cabin, it is the confidence man who ominously leads the way through "the
darkness which ensued." After the war, only Twain would better Melville's synthesis of the river's disparate elements, and his bleak vision of America's progress
along the symbolic Mississippi, but Twain's bitter pills were less difficult to swal-
low. (As Cook has commented, "if *Life on the Mississippi, Huckleberry Finn,* and
the various versions of *The Mysterious Stranger* were somehow imaginatively synthesized, they might create a narrative approximating *The Confidence-Man*.") As

Melville prophesied, "something further may follow of this masquerade." But like other visions of the river's underworld that reached for bleak, difficult truths, his novel was largely ignored. When the river's underworld masquerade next made a significant appearance in American culture, it would be as a happy illusion.[73]

"BEGAD SIR, I WISH I COULD PLAY POKER
WITH YOUR DASH AND SPIRIT"

In 1879, Allen Pinkerton wrote that "the Mississippi River has for many years—more especially since the War—been infested by a class of men who never would try to get an honest living, but would prey upon their neighbours." These "marauders could be seen prowling along the banks of the Mississippi." The river's underworld persisted (New Orleans' famed Storyville, for example, would survive into the twentieth century). Despite the demise of slavery, apparently so vital to the popular conception of the river underworld, the Mississippi never lost its equivocal reputation. Yet as the steamboat slowly waned, the true riverboat gambler became a rare creature. Simultaneously, he emerged as a popular icon.[74]

In the 1870s and 1880s, high-profile gamblers like John Morris (really John O'Connor), Mason Long, Henry Edward Hugunin, and George Devol released autobiographies that immortalized their youthful escapades. They evoked a world that, though dominated by cheating and double-dealing, had enough gallantry, romance, and sentiment to fire the imagination. This process involved an intrinsic sentimentality. Figures like "Canada" Bill Jones emerged from their narratives as icons of honest double-dealing; gamblers who only conned deserving suckers; gamblers who dressed well, spent joyfully, and repented in the morning. Canada Bill, Devol wrote, "resembled an idiot": he "walked with a shuffling, half-apologetic sort of a gait [. . .] He had a squeaking, boyish voice, and awkward, gawky manners, and a way of asking fool questions and putting on a good natured sort of a grin, that led everybody to believe that he was the rankest kind of a sucker—the greenest sort of a country jake." In truth, he was "a regular card shark" who "could turn monte with the best of them." His motto: "suckers had no business with money." And yet, what Bill won from suckers he lost at short cards: legendarily, it was Bill who kept playing in a crooked game, knowing he was being conned, because "it was the only game in town." Devol "found him honest to a fault [. . .] There never lived a better hearted man." He died "a pauper, and God bless him for it," Devol wrote, "for he gave more money to the poor than a thousand professed Christians." The creation of the emblematic riverboat gambler was the last and most enduring con of the old blacklegs who worked the Mississippi.[75]

Concomitantly the potential of the gambler and his daring escapades was discovered—or rediscovered and repackaged—by the dime novelist. Hero-gamblers like "Dan, the River Sport," "Monte Jim," "Gabe Ganderfoot," and "sandycraw," thrilled Gilded Age readers. Antebellum America tried to banish the fearful, destabilizing presence of the gambler. As the twentieth century beckoned, this newly refurbished gambler emerged as a charismatic figure entirely suited to the spirit of the Gilded Age. Ann Fabian has traced his popular proliferation to daydreaming "northern readers," entranced by "the Mississippi Valley's surviving myths of easy wealth" because "increasingly confined to the small and uncertain gains of wage labour." Gambling "allowed the poor to challenge the rich"—and that power resonated, even if the challenge was only imaginary. Unsurprisingly, the hero-gambler, like his folklore predecessors, was often seen to be generous to the poor.[76]

Most notable was Edward Willets's dime novel series, *Flush Fred,* released by the Beadle publishing company in 1884 (the year that *Huckleberry Finn* was published). Willett, a newspaperman, was a resident of St. Louis and was undoubtedly influenced by the reminiscences of gamblers in his milieu. Flush Fred was a true gambler-hero: "an attractive and noticeable young man, with dark hair and eyes, a fine mustache, and a general air of good breeding and good temper." A man beaten by Fred at cards happily exclaims: "I wish I had your nerve and your pluck, and I wish I had your youth and spirit; and begad sir, I wish I could play poker with your dash and spirit." To a young woman, Fred "is just lovely—my ideal of a man [. . .] He could swindle me, I know." From the 1880s onward, therefore, the gambler was assured of an afterlife as an icon of popular culture. The Mississippi—that potent symbol of chance and mutability, both lady luck and the devil in disguise—had bred a water spirit in its own image.[77]

In the 1890s, J. W. Lillard traveled to Mississippi river towns looking for old gamblers who would reminisce about the antebellum river for his collection of *Poker Stories.* Old Mr. Martin of St. Louis was aware of the process of cultural rehabilitation that the Mississippi gambler had undergone in the postwar decades. For him, the river's underworld had been a dark place: "the black-eyed, black-mustached hero gambler that you read about was anything but a hero. There was no chivalry in his nature, and he was ready for any dark deed that would profit him." Tom Ellison—a well-known face on the steamboats before the war, and a tourist attraction in Vicksburg in the 1890s—remembered differently. In memory, for him and his friends and colleagues, the antebellum river had been a gambler's paradise. What he, and others like him, chose to remember and imagine, became the evocative stuff of legend:

There isn't any more gambling now [. . .] and no gamblers either. Look at what they call gamblers now—kids, nothing but kids, who haven't got either sense or manners. There ain't many of us old fellows left, and it is hard scratching most of the time to make regular connections with meals. The river used to be the place for gambling [. . .] It was dead easy money, too, all the time. Everyone who travelled had lots of stuff, and everyone was willing to bet, and bet high [. . .] but that's been dead over twenty years, and I don't guess it'll ever come to life again. But those were the days, my boy—great days for the town, with thirty-six steamboats all at the wharf at once, the levee covered with drays, and every sport with stuff in his pockets and lots of good clothes.[78]

The Civil War and Mark Twain

There is the great Mississippi, bond of union made by nature herself. She will maintain it forever.
SENATOR J. H. HAMMOND, 1858

M-a-r-k three! . . . . M-a-r-k three! . . . . Quarter-less-three! . . . . Half twain! . . . . Quarter twain! . . . . M-a-r-k twain!
MARK TWAIN, 1883

In the years before the Civil War, the Mississippi was hopefully afforded powers for the preservation of the Union—its final antebellum flourish. In 1850, Cora Montgomery had written about the river's unifying properties: "That matchless tide is the magic cestus which ensures the harmony of the sovereign sisters of the Union, and no peevish eruption of unsisterly jealousy can disport the silver zone that so firmly and graciously binds their varied climes and products into one common interest [. . .] The Mississippi is the most persuasive mediator, the most energetic arbiter, and the most vigilant defender of the federal compact." Such visions proved delusive. When war commenced, the Mississippi's role as simultaneous borderline and connective tissue—between North and South, between free and slave—was no longer symbolic. Dividing and connecting combatants, the practical value of possession and control of the river was immediately understood by all involved in the conflict, military and civilian. General Frémont—the western pathfinder turned Union soldier—said it early and said it best: whoever controlled the river "would hold the country by the heart." The "great object" of the Union force in the West was therefore to be "the descent of the Mississippi River." Such plans, and such rhetoric, echoed the quasi-military illusions of the early nineteenth century; so did the second prong of the Union's river plan—an upriver invasion force to capture New Orleans and all points north. These were no specters. War had come again to the Mississippi, and when it ended it would not be too strong to state that it "was largely on the river that the ultimate outcome of the Civil War was decided."[1]

The lives of two men stand as emblems of the Mississippi's divisions before, during and after the war. Jefferson Davis and Abraham Lincoln were both intimately connected to life on the Western Waters; they represented the disparate worlds of the river, embodying the "staple-crop plantation South": and the "small-farm, agricultural Northwest." Jefferson Davis, named for the third president, was born to a yeoman farmer in a cabin in western Kentucky in 1808. His father was a Revolutionary veteran. Two of his brothers served in the War of 1812. The family moved south to Louisiana, then to Mississippi, where they settled. They turned to King Cotton: their plantation thrived, and the Davises slowly became self-made southern aristocracy. The Western Waters were the vibrant arteries of Davis's youth. Sent to school in Kentucky at the age of eight, Davis journeyed there with a family friend, traveling along the Natchez Trace. The trip incorporated an extended visit with Andrew Jackson at the Hermitage at Nashville. Two years later, he returned to Mississippi, on one of the earliest steamboats to ply the Western Waters. He attended a college in Natchez and local schools, then Transylvania University, then West Point. As a young officer, Davis was posted to St. Louis, Fort Winnebago, and Fort Crawford at Prairie du Chien. While serving at Fort Crawford, Davis fell in love with Zachary Taylor's daughter Sarah. Taylor opposed the union, but the couple married in Louisville in 1835 and traveled down the Mississippi to Joseph Davis's plantation, Hurricane, below Vicksburg. Davis's older brother—"the wealthiest planter in the state" of Mississippi—presented the newlyweds with their own adjacent estate. Davis called it Brierfield, and began to live the life of a planter—with a traumatic interruption. He and Sarah were struck down with fever: she was buried on the banks of the Mississippi River; he went to Cuba to convalesce.[2]

After the bereavement, Davis lived in semiseclusion at Brierfield, reading in his brother's library and studying the political developments of his place and time. His plantation grew in size and number: ten slaves in 1835, forty in 1840, sixty-one in 1845—the same year that Davis married Varina Howells, the daughter of a family friend in Natchez. The couple honeymooned for six weeks in New Orleans, staying at the St. Charles Hotel. Varina's arrival in Davis's life coincided with his entry into the public world. He was elected to Congress in 1845. Following Jefferson and Jackson, Davis was a Democrat—at a time when most wealthy southerners, like Varina's family, were Whigs. But as Shelby Foote has described, change was in the air. Cotton capitalists like Davis had "thought their interests coincided with the interests of capitalists in general. Now antislavery and pro-tariff agitation was beginning to teach them otherwise [. . .] Repudiating Jefferson and Jackson, the Democrats [like Davis] went over to the Whigs, who came to meet them, creating what Calhoun had been after from the start: a solid South. Davis caught the movement at its outset." His youthful travels had made him particularly knowledgeable about the Mississippi Valley as a single entity. This, compounded by his heroic service in the Mexican War and his vocal defense of southern institutions, made him conspicuous in Congress, during his two terms in the Senate, and during his period as secretary of war in Pierce's administration, 1853–57. It would promote him to the presidency of the rebel states.[3]

In 1809, Abraham Lincoln was born—less than a year after Davis, and less than one hundred miles away. Both were Kentucky log-cabin boys. While the Davises went south to Mississippi, the Lincolns went north: to Indianapolis in 1816, then Illinois. Whereas Davis entered early into the urbane world of the steamboat cabin, young Lincoln was an alligator-horse. At the age of sixteen, he immersed himself in life on the river by operating a ferry "at the confluence of the Anderson and Ohio rivers." In 1828—the year that Jackson entered the White House and the year that Mike Fink entered print—he became one of the thousands of farmer flatboatmen who embarked on the Mississippi to transport their crops to market. Employed by local farmer James Gentry, Lincoln and Gentry's son Allen packed a flatboat (which Lincoln helped construct) with "pork, flour, meal, bacon, potatoes" to trade downriver. The two boys reached New Orleans and returned home, three months later, by steamboat. In 1831, after the Lincolns had relocated to Illinois, young Abraham set off for the Crescent City again. This time he hired out to Denton Offutt, "a hard drinker, a hustler, and a talker shrewd with his tongue." Denton had promised the crew—John Johnston and John Hanks were Lincoln's shipmates—a flatboat, but when one failed to materialize Lincoln himself turned boatwright before they took to the waters.[4]

Little is known of these thousand-mile journeys to New Orleans and their effect on Lincoln. Only one authentic snippet survives. Below Baton Rouge on his first trip to New Orleans, Lincoln tied up at a Madame Duquesne's plantation. While Lincoln and Allen slept, seven slaves crept on to the flatboat attempting to steal their cargo. The Hoosiers fought them off and swiftly cast off for New Orleans. Lincoln picked up a scar above his right eye that stayed with him for life. Fiction filled in the gaps. Stories of the time "when Uncle Abe plied the flatboat business" on the Mississippi—all quite possibly apocryphal, and reminiscent of the sketches told about other literary boatmen—were central to the mythology that grew around him, in life and after death.[5]

One story, told by Lincoln's cousin and shipmate John Hanks, described Lincoln's reaction to "the true horrors of human slavery" that he encountered at a slave auction during his first trip to New Orleans: a "vigorous and comely mulatto girl" underwent "a thorough examination at the hands of the bidders." Lincoln walked away from the scene in disgust: "Boys, let's get away from this.

If I ever get a chance to hit that thing, I'll hit it hard!" Another story told of Lincoln's second flatboat trip. A "drove of hogs was to be taken on board," and as the hogs ran wild at that time, they needed to be rounded up and transferred to the flatboat. Lincoln "actually carried them on board, one by one," with his "long arms and great strength." On the same journey, he impressed the inhabitants of New Salem—soon to be his home—with the manner in which he extricated his flatboat from a precarious position. Balanced on a milldam and filling with water, Lincoln helped his colleagues to unload some of the cargo, and then had an idea. Rather than bailing, "he bored a hole in the bow to let water out, plugged the hole, and eased the boat across the dam."[6]

Other stories were more frivolous. In the satirical *Lincolniana: or The Humors of Uncle Abe* (1864), Andrew Adderup related the story "Uncle Abe As A Pilot." The "tall, gaunt Sucker" applied for the position of Mississippi steamboat pilot. The uncertain captain asked whether Lincoln was "acquainted with the river," and whether he knew "where the snags" were?

> "Well, ye-as," responded Uncle Abe rather hesitantly, "I'm pretty well acquainted with the river, but the snags, I don't know exactly so much about them."
>
> "Don't know about the snags?" exclaimed the captain, contemptuously, "don't know about the snags! You'd make a pretty pilot!"

Lincoln explained himself: "What do I want to know where the snags are for, old sea-hoss? I know where they ain't, and that's where I do my sailing!" Lincoln "proved himself one of the best pilots on the river." But Adderup concluded the story with his own aside: "Wonder if Uncle Abe has forgotten how to sail in clear water?"[7]

At two important antebellum moments the disparate careers of these young men of the Western Waters touched. Jefferson Davis was on a furlough during the Black Hawk War and missed the Bad Axe Massacre in which his company was involved. He did, however, oversee the transportation of the captured Black Hawk down the Mississippi, from Fort Crawford to St. Louis. In his autobiography, Black Hawk was appreciative of the efforts Davis made to shield him from "a gaping crowd." In Illinois, Abraham Lincoln enlisted as a volunteer. His friends put him up for the position of captain, and Lincoln was the men's popular choice. His first order to the rag-tag company met with the response: "Go to hell." They never saw action.[8]

Lincoln and Davis were also closely involved—on separate sides—in what was the most important river issue of the late antebellum years: the railroad. The

1850s would be the critical decade for the future of steamboating; the coming of the railroad slowly eroded the river's supremacy. Other factors contributed. Increasing competition from the railroads was exacerbated by increasing competition between steamboat operators. Before the 1850s, demand for steamboat tonnage kept ahead of the supply. By the critical decade, steamboatmen were facing what "for them was becoming a static economy." The river itself exacerbated the situation. A series of "low-water depressions"—where the river was too shallow for steamboat travel—closed the Mississippi for months at a time. In 1854 and 1856, for example, the river's seasonal "fall rise" was delayed almost until winter—only two weeks before the appearance of ice again closed the river to traffic. The railroad was not subject to seasonal fluctuations.[9]

On February 22, 1854, the railroad reached the river, bringing with it the Grand Excursion party. The *Rock Island Advertiser*, in celebratory mood, announced "the nuptial feast of the great Atlantic Ocean to the mighty Father of Waters." The steamboatmen understood what damage the progeny of this union would wreak. The coming of the railroad oriented the country along two metal tracks running from east to west. As it had been for Lewis and Clark many years before—and as it had been more recently for Francis Parkman and all those embarking on the California and Oregon Trail—the Mississippi was to be relegated to a stopover, a crossing-point, a jump-off: "Almost every day," Parkman described, "steamboats were leaving the levee and passing up the Missouri, crowded with passengers on their way to the frontier." And as *De Bow's Southern and Western Review* lamented, as early as 1852, "the commercial patronage of the interior is immediately transferred to the most rapid and direct lines of outlet and intercommunication. It is thus that the great cities of the North have severally penetrated the interior with artificial lines, until they have taken from the open and untaxed current of the Mississippi the commerce produced upon its borders." The title of Albert Richardson's popular transcontinental travel book, *Beyond the Mississippi* (1867), succinctly stated the matter: both physically and symbolically, America was leaving the river behind.[10]

The steamboatmen were not willing to let their world die quietly. The railroad had reached the river; it had not crossed it. The bridge that Henry Farnam (the entrepreneur behind the railroad) planned to build across the Mississippi at Rock Island on the way to Omaha was the sticking point. The steamboatmen claimed that the bridge was "unconstitutional, an obstruction to navigation, dangerous," and they urged "every western state, river city, and town to take immediate action." Jefferson Davis was sympathetic to their needs (especially since he was seeking a southern route for the transcontinental railroad). As secretary of war, he blocked the bridge: the island in the Mississippi that was going to act as a stepping-stone had been used as a military reservation. In court, his decision was overturned. The bridge was completed in 1856. On April 22, the first train crossed the Mississippi—"in solemn silence," a newspaperman reported. As the *Philadelphia Bulletin* wrote: "Civilization took a railroad trip across the Mississippi." That was not the end of the matter. On May 6, in suspicious circumstances, the steamboat *Effie Alton* drifted into a collision with the bridge (accompanied by cheers, whistles. and bells). The bridge burned down. This time it was Farnam who needed legal support. He hired Abraham Lincoln.[11]

Lincoln's arguments in support of the bridge were reminiscent of Jefferson's arguments for the free navigation of the Mississippi decades before. He stressed the need to recognize that "there is a travel from east to west whose demands are not less than that of those of the river. It is growing larger and larger, building up new countries with a rapidity never before seen in the history of the world." The *Rock Island Magazine* reported that, "Mr Lincoln [. . .] claimed that rivers were to be crossed and that it was the manifest destiny of the people to move westwards." The jury failed to agree with him. The matter was not finally settled in favor of the railroads until 1862. By that time, attention was focused on other matters.[12]

As 1860 turned into 1861, a period of "feverish activity" marked the Mississippi's preparations for war, all along its length. Merchants from the Upper Mississippi hastened to ship their goods to the South before the expected river embargo was enforced. Steamboats making their final peacetime journeys upriver came, as a Davenport editor described, "loaded to the guards with Southern passengers fleeing from the wrath to come. They were mostly of the labouring class, and probably some of those which left this country for the South when hard times came on here [. . .] We are glad to see it. This is the country for labouring people." In New Orleans, George Devol and his gambling colleagues (he claimed) "got up a cavalry company, and named it the Wilson rangers." They outfitted themselves in "fine uniforms," rode "good horses," and left the city each day to drill: "Dismount! Hitch horses! March! Hunt shade! Begin playing!" At the first suggestion of a Union advance on the city, the gamblers "cut the buttons off our coats [. . .] buried our sabres" and "tried to make ourselves look as much like peaceful citizens as possible." In June 1861, Federal authorities set up a blockade at Cairo. Confederates employed the same measures at Memphis.[13]

Upper and Lower Mississippi towns were united in a lament for commerce. By July, twenty thousand steamboatmen were out of work at St. Louis. Ironically, the war provided Mississippi steamboating with its last boom. Lucrative government contracts—and some revival of civilian trade when the river was finally reopened—meant that steamboatmen were kept busy with diverse cargoes: "troops, munitions, and equipment, food and forage supplies of all kinds, draft animals, and livestock [. . .] wounded soldiers, prisoners of war, soldiers on furlough, captured equipment and contraband goods." The boom was unsustainable, but as the *Missouri Democrat* announced early in 1862: "The mania at present is for investment in floating property. Everybody wants an interest in a steamboat [. . .] Youths and men who hardly ever saw a steamboat, are tremblingly eager to invest."[14]

When battle finally came to the river, its fate was, for the most part, swiftly decided. The Federalists presciently limited the high-water mark of the Confederate Mississippi by securing Cairo soon after the fall of Fort Sumter. Cairo was an important military base—"the great fountainhead of ammunition, materiel, weapons and personnel for the coming Mississippi campaigns." Anthony Trollope reached the river in the dramatic winter of the first year of the war. He noted that "men of the Northern States" all returned to the same point "with the greatest firmness": "We will never abandon the right to the mouth of the Mississippi." He visited Cairo to witness "all the pomps and circumstance of glorious war" that were massing on the Federal banks of the Mississippi. Cairo lived up to its "desolate" reputation and the renown for "mud" that Dickens had awarded it as "Eden" in *Martin Chuzzlewit*. The bulk of the army had been moved the day before he arrived, but "a squadron of gunboats [. . .] formidable weapons for river warfare" remained. More formidable were the "thirty-eight mortar-boats." The guns were of "enormous weight": "twenty-three pounds of powder" were used to fire them, and the shell could travel "three miles" with "absolute precision." As Trollope imagined the effect that their bombardment could produce, the river evoked a terrifying biblical resonance: "it seemed as though the fate of Sodom and Gomorrah could not be worse than the fate of that city"; the "grandeur of the idea is almost sublime."[15]

The Union river fleet was pioneering. Both sides modified existing steamboats into gunboats, but under the guiding talents of Samuel Pook and James Buchanan Eads, the Federal river force was amplified with an entirely new weapon: the ironclad. A vital figure in the river's history, in the antebellum years Eads had worked on steamboats and invented a diving bell to salvage wrecks and remove snags; after the war he would build the first iron bridge to cross the Mississippi, at St. Louis. In August 1861, Eads was responsible for the practical interpretation of Samuel Pook's revolutionary designs. The ironclads were a novel concept: steam-powered warships designed with a low draft for the treacherous Western Waters, fortified with thirteen guns and two-and-a-half-inch-thick armor plating. They were the precursors of modern navies worldwide. By the end of November, having worked four thousand men around the clock in boatyards at St. Louis and Illinois, supplementing the insufficient government budget with his own funds, Eads had eight ironclads ready for service. The Confederates' own ironclads—to be built at Memphis and New Orleans—were planned too late to help on the Western Rivers (though the famous *Arkansas* saw successful action). The South did, however, develop torpedoes and mines, which sank two of Eads's ironclads. (In many regards, these advances in military technology were another culmination of Robert Fulton's work. With a mind "animated by war," he had obsessively worked on the development of submarines, torpedoes and steam-powered warships.)[16]

Confederate forces secured their positions on the Lower Mississippi. Only fifteen miles downriver from Cairo, General Leonidas Polk waited at Columbus, Kentucky. A string of forts, under the command of Albert Sidney Johnston, ran down to New Orleans. As McPherson has argued, 'the Mississippi loomed [. . .] large in southern consciousness." But forts Henry and Donelson on the vital Tennessee and Cumberland rivers were "poorly sited and unfinished at the end of 1861." Under the combined attack of Commodore Foote and General Grant, and the formidable ironclads, these forts fell to the Union in February 1862. Columbus was evacuated; New Madrid was captured by a ground assault in March; the batteries at Island Ten followed in April. General Beauregard—a Creole who had an intimate knowledge of the river system—had feared that the fall of New Madrid and Island Ten would "be followed immediately by the loss of the whole Mississippi Valley to the mouth of the Mississippi River." For Beauregard, that meant the end of the war. He was almost correct. Plum Run Bend was a minor Confederate river victory; but soon, Fort Pillow was evacuated; then, in June, as its inhabitants witnessed the destruction of the rebel navy, Memphis fell.[17]

Arguably the most decisive victory had already taken place downriver. New Orleans, blockaded since May 1861, fell to the Union in April 1862. (Kate Stone, a Louisianan diarist, described the Union gunboats "polluting the waters of the grand old Mississippi.") At the time of the attack, the Confederate ironclads had not been completed; Farragut's battleships were too powerful for the defending force. Confederate batteries on the old Chalmette battlefield could not repeat Andrew Jackson's miracle. George Washington Cable was there as a young boy and remembered that "the crowds on the levee howled and screamed with rage." Mary Chesnut lamented: "New Orleans is gone, and with it the Confederacy!

Are we not cut in two? The Mississippi ruins us if it is lost." The completion of the Confederate ironclads, the *Mississippi* and the *Louisiana,* might have provided the chance to break the Union blockades. The absolute loss of the South's major port seemed to spell the end of a Confederate Mississippi; it also made the possible recognition of the Confederacy by England or France unlikely. Benjamin "Beast" Butler took control of New Orleans; when not allegedly stealing spoons, he closed the gambling houses. Devol was imprisoned, but took revenge by winning $19,000 from a "sucker paymaster." He became friendly with Butler—who, Devol wrote, gave him "two silver spoons to remember him by." Farragut sailed up the river and received the surrender of Baton Rouge, then Natchez.[18]

Only Vicksburg and Port Hudson remained. For Davis, Vicksburg was "the nailhead that held the South's two halves together." Said Lincoln:

> See what a lot of land these fellows hold, of which Vicksburg is the key [. . .] I am acquainted with that region and know what I am talking about, and valuable as New Orleans will be to us, Vicksburg will be more so. We may take all northern ports of the Confederacy, and they can still defy us from Vicksburg. It means hog and hominy without limit, fresh troops from all states of the far South and a cotton country where they can raise the staple without interference [. . .] The war can never be brought to a close until that key is in our pocket.

The extraordinary events of the war grafted a new mythological layer on to the Mississippi. Names and events associated with the decisive river battles that split the Confederacy would linger long in the collective memory. Vicksburg would linger longest.[19]

"A queer place this," wrote war correspondent Franc Wilkie from the Union Camp at Milliken's Bend, "miles of steamers extending along the bend of the Mississippi [. . .] in the foreground, scattered groups of blue-coats." Vicksburg, perched on a two-hundred-foot bluff above the river, was trapped between the two prongs of the Union river force. Geography was in its favor. River traffic was vulnerable to the batteries on the bluff; the surrounding countryside was, according to Foote, a "flat and swampy expanse"—a maze of tributaries, swamps, and bayous—"impenetrable to all but the smallest of military parties [. . .] the exclusive domain of moccasins, bears, alligators and panthers." Seven times, in seven separate ways, Grant attempted to breach the river fortress with frontal assaults, tunnels, mines; twice, he even tried to divert the course of the Mississippi. The first was abandoned when Sherman—described by his friend Admiral David Porter as "half-sailor, half-soldier, with a touch of the snapping turtle"—complained that the rising Mississippi "threatens to drown us out." The second was more pleasant: "McPherson and his staff [. . .] enjoyed something of a holiday, taking a regimental band aboard the little steamer for moonlight excursions, to and from the landing at one of the lakeside plantation houses which turned out to have a well-stocked cellar." (In 1876, the capricious river achieved what Grant could not: the Mississippi cut itself a new path, west of Vicksburg, leaving the river town high and dry. The Army Corps of Engineers diverted the Yazoo past the city in 1903.)[20]

The eighth attempt proved successful. A grinding siege lasted from the end of May until the fateful Independence Day when Vicksburg fell and Gettysburg was decided. Cut off from supplies, soldiers and civilians inside the town suffered under the Union bombardment and increasing deprivations—descending from half rations, to quarter rations, to mule meat. (One bored soldier found some bleak humor in the situation, producing a "Bill of Fare" for the "Hotel de Vicksburg" that consisted solely of mule variations: "Mule head stuffed a-la-Mode.") A Texas colonel complained that his men had "symptoms of incipient scurvy." Surrender became inevitable. The Mississippi fully passed into Union hands. Seventeen thousand casualties of war lay in the National Cemetery at Vicksburg.[21]

Of July 4, 1863—sixty years to the day that Jefferson announced the Louisiana Purchase—Lincoln declared: "The Father of Waters again goes unvexed to the sea." William Tecumseh Sherman—who developed a deep connection to what he called "the great artery" of America, writing to a friend soon after Vicksburg: "I want to live out here and die here also, and I don't care if my grave be like De Soto's in its muddy waters"—wrote, "Now the river of our greatness is free, as God made it." Admiral David Porter expressed the matter most fully: "The Father of Waters flowed peacefully to the sea, free and untrammelled [. . .] The great chain of slavery was broken, never to be again united. The work of setting free the great artery of the North and South, so essential to our nationality, had been accomplished." Nathaniel Hawthorne was less impressed. He thought the "dead old Union" was still a lost cause, writing on July 20: "The best thing possible, as far as I can see, would be to effect a separation [. . .] giving us the West bank of the Mississippi, and a boundary line affording as much Southern soil as we can hope to digest into freedom in another century." Stonewall Jackson had died a month earlier on May 10, having been fatally wounded at Chancellorsville, and the South felt his loss almost as keenly as that of the river itself. Jackson himself had spent a significant portion of his orphaned childhood on the Mississippi, floating down the Ohio by raft before selling wood to passing steamboats; his last words were of a peace that, for America and the Mississippi, still seemed distant: "Let us cross over the river, and rest under the shade of the trees."[22]

Posterity would indelibly connect the men who fought for control of the Mississippi to its waters. When Frederick Douglass paid tribute to Lincoln in 1876, at the unveiling of the Freedmen's Monument in Washington, D.C., he represented him in an iconic pose: "at home on water, with his oars, with his poles, with his planks, and with his boat-hooks [. . .] Whether in his flat-boat on the Mississippi river, or at the fireside of his frontier cabin, he was a man of work. A son of toil himself, he was linked in brotherly sympathy with the sons of toil in every loyal part of the republic. This very fact gave him tremendous power with the American people." Jefferson Davis, on the other hand, was shaped into a very different role. As Gilbert Haven declared, in a sermon delivered in Boston in 1865, "none so strikingly in their rise, rule, and fall resemble each other as Pharaoh and Jefferson Davis." Though living "thousands of years apart," as the rulers of riverine slave empires they "have had a history and will have a fame nigh identical." The lesson to be learned was the same; the American Nile had played its part to the end: "Thus has God shown that he is the perpetual Master of the world. Whether on the banks of the Nile or the Mississippi, whether thousands of years ago or to-day, whoever of his oppressed people calls upon Him, He will hear, He will answer." If Davis was Pharaoh, Lincoln and Grant, for Haven, were "our Aaron and Moses." Grant, like Jackson before him, would reach the White House in large part because of his victories on the Mississippi. The popular association, even the quality of the language, had a profound sense of déjà vu—as in the song, to the tune of "Benny Havens," reported by the pseudonymous Private Miles O'Reilly:

> Oh, a bumper to Ulysses Grant,
> A chief whose worth we know;
> Our banner in his stalwart hands,
> What reck we of the foe?
> He's the Mississippi river horse—
> Resistless as its flow,
> And all its length of waters
> With his victories are aglow.[23]

The fall of Vicksburg did not mean that the river war was over. Like the incarnation of antebellum mystery novels, the secret plots of Confederate mail runners and boat burners haunted the river. The memoirs of Absalom C. Grimes, a self-professed Confederate mail runner, provide the most remarkable account of the clandestine river war. Before the war, Grimes worked as a steamboat pilot. When war came, he left the river and joined a Confederate militia back in Missouri—with his friends and fellow pilots Sam Bowen and Samuel Clemens. His covert career began soon after his first capture by Federal troops. While being transported to a Union prison via steamboat, Grimes hid himself away and pretended to be an engineer: "I rolled up my sleeves, grabbed an oil can in one hand and wrench in the other, smeared my face and hands with grease." After his escape, he "conceived the idea of gathering up all the letters I could and carrying them south to the Missouri boys in the army." Assisted by a team of "lady assistants," he successfully carried mail to and from Confederate troops—even running the Vicksburg blockade—and was equally successful at escaping Union prisons. Horace Bixby—Sam Clemens's old mentor—was a solid Union man who said of Grimes: "That notorious devil [. . .] is here for no good to us." Though Grimes mentioned only one aborted attempt at boat burning in which he was personally involved, he paid tribute to his sometime partner, Robert Louden, who spent much of the war "amusing himself burning government steamboats."[24]

The covert nature of the river war fascinated those who attempted to work popular fictions from the hard realities of the conflict. Charles Fosdick wrote a successful series of books for boys that mingled natural history with war on the Mississippi. In three of his six adventures, Frank Nelson fought in a Union gunboat on the western river campaigns and rose through the ranks. The bulk of his adventures were clandestine missions. Frank could be found escaping from Confederate prisons or taking on a "guerilla station" and accosting mail runners like Absalom Grimes. The same was true of another popular wartime figure, Pauline D'Estraye, who was featured in adventure novels by Charles Wesley Alexander, *Pauline of the Potomac* and *Maud of the Mississippi*. A southern belle turned Union spy, Pauline provided valuable assistance to Grant at the siege of Vicksburg—infiltrating the town where "the most ample promises of reward have failed to induce the most daring of my scouts or spies to penetrate into the city itself." As ever with the Mississippi, it was the secret history that lingered.[25]

The finale of the Mississippi's war came almost three weeks after Appomattox. The steamboat *Sultana* had been built in January 1863, a product of the midwar Mississippi boom. Throughout the war years it operated along the Western Waters, fulfilling government contracts and dodging sporadic Confederate sniper fire. In the momentous month of April 1865, the boat was still involved in the lucrative war trade. Since telegraphic communications with the South remained disrupted, the *Sultana* was the first downriver boat to carry news of Lincoln's assassination. On its return voyage, the *Sultana* steamed toward Vicksburg to secure one of the last valuable contracts of the war. The Union prisoners who had survived the horrors of the Andersonville and Cahaba prisoner-of-war camps had been transported to Camp Fisk, four miles from Vicksburg. They awaited transportation to the North along the Mississippi.

The *Sultana* arrived at Vicksburg on April 23. A combination of greed, impatience, bureaucratic incompetence, and, perhaps most important, the desire to return the afflicted prisoners to their homes meant that when it steamed away on the evening of April 24, the *Sultana* was carrying "probably [. . .] more than 2500" passengers. This was more than "six times the *Sultana*'s legal carrying capacity of 376." The liberated men did not complain about the cramped and unsanitary conditions. As William Dixon later wrote: "We were all talking of home and friends and the many good things we would have to eat. We consoled ourselves that we had lived through it all and now were in the land of the free." Then, on the night of April 27, as the men slept where they could, the *Sultana*'s four boilers exploded. The explosion, shrapnel, fire, steam, scalding water, and the swollen spring river took an almost unbelievable toll. Approximately 1,800 of the *Sultana*'s passengers were killed. The river's war ended in all-consuming fire.[26]

"VERILY ALL IS VANITY AND LITTLE WORTH—SAVE PILOTING"

But the change of changes was on the "levee" [. . .] Half a dozen sound-asleep steamboats where I used to see a solid mile of wide-awake ones! This was melancholy, this was woful. The absence of the pervading and jocund steamboatman from the billiard-saloon was explained. He was absent because he is no more. His occupation is gone, his power has passed away, he is absorbed into the common herd [. . .] Mississippi steamboating was born about 1812; at the end of thirty years, it had grown to mighty proportions; and in less than thirty more, it was dead! [. . .] Of course it is not absolutely dead; neither is a crippled octogenarian who could once jump twenty-two feet on level ground; but as contrasted with what it was in its prime vigor, Mississippi steamboating may be called dead [. . .] A strangely short life for so majestic a creature.

When war came to the Mississippi, one young steamboat pilot was forced to leave the river, and the career that he had long sought to pursue. Possibly conceived on a steamboat traveling west, he had grown up in Hannibal, Missouri. It was a town—like its state—that geographically and culturally blended aspects of North and South. Hannibal had been laid out in the pre-Jacksonian years of speculation, imagined into existence from the bare bones of a small trading post in 1819. Incorporated in 1839, the year before the boy's arrival, the town had risen to a healthy population of one thousand, of which a small but significant proportion were slaves. Hannibal was part of the slave economy; it was also increasingly industrial, with sawmills, hotels, factories, and ambitions for a railroad. The river was its animating spirit. As the boy would later describe, Hannibal was a "white town drowsing in the sunshine of a summer's morning [. . .] glorious with expectancy" for the daily visitation of a steamboat: "the scene changes! The town drunkard stirs, the clerks wake up, a furious clatter of drays follows, every house and store pours out a human contribution, and all in a twinkling the dead town is alive and moving." After its departure, "the day was a dead and empty thing."[27]

The young boy—like his peers—had "one permanent ambition [. . .] That was, to be a steamboatman." It suffused their games, and his memories of childhood. A boy might pretend to be the steamboat *Big Missouri:* "Let her go back on the labboard! Ling-a-ling-ling! Chow-ch-chow-chow!" The children knew the river as the scene of games, license, magic—perhaps the scene for a piratical raft adventure, since the river's undercurrents entered their games, and it was believed "that Murrel's gang used to be around here one summer." The boy would have seen the remaining alligator-horses on the waterfront—those "heavy drinkers, coarse frolickers [. . .] heavy fighters, reckless fellows'—and witnessed their fights and boasts: "Look at me! I take nineteen alligators and a bar'l of whiskey for breakfast when I'm in good health, and a bushel of rattlesnakes and a dead body when I'm ailing." But he would also learn that the Mississippi could be a mortal enemy. A friend, Lem Hackett, "fell out of an empty flat-boat, where he was playing. Being loaded with sin, he went to the bottom like an anvil." "Dutchy" drowned too, during a diving game, and the boy was chosen to be the one to locate his body: "I felt among the hoop poles, and presently grasped a limp wrist." The boy himself once came close to a watery death; but as his mother comforted him, "People who are born to be hanged are safe in the water."[28]

Then there were the slaves. The boy's family owned a young girl named Jennie, who nursed him through many childhood illnesses. He knew more slaves at his uncle John's farm, "a heavenly place for a boy." He would listen to the "bedridden white-headed slave woman" Hannah, who told of "witches" and had remedies against their work. On "privileged nights" he would join the cluster of "white and black children grouped on the hearth, with the firelight playing on their faces and the shadows flickering upon the walls" to hear Dan'l, a slave known to all as Uncle, "telling the immortal tales." He came to know their Mississippi, the artery of enslavement, and their ever-present terror of being transported from the comparative comforts of Hannibal, along the river's length, to the grinding work of a plantation: "Oh, de good Lord God have mercy on po' sinful me—*I's sole down the river!*" When the boy's family hit hard times, Jennie was sold: "she wanted to be sold to Beebe," the boy remembered, or chose to remember, "and was. He sold her down the river. Was seen, years later, ch.[ambermaid] on steamboat." One of the boy's friends found and helped a slave who was trying to escape, hiding on an island in the Mississippi just across from Hannibal. Word got out, and a party of men went to investigate. The slave supposedly drowned, "trying to cross a drift." A few days later, the boy and his friends were playing on the island. The corpse abruptly resurfaced: "the negro rose before them, straight and terrible, about half his length out of the water. He had gone down feet foremost, and the loosened drift had released them."[29]

There was music, too. The river was always a river of song. The *Index*, a Confederate newspaper, claimed that "Dixie" was first sung by "free Negroes of the North, especially those employed on board the steamers on the western rivers." The "negro minstrel show" often played in Hannibal. If, as they surely did, the minstrels performed the work of Stephen Foster, then the Mississippi featured prominently: "Down on de Mississippi floating / Long time I trabbel on de way / All night de cotton wood a toting / Sing for my true lub all de day." The slaves had their own music, with a "double-level meaning" often elusive to contemporary commentators—but perhaps no mystery to the boy who memorized and recited their spirituals throughout his life. An observer described him singing one in 1874: "his voice was low and soft, a whisper of wind in the trees; his eyes were closed, and he smiled strangely."

> O, Jordan bank was a great old bank,
> Dere ain't but one more river to cross.
> We have some valiant soldier here,
> Dere ain't but one more river to cross.
> O, Jordan stream will never run dry,
> Dere ain't but one more river to cross.
> Dere's a hill on my left, and he catch on my right.
> Dere ain't but one more river to cross.

Thomas Higginson, who commanded the first black regiment in the Civil War, recorded that spiritual but, disconnected from the Western Rivers, "could get no explanation of this last riddle." The boy knew that it signified the river as the road to freedom, directions to the Promised Land.[30]

Still, the boy did not take to the water immediately. Family privation meant that he had to work from an early age. At twelve, he became a printer's devil, immersing himself in the burgeoning world of print. Southwestern vernacular sketches filled the papers that came into the newspaper office. He tried his own hand at writing. His first sketch, written at the age of sixteen, was entitled "The Dandy Frightening the Squatter" (1852). It involved comic and violent interaction between two different social types on the river. The dandy ended up the loser, "floundering in the turbid waters of the Mississippi." The earliest surviving image of the boy was taken at this time, too, a photograph of youthful pride that resembles the pictures that would soon be taken of young soldiers. Rather than their ubiquitous guns, he proudly displayed his name in type, reversed by the photographic procedure so that it appeared: MAS. In 1853, Sam left his hometown and lived the peripatetic life of a journeyman printer. In 1857, the river finally called him. He fell into his "permanent ambition" almost by accident, on his way down the Mississippi to try and book passage for South America to make his fortune from cocaine. Horace Bixby indulged his desire to steer the boat. In New Orleans, they came to an arrangement: $500 for tuition in the art of steamboat piloting, $100 in advance. Sam became a steamboatman.[31]

That meant learning a new and unfamiliar language: that of the Mississippi. Bixby, revelation by revelation, initiated him into the mysteries of the river. A pilot had to "get this entire river by heart. You have to know it just like ABC." And a pilot had to know two rivers—one upstream, one down—and twice again, by day and by night: "My boy, you've got to know the *shape* of the river perfectly. It is all there is left to steer by on a very dark night. Everything else is blotted out and gone." Appearances were not only useless, they were positively misleading. The river had to be learned "with such absolute certainty that you can always steer by the shape that's *in your head,* and never mind the one that's before your eyes." In the end, it came down to "instinct." The only Mississippi that mattered was the imagined Mississippi of the mind, and a "true pilot" cared "nothing about anything on earth but the river."[32] He learned:

> The face of the water, in time, became a wonderful book—a book that was a dead language to the uneducated passenger, but which told its mind to me without reserve, delivering its most cherished secrets as clearly as if it uttered them with a voice. And it was not a book to be read once and thrown aside, for it had a new story to tell every day. Throughout the long twelve hundred miles there was never a page that was void of interest, never one that you could leave unread without loss, never one that you would want to skip, thinking you could find higher enjoyment in some other thing. There never was so wonderful a book written by man;

never one whose interest was so absorbing, so unflagging, so sparklingly renewed with every re-perusal.

He lost something, too—an innocent eye. Learning the practical lessons of the river meant that "the grace, the beauty, the poetry had gone out of the majestic river!" (He would imagine it and conjure it for others, though; in time he would learn it again. In 1902, on his last trip to his boyhood home, the last time that he would see the Mississippi, he declared in a birthday speech that he was "seeing now the most enchanting river view the planet could furnish. I never knew it when I was a boy; it took an educated eye that had traveled over the globe to know and appreciate it.") He learned other lessons in recompense. Like Thorpe's narrator in "The Big Bear," he used his time on the heterogeneous river to learn another language: "I got personally and familiarly acquainted with about all the different types of human nature that are to be found [. . .] When I find a well-drawn character in fiction or biography, I generally take a warm personal interest in him, for the reason that I have known him before—met him on the river." His apprenticeship lasted two-and-a-half years, his piloting career one and a half more—a time about which, ironically, little is known. Only fourteen letters survive from the four-year period of his life on the Mississippi, the time when he was a steamboat pilot and therefore "the only unfettered and entirely independent human being that lived in the earth." The river's pervasive secrecy drew a veil.[33]

Then the river took its tribute. Sam's brother had joined him on the river-road to wealth, encouraged by his older sibling: "Henry was doing little or nothing here, and I sent him to our clerk to work his way for a trip, by measuring woodpiles, counting coal boxes, and other clerkly duties, which he performed satisfactorily. He may go down with us again, for I expect he likes our bill of fare better than that of his boarding house." Henry made a number of trips on Sam's boat, the *Pennsylvania,* until disaster struck. Horace Bixby was the pilot idealized; William Brown of the *Pennsylvania,* on the other hand, was an "ignorant, stingy, malicious, snarling, fault-hunting, mote-magnifying tyrant." When Brown's wrath was turned toward Henry, violence ensued: "Brown, with a sudden access of fury, picked up a ten-pound lump of coal and sprang after him; but I was between, with a heavy stool, and I hit Brown a good honest blow which stretched him out." For the next upriver journey, therefore, Sam was obliged to ship on another steamboat while Henry remained on the *Pennsylvania.* They were to be reunited in St. Louis. On that trip, the *Pennsylvania* exploded, and Henry was fatally injured. After six days, "we bore him to the death-room." Sam stayed on the river until the war came.[34]

After his brief "taste" of war in the Confederate militia with Absalom Grimes, he "stepped out again permanently." He did not participate in or witness the brutal guerrilla war that tore apart his home state, making an icon out of Jesse James. He did not fight on the Mississippi. Since he stayed away so long, neither did he see the slow decline of the river and its economy. If he had stayed on the river—burning boats with Grimes and Robert Louden, bushwhacking with fellow-Missourian Jesse James, piloting a gunboat with Horace Bixby, or fighting off his future friend, Ulysses Grant, at Vicksburg—or if he had returned to the river after the war, piloting a boat in the declining passenger trade, then the cultural history of the Mississippi would have been profoundly, unthinkably, different. If he had died in the war, no other writer would conceivably have stepped into the breach and stamped their own defining imprint on the river. If he had lived, the war would have altered his vision of the river. He had no war stories to tell, but he had something else to offer: memory; and "a pilot's memory," after all, was "the most wonderful thing in the world." The Hannibal of his childhood, the Mississippi of his youth, remained alive to him—as it would, soon, to the rest of the world, forever. Sam lit out for the territory and carried on writing. In 1863, at the turning point of the Civil War, the year of Vicksburg and Gettysburg, Samuel Clemens gave birth to Mark Twain.[35]

The antebellum years were the Heroic Age of the Mississippi. Countless stories were told in countless ways about the giant river that bisected America, and the Mississippi meandered into the national consciousness as an ever-shifting symbol—of the West, its strange and unfamiliar waters threatening and full of promise; of American nationalism, its waters a melting pot that brought forth new and distinct types; of European disapprobation, its waters a murky embodiment of the republican experiment; of technological advancement, its waters the crucible of steam and the subject of new industrial images; of unsettling undercurrents, its waters the home of dark, hidden, uncontrollable forces; of union, slavery, internal division, conflict, liberation, and decline, its waters dividing and connecting in blood; and, through everything, of possibility: the chance of transformation, the prospect of change, the hope of improvement and the risk of destruction. For all the advancements made in the antebellum years, the Mississippi remained what it had always been: ultima Thule, a limit almost to the range of thought—a river of dreams. Without Mark Twain, this is how the cultural Mississippi would have remained: a disparate mélange of representations, competing and complementing in equal measure. A Heroic Age needs a single poet's singular vision; the Mississippi needed Mark Twain.

His great river books have often been taken as autobiography. In many aspects, they were; but they were also, more truthfully, biography: he told the life of the Mississippi, each book representing a different age. From the beginning, the river was there as a literary possibility, running as deep in his work as it did in his life. In 1866, he wrote to his mother and sister from San Francisco, wishing that he "was back there piloting up & down the river again." He also dropped hints that he was planning a book on the Mississippi: "the last hundred [pages] will have to be written in St. Louis, because the materials for them can only be got there." In 1871, he wrote to wife, Olivia: "when I come to write the Mississippi book, *then* look out! I will spend 2 months on the river & take notes, & I bet you I will make a standard work."[36]

Not a single standard work, but many: *The Adventures of Tom Sawyer* (1876) was the innocent, ignorant river of childhood; "Old Times on the Mississippi" (1875), the river of youthful instruction; *Adventures of Huckleberry Finn* (1884), the river of troubled adolescence; *Pudd'nhead Wilson,* the resolutely, bitterly adult river; and *Life on the Mississippi* (1883), the tired and run-down river of old age. Twain's vision of the Mississippi, in its youth at least, might persuasively be taken as a paradise. But he knew the river too well—had suffered on it too much—to think so simply. Dark intimations accompanied his river from the very start: murder and mortality in *Tom Sawyer;* slavery, deception, and violence in *Huck Finn;* the cruel and uncaring social world of the bitter *Pudd'nhead Wilson;* loss and deterioration in *Life on the Mississippi.* In one of his blackest moments, he imagined the afterlife of his childhood heroes: "Huck comes back, 60 years old, from nobody knows where—& crazy [. . .] Tom comes, at last, 60 from wandering the whole world & tends Huck, & together they talk the old times; both are desolate, life has been a failure, all that was lovable, all that was beautiful is under the mould. They die together."[37]

And yet, for all that, Twain knew the river's undercurrents, knew that its course was a powerful conduit for the worst of humanity's failings, knew that its waters all too clearly reflected the degeneration and decline of a human life, the broken promises of America, his other, imagined Mississippi was ultimately more potent. It was a bond of union after all:

> We said there warn't no home like a raft, after all. Other places do seem so cramped up and smothery, but a raft don't. You feel mighty free and easy and comfortable on a raft [. . .] Two or three days and nights went by; I reckon I might say they swum by, they slid along so quiet and smooth and lovely [. . .] Soon as it was night, out we shoved; when we got her

out to about the middle, we let her alone, and let her float wherever the
current wanted her to; then we lit the pipes, and dangled our legs in the
water and talked about all kinds of things—we was always naked, day
and night, whenever the mosquitoes would let us [. . .] Sometimes we'd
have that whole river all to ourselves for the longest time.

At such moments, his vision was a vision for the ages—a Mississippi that, if it
never truly was, might have been: the river of lazy dreams; the river of liberation
and unfettered freedom; the river as eternal and unchanging Eden, always gone
too soon.[38]

Notes

THE AMERICAN NILE: "ULTIMA THULE"

Epigraph 1. Quoted in Timothy Flint, *Recollections of the Last Ten Years in the Valley of the Mississippi* (1826; Carbondale: Southern Illinois University Press, 1968), 64–66.

Epigraph 2. Zadok Cramer, *The Navigator* (Pittsburgh: Cramer, Spear, and Eichbaum, 1814; repr. 1966), 145.

1. Charles Gayarré, *History of Louisiana: The Spanish Domination* (New York: Redfield, 1854), 601–3.

2. Frederick Jackson Turner, *The Frontier in American History* (1920; Tucson: University of Arizona Press, 1994), 198–99.

3. Wyman H. Herendeen, *From Landscape to Literature: The River and the Myth of Geography* (Pittsburgh: Duquesne University Press, 1986), 5–6.

4. Mark Twain, *Life on the Mississippi* (Boston: James R. Osgood and Co., 1883), 1; John Sears, *Sacred Places: American Tourist Attractions in the Nineteenth Century* (Amherst: University of Massachusetts Press, 1998), 4.

5. Herendeen, *River,* 11.

6. Thomas Buchanan, *Black Life on the Mississippi* (Chapel Hill: University of North Carolina Press, 2004), 20.

7. R. E. Garczynski, "The Upper Mississippi," in William Cullen Bryant, ed., *Picturesque America,* 2 vols. (New York: D. Appleton and Co., 1874), 2:318; Edmund Blunden, *Leigh Hunt: A Biography* (London: Cobden-Sanderson, 1930), 119.

8. Rev. T. W. Aveling, *Rivers of Many Waters; or, Travels in the Lands of the Tiber, the Jordan, and the Nile* (London: John Snow, 1855), 2; Philip Henry Gosse, *Sacred Streams: The Ancient and Modern History of the Rivers of the Bible* (London: Cox, 1850), 355; John T. Irwin, *American Hieroglyphics: The Symbol of the Egyptian Hieroglyphics in the American Renaissance* (Baltimore: Johns Hopkins University Press, 1983), 72.

9. George Gale, *Upper Mississippi: or, Historical Sketches of the Mound Builders* (New York: Oakley and Mason, 1867), 22; Angie Debo, *The Rise and Fall of the Choctaw Republic* (Norman: University of Oklahoma Press, 1961), 1–2; James Adair, *The History of the American Indians* (London: Edward and Charles Dilly, 1775), 13–14.

10. Mrs. Houstoun, *Hesperos, or Travels in the West,* 2 vols. (London: J. W. Parker, 1850), 2:42; Neil Brody Miller, "'Embalmed in Egyptian Ethnology': Racial Discourse and Antebellum Interest in the Ancient Near East" (paper presented at the Midwest Popular Culture Association meeting, Cleveland, Ohio, October 10, 2004), 2–3; James D. Davis, *The History of the City of Memphis* (Memphis: Hite, Crumpton, and Kelly, 1873), 29.

11. Miller, "Egyptian," 3; Augustin Cochin, *The Results of Slavery,* trans. M. L. Booth (Boston: Walker, Wise, and Co., 1863), 294; Harriet Beecher Stowe, *Uncle Tom's Cabin* (London: C. H. Clarke and Co., 1852), 120.

12. Andrew Jackson, *Narrative and Writings of Andrew Jackson, of Kentucky* (Syracuse: Daily and Weekly Star Office, 1847), 13; Josiah Henson, *Truth Stranger Than Fiction: Father Henson's Story of His Own Life* (Boston: John P. Jewett and Co., 1858), 86–87; Charles Alexander, *Battles and Victories of Allen Allensworth* (Boston: Sherman, French, 1914), 19.

13. John Joseph, *The Life and Sufferings of John Joseph* (Wellington: J. Greedy, 1848), 7.

14. Buchanan, *Black Life*, 102; William Wells Brown, *The Black Man, His Antecedents, His Genius, and His Achievements* (New York: Hamilton, 1863), 20; Brown, *Black Man*, 281, 35.

1. EMPIRE: JEFFERSON AND "THE MISSISSIPPI WE MUST HAVE"

Epigraph 1. An address to Congress from the sixth Kentucky convention, 1788. From *Littell's Political Transactions in and Concerning Kentucky*, ed. with an introduction by Temple Bodley (1806, repr., Louisville: John P. Morton, 1926), 104–5.

Epigraph 2. "The Travel Diary of Elizabeth House Trist," in William L. Andrews et al., eds., *Journeys in New Worlds: Early American Women's Narratives* (Madison: University of Wisconsin Press, 1990), 183–232, 224.

1. Thomas Jefferson to M. Dupont de Nemours, Washington, February 1, 1803, in H. A. Washington, ed., *The Writings of Thomas Jefferson*, 9 vols. (New York: Taylor and Maury, 1853), 4:456–60.

2. Timothy Severin, *Explorers of the Mississippi* (Minneapolis: University of Minnesota Press, 2002), 147. To distil a convoluted history: de Soto and his men reached the river on May 8, 1541. It wasn't for over one hundred years that the Mississippi became the focus of colonial attention. La Salle claimed the river and the land drained by its tributaries (Louisiana) for France in 1682. France secretly ceded Louisiana to Spain in November 1762. The Treaty of Paris, at the end of the Seven Years' War, awarded Britain all French lands east of the Mississippi (sometimes referred to as Georgiana) with the exception of New Orleans. The Revolutionary War saw the British possessions become American (though Florida was returned to Spain by Britain in 1783). In 1800, in the Treaty of St. Ildefonso, Napoleon reclaimed Louisiana for France—in whose grasp it remained (although France only officially took possession in December 1802) until the Louisiana Purchase in 1803.

3. Henry Savage Jr. and Elizabeth J. Savage, *André and François André Michaux* (Charlottesville: University Press of Virginia, 1986), 155; John W. Reps, *Cities of the Mississippi: Nineteenth-Century Images of Urban Development* (Columbia: University of Missouri Press, 1994), 5.

4. Frederick Jackson Turner, *The Frontier in American History* (1920; Tucson: University of Arizona Press, 1994), 182; John Buchanan, *Jackson's Way: Andrew Jackson and the People of the Western Waters* (Hoboken, N.J.: Wiley, 2001), 14.

5. Thomas Jefferson to George Rogers Clark, Richmond, December 25, 1780, in Julian P. Boyd, ed., *The Papers of Thomas Jefferson* (Princeton: Princeton University Press, 1951), 4:237.

6. Alexis de Tocqueville, *Democracy in America* (1835–40; London: Folio Society, 2002), 21, 27, 50. Bodley, *Littell's*, 183; Turner, *Frontier*, 183.

7. Saul K. Padover, ed., *The Complete Jefferson: Containing His Major Writings, Published and Unpublished, Except His Letters* (New York: Duell, Sloan, and Pearce, 1943), 570; Boyd, *Papers*, 2:408; Thomas Perkins Abernethy, *Western Lands and the American Revolution* (New York:

Appleton-Century, 1937), 295. See also Frederic Austin Ogg, *The Opening of the Mississippi: A Struggle for Supremacy in the American Interior* (New York: Macmillan, 1904), 419–20. Jay was unsuccessful in his negotiations, and the matter was not resolved for another decade (then, only until 1802). Pinckney's Treaty of 1795 secured for America the navigation of the Mississippi and the right of deposit at New Orleans.

8. Jared Sparks, ed., *The Writings of George Washington*, 12 vols. (Boston: American Stationers' Co., 1833–37), 9:63.

9. James Madison to Thomas Jefferson, August 20, 1784, in Boyd, *Papers*, 7:401–8.

10. Trist, "Diary," 187.

11. Ibid., 224–32; 195.

12. Thomas Jefferson to Archibald Stewart, Paris, January 25, 1786, in Washington, *Writings*, 1:518; Thomas Jefferson to James Madison, Paris, January 30, 1787, in Washington, *Writings*, 2:105–6; Charles A. Miller, *Jefferson and Nature* (Baltimore: Johns Hopkins University Press, 1988), 229.

13. Thomas Jefferson to William Carmichael, August 22, 1790, in Gilbert L. Lycan, ed., *Alexander Hamilton & American Foreign Policy: A Design for Greatness* (Norman: University of Oklahoma Press, 1970), 130.

14. Thomas Jefferson, *Spain and the Mississippi*, in Padover, *Jefferson*, 240–56.

15. Thomas Jefferson to William Dunbar, Washington, March 13, 1804, in Washington, *Writings*, 4:537–39; Thomas Jefferson to James Madison, Paris, May 3, 1788, in Washington, *Writings*, 2:378–79.

16. From a letter accompanying the presentation of the manuscript of Jefferson's *Examination into the Boundaries of Louisiana* to the American Philosophical Society in 1817, quoted in Padover, *Jefferson*, 259. For more detailed records of these works, see E. Millicent Sowerby, *Catalogue of the Library of Thomas Jefferson*, 5 vols. (Washington: Library of Congress, 1959), passim; John Logan Allen, *Lewis and Clark and the Image of the Northwest* (New York: Dover, 1991), 61.

17. General James Wilkinson, *Expatriation Declaration*, September 1787, in Bodley, *Littell's*, cxxxvii; John Seelye, *Beautiful Machine: Rivers and the Republican Plan, 1755–1825* (New York: Oxford University Press, 1991), 213; William C. Davis, *Three Roads to the Alamo* (New York: Harper Perennial, 1999), 106.

18. Buckner F. Melton, *Aaron Burr: Conspiracy to Treason* (New York: Wiley, 2002), 14; Henry Adams, *History of the United States of America during the Administrations of Thomas Jefferson* (New York: Library of America, 1889–91; repr. 1986), 6.

19. Thomas Jefferson to Archibald Stewart, Paris, January 25, 1786, in Washington, *Writings*, 1:518; Bodley, *Littell's*, xi; General James Wilkinson, *Memoirs of My Own Times*, 3 vols. (Philadelphia: Abraham Small, 1816), 2:110.

20. Thomas Robson Hay and M. R. Werner, *The Admirable Trumpeter: A Biography of General James Wilkinson* (New York: Doubleday, Doran, 1941), 83. See also Bodley, *Littell's*, xxxix–xl; John Bakeless, *Background to Glory: The Life of George Rogers Clark* (New York: Lippincott, 1957), 334; Temple Bodley, *George Rogers Clark: His Life and Public Services* (Boston: Houghton Mifflin, 1926), 316.

21. "Wilkinson's Memorial," in Bodley, *Littell's*, cxix–cxxvii, lx, xl.

22. Bodley, *Littell's*, lviii–lix; the proceedings of the sixth Kentucky convention, printed in the *Kentucky Gazette*, January and February 1789, reprinted in Bodley, *Littell's*, 103; Gilbert Imlay, *A Topographical Description of the Western Territories of North America* (London: J. Debrett, 1792), ix; Robert McColley, ed., *Federalists, Republicans, and Foreign Entanglements* (Englewood Cliffs, N.J.: Prentice-Hall, 1969), 57.

23. McColley, *Federalists*, 14–17.

24. J. P. Brissot de Warville, *New Travels in the United States of America Performed in 1788*, trans. Joel Barlow (Dublin: W. Corbet, 1792), 479–80; Moncure Daniel Conway, *The Life of Thomas Paine*, 2 vols. (New York: G. P. Putnam's, 1892), 2:93.

25. Constantin-François Chasseboeuf Comte de Volney, *A View of the Soil and Climate of the United States of America*, trans. Charles Brockden Brown (Philadelphia: J. Conrad, 1804, repr. 1968), 325. In 1797, much to his chagrin, Volney—who had only just escaped the guillotine—was himself believed to be "engaged in a conspiracy (*me*, a single solitary Frenchman) to throw Louisiana into the hands of the directory." Joel Barlow, "A Poem, Spoken at the Public Commencement at Yale College, in New Haven, September 1, 1781," in William K. Bottorff and Arthur L. Ford, eds., *The Works of Joel Barlow*, 2 vols. (Gainesville, Fla.: Scholar's Facsimiles & Reprints, 1970), 2:33; Frederick Jackson Turner, ed., "Documents on the Relations of France to Louisiana, 1792–1795," *American Historical Review* 3, no. 3 (1897): 490–517, 495. See also James Woodress, *A Yankee's Odyssey: The Life of Joel Barlow* (New York: Greenwood, 1958; repr. 1968).

26. For Imlay's relationship with Wollstonecraft, see Janet Todd, *Mary Wollstonecraft: A Revolutionary Life* (London: Weidenfeld and Nicolson, 2000); Imlay, *Topographical*, 39–40, 108.

27. Gilbert Imlay, *The Emigrants*, ed. W. M. Verhoeven and Amanda Gilroy (1793; New York: Penguin, 1998), 192, xxv; Ralph Leslie Rusk, "The Adventures of Gilbert Imlay," *Indiana University Studies* 10, no. 57 (1923): 20.

28. Rusk, "Adventures," 20; Jefferson to George Rogers Clark, December 4, 1783, in Frederick Jackson Turner, "The Origin of Genet's Projected Attack on Louisiana and the Floridas," *American Historical Review* 3, no. 4 (1898): 673.

29. See John Carl Parish, "The Intrigues of Doctor James O'Fallon," *Mississippi Valley Historical Review* 17, no. 2. (September 1930): 230–63.

30. Louise Phelps Kellogg, "Letter of Thomas Paine, 1793," *American Historical Review* 29, no. 3 (1924): 501–5.

31. Harry Ammon, *The Genet Mission* (New York: Norton, 1973), 26; Turner, "Origin," 665.

32. From the documents pertaining to the Genet conspiracy in the "Report of Historical Manuscripts Commission," *Annual Report of the American Historical Association*, 2 vols. (Washington: Government Printing Office, 1896), 1:985; Turner, "Origin," 669.

33. Allen, *Lewis*, 66; Savage and Savage, *Michaux*, 138.

34. Ammon, *Genet*, 86.

35. William H. Masterson, *William Blount* (Baton Rouge: Louisiana State University Press, 1945), 307; Melton, *Burr*, 20.

36. Arthur Preston Whitaker, *The Mississippi Question, 1795–1803: A Study in Trade, Politics and Diplomacy* (New York, Appleton-Century, 1934), 117; Lycan, *Hamilton*, 374; Melton, *Burr*, 40; Lycan, *Hamilton*, 388.

37. Whitaker, *Mississippi*, v; Thomas Jefferson to Robert Livingston, Washington, April 18, 1802, in Washington, *Writings*, 4:434; James Madison to Charles Pinckney, November 27, 1802, in Melton, *Burr*, 41; Poplicola [Charles Brockden Brown], *Monroe's Embassy, or, the Conduct of the Government, in Relation to our Claims of Navigation of the Mississippi* (Philadelphia: John Conrad, 1803), 4–7. See also [Charles Brockden Brown], *An Address to the Government of the United States, on the Cession of Louisiana to the French* (Philadelphia: John Conrad, 1803).

38. Whitaker, *Mississippi*, 176; Lawrence S. Kaplan, *Thomas Jefferson: Westward the Course of Empire* (Wilmington: S. R. Books, 1999), 138–39; Jack Fruchtman Jr., *Thomas Paine: Apostle of Freedom* (New York: Four Walls Eight Windows, 1994), 399–400.

39. Pichon to Talleyrand, January 24, 1803, in Adams, *History*, 295.

40. George Dangerfield, *Chancellor Robert R. Livingston of New York, 1746–1813* (New York: Harcourt, Brace, 1960), 336; Robert Livingston to James Madison, August 10, 1802. In *State Papers and Correspondence Bearing upon the Purchase of the Territory of Louisiana*, House of Representatives, House Documents, 57th Cong., 2nd sess., vol. 92, doc. no. 431 (Washington: Government Printing Office, 1903), 36–44.

41. *State Papers and Correspondence Bearing upon the Purchase of the Territory of Louisiana*, House of Representatives, House Documents, 57th Cong., 2nd sess., vol. 92, doc. no. 431 (Washington: Government Printing Office, 1903), 36–44.

42. Dangerfield, *Livingston*, 371; E. Wilson Lyon, *The Man Who Sold Louisiana: The Career of François Barbé-Marbois* (Norman: University of Oklahoma Press, 1942; repr. 1974), 120–21; François Barbé-Marbois, *The History of Louisiana* (Philadelphia: Carey and Lea, 1830), 263, 274.

43. Stephen E. Ambrose and Douglas G. Brinkley, *The Mississippi and the Making of a Nation: From the Louisiana Purchase to Today* (Washington: National Geographic, 2002), 14; Wilkinson, *Memoirs*, 1: vii; Lycan, *Hamilton*, 416; Eric Homberger, *Historical Atlas of North America* (London: Penguin, 1995), 53.

44. Whitaker, *Mississippi*, 131; Thomas Buchanan, *Black Life on the Mississippi* (Chapel Hill: University of North Carolina Press, 2004), 6; Davis, *Alamo*, 52; Buchanan, *Black Life*, 10; Turner, *Frontier*, 198.

45. Thomas Boyd, *Poor John Fitch* (New York: Putnam's, 1935), 144; Seelye, *Machine*, 80; Louis Hunter, *Steamboats on the Western Rivers: An Economic and Technological History* (1949; New York: Dover, 1993), 6; Imlay, *Topographical*, 99–100.

46. Charles Mead, *Mississippian Scenery; A Poem, Descriptive of the Interior of North America* (Philadelphia: S. Potter, 1819), frontispiece, 13–18. For more on the machine in the Jeffersonian garden, see Leo Marx, *The Machine in the Garden: Technology and the Pastoral Ideal in America* (New York: Oxford University Press, 1964).

47. Boyd, *Fitch*, 127.

48. Ibid., 137; Seelye, *Machine*, 239; John Fitch, *The Autobiography of John Fitch*, ed. Frank D. Prager (Philadelphia: American Philosophical Society, 1976), 176.

49. Kirkpatrick Sale, *The Fire of His Genius: Robert Fulton and the American Dream* (New York: Free Press, 2001), 79–82.

50. Livingston to Thomas T. Tillotson, November 12, 1802, in Dangerfield, *Livingston*, 404; Sale, *Fulton*, 90–93.

51. Sale, *Fulton*, 92, 119–20; Padover, *Jefferson*, 425.

52. Severin, *Explorers*, 227–28; Edgar Allan Poe, *Works of Edgar Allan Poe*, ed. Edmund Clarence Stedman and George Edward Woodberry, 10 vols. (London: Lawrence and Bullen, 1895), 5:257–59.

53. Henry Nash Smith, *Virgin Land: The American West as Symbol and Myth* (1950; New York: Vintage, 1970), 11. Quotation from the Loyal Land Company charter in Allen, *Lewis*, 60; Stephen Ambrose, *Undaunted Courage: Meriwether Lewis, Thomas Jefferson and the Opening of the American West* (New York: Touchstone, 1997), 68.

54. Severin, *Explorers*, 208–9; Allen, *Lewis*, 26; Carver's original Mississippi notebooks are in the British Library, having come to light at the beginning of the twentieth century. See the Manuscripts collection, catalogue numbers 8949 and 8950.

55. Allen, *Lewis*, xix; Ambrose, *Courage*, 119, 131; "Lewis and Clarke's *American Travels*," *Quarterly Review* 12 (1815): 317–68, 319; Allen, *Lewis*, 183.

56. Milton Lomask, *Aaron Burr: The Conspiracy and Years of Exile* (New York: Farrar, Straus, Giroux, 1982), 85; Adams, *History*, 771; Melton, *Burr*, 122.

57. Melton, *Burr*, 120; Roger G. Kennedy, *Burr, Hamilton, and Jefferson* (New York: Oxford University Press, 2000), 297; Lomask, *Burr*, 120, 165; Kennedy, *Burr*, 302, 281; Lomask, *Burr*, 112.

58. Henry Whiting, "Life of Z. M. Pike," in Jared Sparks, ed., *The Library of American Biography* (Boston: Charles C. Little and James Brown, 1844), second series, 5:225; W. Eugene Hollon, *The Lost Pathfinder: Zebulon Montgomery Pike* (Norman: University of Oklahoma Press, 1949), 88; Seelye, *Machine*, 218; Whiting, "Pike," 225; Thomas Jefferson to William Dunbar, Washington, March 13, 1804, in Washington, *Writings*, 4:537–39.

59. James Wilkinson to Zebulon Montgomery Pike, St. Louis, July 30, 1805, in Elliott Coues, ed., *The Expeditions of Zebulon Montgomery Pike*, 3 vols. (New York: Francis P. Harper, 1895), 2:842–43.

60. From Pike's journal, in Coues, *Pike*, 1:152–54; Constantin François de Volney, *Travels through Egypt and Syria*, 2 vols. (New York: Evert Duyckinck and Co., 1798), 1:17–18.

61. Coues, *Pike*, 1:254–56; Thomas Jefferson to William Henry Harrison, Washington, February 27, 1803, in Washington, *Letters*, 4:473.

62. Hollon, *Pike*, 88; Padover, *Jefferson*, 424; Hollon, *Pike*, 58; Joel Barlow, *The Columbiad* (Philadelphia: Fry and Kammerer, 1807), 363.

2. FRONTIER: JACKSON AND THE "HALF-HORSE, HALF-ALLIGATORS"

Epigraph 1. Thomas Clark, *The Rampaging Frontier* (New York: Bobbs-Merrill, 1939), 79.

Epigraph 2. James Kirke Paulding, *The Lion of the West (The Kentuckian, or, A Trip to New York)*, ed. James N. Tidwell (Stanford: Stanford University Press, 1954), 21.

1. B. M. Dusenberry ed., *Monument to the Memory of General Andrew Jackson* (Philadelphia: Walker and Gillis, 1846), iii; Washington McCartney, "Eulogy for Andrew Jackson," delivered in Pennsylvania in June 1845, in Dusenberry, *Monument*, 281; Dr. Samuel A. Cartwright, "Eulogy for Andrew Jackson," delivered in Natchez in July 1845, in Dusenberry, *Monument*, 292.

2. Carroll Smith-Rosenberg, *Disorderly Conduct: Visions of Gender in Victorian America* (New York: Oxford University Press, 1986), 92–93.

3. John Buchanan, *Jackson's Way: Andrew Jackson and the People of the Western Waters* (Hoboken, N.J.: Wiley, 2001), 50; Robert V. Remini, *Andrew Jackson and the Course of American Empire, 1767–1821* (New York: Harper and Row, 1977), 43.

4. Buchanan, *Jackson,* 119; Cartwright, "Eulogy," in Dusenberry, *Monument,* 305; Buchanan, *Jackson,* 167. The ramifications of the Jacksons' unorthodox courtship and marriage were long-lasting, compounded when it emerged that Robards did not actually file for divorce until 1793.

5. Remini, *Empire,* 55; Burke Davis, *Old Hickory: A Life of Andrew Jackson* (New York: Dial, 1977), 19; Remini, *Empire,* 49.

6. Remini, *Empire,* 54, 106; Buchanan, *Jackson,* 172; Remini, *Empire,* 132.

7. David S. Heidler and Jeanne T. Heidler, *Old Hickory's War: Andrew Jackson and the Quest for Empire* (Mechanicsburg, Pa.: Stackpole, 1996), 2; Buckner F. Melton, *Aaron Burr: Conspiracy to Treason* (New York: Wiley, 2002), 117.

8. Heidler and Heidler, *Hickory,* 4; Frederic Austin Ogg, *The Reign of Andrew Jackson: A Chronicle of the Frontier in Politics* (New Haven: Yale University Press, 1920), 24.

9. Washington Irving, *Astoria; or, Enterprise beyond the Rocky Mountains,* 3 vols. (London: Richard Bentley, 1836), 1:220–22; Michael Allen, *Western Rivermen, 1763–1861* (Baton Rouge: Louisiana State University Press, 1990), 94. Allen defines the presteamboat period as 1763 to 1823. His start date is the beginning of Spanish occupation. This date certainly marked a change in life on the Western Waters and a development in the life of the boatman. Men were, of course, plying the rivers before 1763. Allen admits that his end date has "an arbitrary element" (4). Its value is symbolic, since it was the year of Mike Fink's death. More accurately, the dominance of the steamboat slowly developed throughout the decade 1820 to 1830. The 1830s were the beginning of steam's golden age, even if flatboats persisted. Using Louis Hunter's figures, it can be seen that the number of western steamboats jumped from 17 in 1817 to 69 in 1820. In 1823 and 1825, they remained stable at 75 and 73 respectively. By 1830, they had increased to 187. The appearance of the first elegiac Mike Fink story in 1828 also suggests that change. Louis Hunter, *Steamboats on the Western Rivers: An Economic and Technological History* (1949: New York: Dover, 1993), 33.

10. Allen, *Rivermen,* 94, 238.

11. Richard E. Oglesby, "The Western Boatman: Half Horse, Half Myth," in John Francis McDermott, ed., *Travelers on the Western Frontier* (Urbana: University of Illinois Press, 1970), 254; Allen, *Rivermen,* 238; Timothy Flint, *Recollections of the Last Ten Years in the Valley of the Mississippi* (1826; Carbondale: Southern Illinois University Press, 1968), 68.

12. T. B. Thorpe, "Remembrances of the Mississippi," *Harper's New Monthly Magazine* 12, no. 67 (December 1855): 25–41, 29.

13. Richard M. Dorson, *America in Legend: Folklore from the Colonial Period to the Present* (New York: Pantheon, 1973), 57, 81; Thorpe, "Remembrances," 29; Henry Adams, *History of the United States of America during the Administrations of Thomas Jefferson* (New York: Library of America, 1889–91; repr. 1986), 40; Constance Rourke, *American Humor: A Study of the National Character* (New York: Harcourt, Brace, 1931; repr. 1953), 44; Allen, *Rivermen,* 2.

14. Stephen Ambrose, *Undaunted Courage: Meriwether Lewis, Thomas Jefferson and the Opening of the American West* (New York: Touchstone, 1997), 122.

15. Christian Schultz, *Travels on an Inland Voyage*, 2 vols. (New York: Isaac Riley, 1810), 2:99, 114, 133–36, 145.

16. Arthur Palmer Hudson, ed., *Humor of the Old Deep South* (New York: Macmillan, 1936), 58–60; Allen, *Rivermen*, 51; Hudson, *Humor*, 296.

17. Thomas Buchanan, *Black Life on the Mississippi* (Chapel Hill: University of North Carolina Press, 2004), 36; J.H.B. Latrobe, *The First Steamboat Voyage on the Western Waters* (Baltimore: Maryland Historical Society, 1871), 24. Latrobe was not a member of the party but wrote of the events—"The stories I listened to in my childhood"—years later (3–4).

18. John Francis McDermott, ed., *Before Mark Twain: A Sampler of Old, Old Times on the Mississippi* (1968; Carbondale: Southern Illinois University Press, 1998), 150; Hunter, *Steamboats*, 16; Mary Helen Dohan, *Mr. Roosevelt's Steamboat* (New York: Dodd, Mead, 1981), 61.

19. David S. Heidler and Jeanne T. Heidler, *The War of 1812* (Westport, Ct.: Greenwood, 2002), xiii.

20. S. G. Heiskell, *Andrew Jackson and Early Tennessee History*, 3 vols. (Nashville: Ambrose, 1920), 1:460; Remini, *Empire*, 173; Buchanan, *Jackson*, 200.

21. Remini, *Empire*, 175.

22. Ibid., 191; David Crockett, *Narrative of the Life of David Crockett* (Philadelphia: E. L. Carey and A. Hart, 1834), 88; Buchanan, *Jackson*, 300.

23. Buchanan, *Jackson*, 305; Robert V. Remini, *The Battle of New Orleans* (London: Pimlico, 2001), 42; Jane Lucas de Grummond, *The Baratarians and the Battle of New Orleans* (Baton Rouge: Louisiana State University Press, 1961), 56.

24. Jefferson to the Marquis de Lafayette, Monticello, February 14, 1815, in H. A. Washington, ed., *The Writings of Thomas Jefferson*, 9 vols. (New York: Taylor and Maury, 1853), 6:425–27; John William Ward, *Andrew Jackson: Symbol for an Age* (New York: Oxford University Press, 1955), 7; *Washington National Intelligencer*, Saturday, February 25, 1815, vol. 16, no. 2251.

25. Buchanan, *Jackson*, 351–52; Ward, *Jackson*, 26. Ward also cites the friendly shooting competition held between the frontiersman and the local Creoles in the days after the battle: the Creoles were victorious.

26. Leland Baldwin, *The Keelboat Age on Western Waters* (Pittsburgh: University of Pittsburgh Press, 1941; repr. 1980), 105, 217; William Petersen, *Steamboating on the Upper Mississippi* (1937; New York: Dover, 1995), 70; Hunter, *Steamboats*, 552.

27. Richard C. Wade, *The Urban Frontier: Pioneer Life in Early Pittsburgh, Cincinnati, Lexington, Louisville, and St. Louis* (Chicago: University of Chicago Press, 1964), 40; Walter Blair and Franklin J. Meine, eds., *Half-Horse, Half-Alligator: The Growth of the Mike Fink Legend* (1956; Lincoln: University of Nebraska Press, 1981), 20. Recorded in James Keyes's *Pioneers of Scioto County* (1880).

28. Allen, *Rivermen*, 115; Major Jack Downing [Seba Smith], *Life of Andrew Jackson* (Philadelphia: T. K. Greenbank, 1834), 92.

29. Woodward was also known as Woodworth. Ward, *Jackson*, 15, 218; Noah Ludlow, *Dramatic Life As I Found It* (St. Louis: G. I. Jones and Co., 1880), 237–38, 250.

30. The first two figures are from Timothy Flint's *History and Geography of the Mississippi Valley*, 2 vols. (Cincinnati: E. H. Flint and L. R. Lincoln, 1832), 1:135. The last, from James Hall's

The West: Its Commerce and Navigation (Cincinnati: H. W. Derby and Co., 1848), 28; Hunter, *Steamboats,* 27.

31. Wade, *Frontier,* 140; Zadok Cramer, *The Navigator* (Pittsburgh: Cramer, Spear, and Eichbaum, 1814; repr. 1966), iii; Charles W. Dahlinger, *Pittsburgh: A Sketch of Its Early Social Life* (New York: Putnam's, 1916), 175; Flint, *Recollections,* 17. Flint also relied on Cramer's *Navigator* when writing up his *Recollections.*

32. Cramer, *Navigator,* 34, 176, 225, 202; Flint, *Recollections,* 17.

33. Cramer, *Navigator,* iv, 178; Dohan, *Steamboat,* 57.

34. Cramer, *Navigator,* 33.

35. See, for example, Samuel Cumings, *The Western Pilot* (Cincinnati: N. & G. Guildford, 1832); David Rachels and Edward Watts. eds., *The First West: Writing from the American Frontier, 1776–1860* (New York: Oxford University Press, 2002), 340–41.

36. Flint, *Recollections,* 64–67, 32, 207.

37. Ibid., 273; James K. Folsom, *Timothy Flint* (New York: Twayne, 1965), 54; Timothy Flint, *A Condensed Geography and History of the Western States, or the Mississippi Valley* (Cincinnati: E. H. Flint, 1828), 131; Timothy Flint, *George Mason, The Young Backwoodsman; or "Don't Give Up the Ship!" A Story of the Mississippi* (Boston: Hillard, Gray, Little, and Wilkins, 1829), 16, 124. For an example of just one writer's indebtedness to Flint, see Arlin Turner, "James K. Paulding and Timothy Flint," *Mississippi Valley Historical Review* 34, no. 1 (June 1947): 105–11.

38. From an autobiographical manuscript, in Randolph C. Randall, *James Hall, Spokesman of the New West* (Columbus: Ohio State University Press, 1964), 232. Some of Hall's first publications appeared in Flint's *Western Monthly Review;* the two men fell out over a scathingly bad review that Hall gave to Flint's *Lectures upon Natural History* (1833).

39. Folsom, *Flint,* 57; Hall, *Commerce,* 10–12; James Hall, *Letters from the West* (London: Henry Colburn, 1828), 165, 47, 91, 94, 182.

40. Rachels and Watts attribute this story to Hall in their collection, *The First West.* The story is signed "Bluffdale." An internal joke—regarding the posterity of *The Western Souvenir*—specifically addresses Hall in the third person, and Randall does not include it in his bibliography of Hall's works. He does, however, note that Hall was "personally responsible for three-fifths of the first volume" of his *Illinois Monthly Magazine,* and "half of the second." (Randall, *Hall,* 175). "Three Hundred Years Hence" was published in the *Illinois Monthly Magazine* in its first months of publication (November 1830). It is therefore possible that Hall could have adopted a different pen name for the sake of variety. Either way, he thought enough of the story to publish it. Rachels and Watts, *First West,* 497–501; Henry David Thoreau, "Walking," in *Civil Disobedience and Other Essays* (1862; New York: Dover, 1993), 60.

41. Fink quotation from the *Crockett Almanac for 1851:* Walter Blair and Hamlin Hill, *America's Humor: From Poor Richard to Doonesbury* (New York: Oxford University Press, 1978), 113; Richard Dorson, *American Folklore* (Chicago: University of Chicago Press, 1959), 39; Allen, *Rivermen,* 8.

42. Blair and Hill, *Humor,* 44–45, 115; Dorson, *American Folklore,* 48; Blair and Meine, *Fink,* 14.

43. William T. Coggeshall, *The Poets and Poetry of the West* (Columbus: Follett, Foster and Co., 1860), 172–73; Baldwin, *Keelboat,* 94; *Western Review* 4, no. 6 (July, 1821): 372–74.

44. Leland Baldwin, *Pittsburgh: The Story of a City* (Pittsburgh: University of Pittsburgh Press, 1938), 181; Blair and Meine, *Fink,* 46; Randall, *Hall,* 147.

45. All quotations from Morgan Neville's "The Last of the Boatmen" are taken from Blair and Meine, *Fink,* 45–55, 260.

46. Timothy Flint, "Mike Fink: The Last of the Boatmen," in his *Western Monthly Review* 3, no 1 (July 1829): 15–19, 16; Charles Cist, "The Last of the Girtys" (1845), in Blair and Meine, *Fink,* 269. Beginning life in a ladies' book, Neville's story was respectively reprinted in three editions of Cumings's *The Western Pilot* (1829, 1832, 1834); an English collection of American sketches, Mary Russell Mitford's *Lights and Shadows of American Life* (1832); a London journal, the *Athenaeum* (1832); an American journal, the *Cincinnati Miscellany* (1845); the pamphlet that accompanied John Banvard's moving panorama of the Mississippi (1847); and an American travel narrative, A. De Puy Van Buren's, *Jottings of a Year's Sojourn in the South* (1859).

47. Hunter, *Steamboats,* 53–55; Clark, *Frontier,* 92.

48. Rourke, *Humor,* 52; Clive Barnett, *The Egyptian Gods and Goddesses* (London, 1992), 122; Barbara Watterson, *Gods of Ancient Egypt* (Stroud, Gloucestershire: Sutton, 2003), 113; Franklin J. Meine, ed., *The Crockett Almanacks: Nashville Series, 1835–1838* (Chicago: Caxton Club, 1955), 150. Between 1828 and 1840, ten known Fink stories were originally published, reprinted, or rewritten; between 1840 and 1850, twenty-four; between 1850 and 1860, twenty-three. For the remaining forty years of the century, only eighteen stories appeared, only one of those between 1860 and 1870. See Blair and Meine, *Fink,* 19.

49. Michael A. Lofaro, ed., *The Tall Tales of Davy Crockett: The Second Nashville Series of Crockett Almanacs, 1839–1841* (facsimile reprints, Knoxville: University of Tennessee Press, 1987), *Almanac for 1839,* 23.

50. Crockett, *Life,* 195–200.

51. William C. Davis, *Three Roads to the Alamo* (New York: Harper Perennial, 1999), 122, 175.

52. Heiskell, *Jackson,* 2:131; George Wilson Pierson, *Tocqueville in America* (1938; Baltimore: Johns Hopkins University Press, 1996), 608–11.

53. Davis, *Alamo,* 171; Meine, *Crockett,* xi–xii; Paulding, *Lion,* 21.

54. Meine, *Crockett,* xi–xii .

55. Ibid., 46, 95–96.

56. Lofaro, *Crockett Almanac for 1839,* 22; Dorson, *American Folklore,* 208; Lofaro, *Crockett Almanac for 1840,* 28.

57. Flint, *Mason,* 133; George P. Burnham, "The Steamboat Captain Who Was Averse to Racing," first printed in the *Spirit of the Times* in March 1846, reprinted in a collection of *Spirit* sketches. William T. Porter, ed., *A Quarter Race in Kentucky* (Philadelphia: Carey and Hart, 1846), 125–30.

58. John Hay, *Pike County Ballads* (Boston: James R. Osgood, 1871), 17–20.

59. J. M. Peck, *A New Guide for Emigrants to the West* (Boston: Gould, Kendall, and Lincoln, 1837), ix; John Regan, *Emigrant's Guide to the Western States of America* (Edinburgh: Oliver and Boyd, n.d.), 30, 25.

60. *View of the Valley of the Mississippi: or the Emigrant's and Traveller's Guide to the West* (Philadelphia: H. S. Tanner, 1832), 323.

61. Lee Benson, *The Concept of Jacksonian Democracy: New York as a Test Case* (Princeton: Princeton University Press, 1961), 330; Edward Pessen, *Jacksonian America: Society, Personality, and Politics* (Homewood, Ill.: Dorsey, 1969), 47, 57; Petersen, *Steamboating,* 353; Hunter, *Steamboats,* 428—from Samuel Ludvigh's *Licht und Schattenbilder republikanischer Zustande.*

62. Rev. Thompson's experiences appear in Daniel Curtiss's *Western Portraiture and Emigrant's Guide* (New York: J. H. Colton, 1852), 336; Mrs. Houstoun, *Hesperos, or Travels in the West,* 2 vols. (London: J. W. Parker, 1850), 2:44.

63. Timothy Flint, writing in his *Western Monthly Review* 1, no. 1 (May 1827): 25–26; Thorpe, "Remembrances," 34; [George Lewis Prentiss], *A Memoir of S. S. Prentiss, Edited by His Brother* (New York: Charles Scribner's Sons, 1879), 176–77.

64. Walter Blair, *Native American Humor: 1800–1900* (New York: American Book Company, 1937), 70. See also Norris W. Yates, *William T. Porter and "The Spirit of the Times": A Study of the Big Bear School of Humor* (Baton Rouge: Louisiana State University Press, 1957); Blair, *Native,* 84–85.

65. Blair and Hill, *Humor,* 201. See also Milton Rickels, *Thomas Bangs Thorpe: Humorist of the Old Southwest* (Baton Rouge: Louisiana State University Press, 1962).

66. All quotations taken from the text of "The Big Bear of Arkansas," as reprinted in McDermott, *Mississippi,* 222–35. McDermott follows the text of its first publication in the *Spirit,* March 27, 1841. When Porter included it in the *Big Bear* anthology, he "revised the text of Thorpe's story, evidently with an eye to making it less colloquial—and thus, perhaps, supposedly more suitable for a general audience." In Thorpe's own collection, *The Hive of the Bee Hunter,* the text of "The Big Bear" followed Porter's amendments and was further revised. See J. A. Leo Lemay's "The Text, Tradition, and Themes of 'The Big Bear of Arkansas,'" in *American Literature* 47, no. 3 (1975): 321–42.

67. Rourke, *Humor,* 59; Randall, *Hall,* 162.

68. Robert V. Remini, *Andrew Jackson and the Course of American Freedom: 1822–1832* (New York: Harper and Row, 1981), 228; Robert V. Remini, *Revolutionary Age of Andrew Jackson* (New York: Harper and Row), 110.

69. Perry A. Armstrong, *The Sauks and the Black Hawk War* (Springfield, Ill.: H. W. Rokker, 1887; facsimile repr. 1979), 277, 467–68. See also Major John A. Wakefield, *Wakefield's History of the Black Hawk War* (Chicago: Caxton Club, 1908). Originally published just after the conflict in 1834.

70. Remini, *The Revolutionary Age,* 118–19; Anthony C. F. Wallace, *The Long, Bitter Trail: Andrew Jackson and the Indians* (New York: Hill and Wang, 1993), 88; Pierson, *Tocqueville,* 597–98.

71. Jean-Marc Serme, "Stormy Weather at Andrew Jackson's Halcyon Plantation, in Coahoma County, Mississippi, 1838–1845," in *Revue française d'études américaines,* no. 98 (December 2003): 32–48, 34.

72. Robert V. Remini, *Andrew Jackson and the Course of American Democracy, 1835–1845* (New York: Harper and Row, 1984), 456, 492.

73. Serme, "Halcyon," 41.

74. Remini, *Democracy,* 461, 522.

3. TRAVEL AND TOURISM: EUROPEANS ON "THIS FOUL STREAM"

Epigraph 1. Ralph L. Rusk, ed., *Letters of Ralph Waldo Emerson,* 6 vols. (New York: Columbia University Press, 1939), 2:394–95.

Epigraph 2. Charles Dickens, *American Notes for General Circulation*, 2 vols. (London: Chapman and Hall, 1842), 2:148.

1. Giacomo Beltrami, *A Pilgrimage in Europe and America*, 2 vols. (London: Hunt and Clarke, 1828) 2:33; George Catlin, *Letters and Notes on the Manners, Customs and Condition of the North American Indians*, 2 vols. (London: self-published, 1841), 2:130.

2. Dickens, *Notes*, 2:111.

3. Herman Melville, *The Confidence-Man: His Masquerade* (London: Longman, Brown, Green, Longman & Roberts, 1857), 6.

4. Lynne Withey, *Grand Tours and Cook's Tours: A History of Leisure Travel, 1750 to 1915* (New York: Morrow, 1997), 117; Brian Dolan, *Ladies of the Grand Tour* (London: Flamingo, 2002), 187; Cesare de Seta, "Grand Tour: The Lure of Italy in the Eighteenth Century," in Andrew Wilton and Ilaria Bignamini, eds., *Grand Tour: The Lure of Italy in the Eighteenth Century* (London: Tate Gallery, 1996), 17; Malcolm Andrews, *The Search for the Picturesque* (Aldershot: Scolar, 1989), 67.

5. Carl Paul Barbier, *William Gilpin: His Drawings, Teaching, and Theory of the Picturesque* (Oxford: Oxford University Press, 1963), 99; T. D. Fosbroke, ed., *The Tourist's Grammar* (London: John Nichols, 1826), 53–57; Archibald Alison, *Essays on the Nature and Principles of Taste* (Edinburgh: Bell and Bradfute, 1790), 15.

6. John Sears, *Sacred Places: American Tourist Attractions in the Nineteenth Century* (Amherst: University of Massachusetts Press, 1998), 14; Dickens, *Notes*, 2:167; Edmund Burke, *A Philosophical Enquiry into the Origin of the Sublime and the Beautiful* (London: R. and J. Dodsley, 1757), 50.

7. Ida Pfeiffer, *A Lady's Second Journey Round the World*, 2 vols. (London: Longman, Brown, Green, and Longman, 1855), 2:301; *Captain Hall in America, by an American* (Philadephia: Carey and Lea, 1830), 58; Wylie Sypher, *Rococo to Cubism in Art and Literature* (New York: Random House, 1960), 110; Frances Trollope, *Domestic Manners of the Americans*, 2 vols. (London: Richard Bentley, 1832), 2:291; Ralph Waldo Emerson, *Selected Essays*, ed. Larzer Ziff (New York: Penguin, 1982), 39. *Nature* originally published in 1836.

8. Margaret Fuller Ossoli, *Life Without and Within; or, Reviews, Narratives, Essays, and Poems*, ed. Arthur B. Fuller (New York: Tribune Association, 1869), 109.

9. Caroline Hale to her sisters, March 14, 1844, Tulane University, Howard-Tilton Memorial Library, Jones Hall, Manuscript Collection, M1055; J. Burt Jr. to his wife, December 31, 1862, Tulane University, Howard-Tilton Memorial Library, Jones Hall, Manuscript Collection, M227.

10. Richard Griffin, ed., *The Domestic Manners of the Americans; or, Characteristic Sketches of the People of the United States* (Glasgow: Richard Griffin and Co., 1836), 1.

11. Trollope, *Manners*, 1: v; 2:216; James Kirke Paulding, "The Mississippi" (ca. 1842), Tulane University, Howard-Tilton Memorial Library, Jones Hall, Manuscript Collection, M227; Mrs. Eliza Steele's *A Summer Journey in the West* (New York: J. S. Taylor, 1841), reprinted in John Francis McDermott, ed., *Before Mark Twain: A Sampler of Old, Old Times on the Mississippi* (Carbondale: Southern Illinois University Press, 1998), 70–83, 81.

12. Griffin, *Domestic*, 45; Frances Kemble, *Journal of a Residence in America* (Paris: A. and W. Galignani, 1835), 211.

13. Trollope, *Manners*, 1:19.

14. Ibid., 2:217; Harriet Martineau, *Autobiography*, 2 vols. (London: Smith, Elder, and Co., 1877), 2:94; Kemble, *Residence*, 86; Godfrey T. Vigne, *Six Months in America*. 2 vols. (London: Whittaker, Treacher, and Co., 1832), 1:59; Frances Anne Kemble, *Records of Later Life*, 3 vols. (London: R. Bentley, 1882), 1:85, 264, 287; 2:267–68.

15. Anthony Trollope, *North America*, 2 vols. (London: Chapman and Hall, 1862; repr. 1987), 1:2; Henry Tuckerman, *America and Her Commentators* (New York: Charles Scribner, 1864), 298; Ida Pfeiffer, *A Lady's Voyage Round the World*, trans. William Hazlitt (London: Routledge and Co., 1852), iii.

16. Dolan, *Ladies*, 5.

17. Priscilla Wakefield, *Excursions in North America, Described in Letters from a Gentleman and His Young Companion to Their Friends in England* (London: Darton and Harvey, 1806), 1–2.

18. Tuckerman, *America*, 215; Wakefield, *Excursions*, iii, 125.

19. Margaret Hall, *The Aristocratic Journey: Being the Outspoken Letters of Mrs. Basil Hall Written during a Fourteen Months' Sojourn in America 1827–8*, ed. Una Pope-Hennessey (New York: Putnam's, 1931), 4, 33, 26, 262.

20. Hall, *Aristocratic*, 252–65.

21. *Lie-ary on America! With Yarns on Its Institutions, By Captain Marry-it, C.B (Common Bloat)* (Baltimore: Turners, 1840), 6, 33; Andrew Dix, "Leaving *Huckleberry Finn* Behind: Belatedness and Authority in Jonathan Raban's *Old Glory*," *Studies in Travel Writing* 5 (2001): 63–83, 79.

22. Kemble, *Journal*, v–vi.

23. Quoted in Pamela Neville-Singleton's introduction to her edition of Frances Trollope's *Domestic Manners of the Americans* (London: Penguin, 1997), xiii; Trollope, *Manners*, 1:10; Stephen Fender, *Sea Changes: British Emigration and American Literature* (Cambridge: Cambridge University Press, 1992), 237; Trollope, *Manners*, 1:1–2.

24. Trollope, *Manners*, 1:3–5, 19.

25. Ibid., 1:10, 24–29.

26. Harriet Martineau, *Retrospect of Western Travel*, 3 vols. (London: Saunders and Otley, 1838), 1:42; Barbara Todd, *Harriet Martineau at Ambleside* (Carlisle: Bookcase, 2002), 19; Kemble, *Records*, 1:17; Barbara Leigh Smith Bodichon, *An American Diary 1857–8*, ed. Joseph W. Reed (London: Routledge, 1972), 27; Kemble, *Records*, 1:27.

27. "Lewis and Clarke's *American Travels*," *Quarterly Review* 12 (1815): 317–68, 319; Martineau, *Retrospect*, 2:161; Joseph Warton, ed., *The Works of Virgil In Latin and English* (London: J. Dodsley, 1778), 171–72; Harriet Martineau, *Society in America*. 3 vols. (London: Saunders and Otley, 1837), 1: viii; Martineau, *Retrospect*, 1: v.

28. Martineau, *Society*, 1:208–12.

29. Martineau, *Retrospect*, 2:194, 178, 172, 187.

30. Martineau, *Society*, 2:101; Martineau, *Retrospect*, 2:193.

31. The *New York Home Journal* of April 1851, as quoted in W. Porter Ware and Thadeus C. Lockard Jr., *P. T. Barnum Presents Jenny Lind: The American Tour of the Swedish Nightingale* (Baton Rouge: Louisiana State University Press, 1980), 73; Frederika Bremer, *The Homes of the New World; Impressions of America*, trans. Mary Howitt, 3 vols. (London: A. Hall, Virtue, 1853), 2:324, 273.

32. Bremer, *Homes,* 2:273, 369, 314.

33. Ibid., 454; Bodichon, *Diary,* 58–65; Pfeiffer, *Second,* 2:241.

34. Pfeiffer, *Second,* 2:241; Victoria Stuart Wortley, *A Young Traveller's Journal of a Tour in North and South America during the Year 1850* (London: T. Bosworth, 1852), 112; Lady Emmeline Stuart Wortley, *Travels in the United States, etc. during 1849 and 1850,* 3 vols. (London: Richard Bentley, 1851), 1:209–10; Amelia M. Murray, *Letters from the United States, Cuba and Canada,* 2 vols. (London: J. W. Parker, 1856), 2:114. The Stuart-Wortleys brought Byron to the river: Emmeline always carried a lock of his hair, a gift from Augusta Leigh.

35. Isabella Lucy Bird, *The Aspects of Religion in the United States of America* (London: Sampson Low, 1859), 129–30; Isabella Trotter, *First Impressions of the New World on Two Travellers from the Old* (London: Longman,1859), 221, 228; Emilie Marguerite Cowell, *The Cowells in America, Being the Diary of Mrs. Sam Cowell during her Husband's Concert Tour in the Years 1860–1861,* ed. M. Willson Disher (London: Oxford University Press, 1934), 78.

36. Thomas Ashe, *Travels in America, Performed in 1806,* 3 vols. (London: Richard Philips, 1808), 1:15–21, 146, 171–83, 289; 3:126.

37. Otto A. Rothert, *The Outlaws of Cave-in-Rock* (Carbondale: Southern Illinois University Press, 1996), 37; Ashe, *Travels,* 3:13–15; Rothert, *Outlaws,* 19–20.

38. Christian Schultz, *Travels on an Inland Voyage,* 2 vols. (New York: Isaac Riley, 1810), 1: iv–v; Rothert, *Outlaws,* 325

39. "Dickens's *American Notes,*" *Edinburgh Review* 76 (1843): 497–522, 499; *Marry-it,* 5–6; Bodichon, *Diary,* 114; "Dickens's *American Notes,*" 502.

40. Basil Hall, *Voyages and Travels of Captain Basil Hall, R.N.* (London: T. Nelson, 1895), 5; *Marry-it,* 31.

41. Hall, *America,* 3:318–19.

42. Ibid., 3:370–79; 2:383; 3:353.

43. Captain Frederick Marryat, *A Diary in America with Remarks on its Institutions,* 3 vols. (London: Longman, 1839), 2:125, 69, 142–43.

44. Marryat, *Diary,* 2:126; Dickens, *Notes,* 2:108–12.

45. Dickens, *Notes,* 2:110–12, 146–48.

46. William Makepeace Thackeray, *The Letters and Private Papers of William Makepeace Thackeray,* ed. Gordon N. Ray, 4 vols. (London: Oxford University Press, 1946), 3:559–96.

47. Richard F. Burton, *The City of the Saints, and Across the Rocky Mountains to California* (London: Longman, Green, Longman, and Roberts, 1861), 20; Alexander Mackay, *The Western World; or, Travels in the United States in 1846–47,* 3 vols. (London: R. Bentley, 1849), 3:3.

48. Maximilian, Prinz von Wied-Neuwied, *Travels in the Interior of North America,* trans. H. Evans Lloyd (London: Ackermann and Co., 1843), 96–100.

49. Sir Charles Lyell, *A Second Visit to the United States of North America,* 2 vols. (London: John Murray, 1849), 2:131, 186, 249–50.

50. Christopher Mulvey, *Anglo-American Landscapes: A Study of Nineteenth-Century Anglo-American Travel Literature* (Cambridge: Cambridge University Press, 1983), 229; Mackay, *Western,* 3:3–6.

51. Mackay, *Western,* 3:3–6.

52. *Conclin's New River Guide or Gazetteer of All the Towns on the Western Waters* (1850; Cincinnati: J.A and U. P. James, 1854), 5; Daniel S. Curtiss, *Western Portraiture and Emigrant's Guide* (New York: J. H. Colton, 1852), xiii, 207.

53. James T. Lloyd, *Lloyd's Steamboat Directory and Disasters on the Western Waters* (Cincinnati: James T. Lloyd, 1856), iii, 89–93.

54. William Petersen, *Steamboating on the Upper Mississippi* (1937; New York: Dover, 1995), 284–86. See also Curtis C. Roseman and Elizabeth M. Roseman, *Grand Excursions on the Upper Mississippi River* (Iowa City: University of Iowa Press, 2004).

55. J. Disturnell, *Tourist's Guide to the Upper Mississippi* (New York: American News Co., 1866), 25.

56. Ibid., 43–59; Henry Wadsworth Longfellow, *Evangeline, The Song of Hiawatha, The Courtship of Miles Standish* (London: George Routledge, 1886), 65–69.

57. Epigraph is from Berquin-Duvallon, *Travels in Louisiana and the Floridas,* trans. John Davis (New York: I. Riley, 1806), 61.

58. Steele in McDermott, *Mississippi,* 74.

59. Charles Dickens, *Martin Chuzzlewit* (New York: Harper and Brothers, 1844), 137.

60. Viscount François René de Chateaubriand, *Chateaubriand's Travels in America,* trans. and ed. Richard Switzer (Lexington: University of Kentucky Press, 1969), xviii; Viscount François René de Chateaubriand, *The Natchez; An Indian Tale,* 3 vols. (London: Henry Colburn, 1827), 1: iii; William Thackeray, "A Mississippi Bubble," in *The Works of William Makepeace Thackeray,* 26 vols. (London: Smith, Elder 1887), 22:145–52, 147.

61. Frances Trollope, *Jonathan Jefferson Whitlaw or Scenes on the Mississippi,* 3 vols. (London: Richard Bentley, 1836), 1:4, 36, 112–13.

62. Trollope, *Whitlaw,* 1:81–82.

63. Ibid. 3:341–42.

64. Dickens, *Chuzzlewit,* 132.

65. Ibid., 142–43; 194–97.

66. Twain's judgments were cut from the original edition of *Life on the Mississippi.* Quotation taken from Mark Twain, *Life on the Mississippi,* ed. James M. Cox (New York: Penguin, 1986), 219.

4. MOVING PANORAMAS: THE "USEFUL ILLUSION" OF THE VISUAL MISSISSIPPI

Epigraph 1. Simon Pugh, ed., *Reading Landscape: country-city-capital* (Manchester: Manchester University Press, 1990), 4.

Epigraph 2. Stephen Oettermann, *The Panorama: History of a Mass Medium* (New York: Zone, 1997), 335.

1. Gordon N. Ray, ed., *The Letters and Private Papers of William Makepeace Thackeray,* 4 vols. (London, 1946), 3:575; Charles Dickens, "American Panorama" (1848), in Michael Slater, ed., *Dickens' Journalism,* 4 vols. (London: Dent, 1997), 2:135–37, 136.

2. John W. Reps, *Cities of the Mississippi: Nineteenth-Century Images of Urban Development* (Columbia: University of Missouri Press, 1994), 28.

3. Perry T. Rathbone, ed., *Mississippi Panorama* (St. Louis: Caledonia, 1950), 33; John James Audubon, "Audubon's Story of His Youth," *Scribner's Magazine* 13, no. 3 (March, 1893): 267–89, 287.

4. Audubon, "Youth," 288; Rathbone, *Panorama,* 34; Irving T. Richards, "Audubon, Joseph R. Mason, and John Neal," *American Literature* 6, issue 2 (May 1934): 122–40, 122; John James Audubon, *Writings and Drawings,* ed. Christopher Irmscher (New York: Library of America, 1999), 21.

5. Audubon, *Writings,* 238–39.

6. Ella M. Foshay, *John James Audubon* (New York: Harry N. Abrams, 1997), 84; John James Audubon, *Delineations of American Scenery and Character,* ed. Francis Hobart Herrick. (London: Simpkin, Marshall, 1926), III, 28–31.

7. Michael Edward Shapiro, "The River Paintings," in Michael Edward Shapiro, ed., *George Caleb Bingham* (New York: Abrams, 1990), 141–75, 142; Michael Edward Shapiro, *George Caleb Bingham* (New York: Abrams, 1993), 20; Angela Miller, *Empire of the Eye: Landscape Representation and American Cultural Politics, 1825–1875* (New York: Cornell University Press, 1996), 120; Barbara Groseclose, "The 'Missouri Artist' as Historian," in Shapiro, ed., *Bingham* (1990), 53–93, 55.

8. Shapiro, *Bingham* (1993), 26; John Francis McDermott, *George Caleb Bingham: River Portraitist* (Norman: University of Oklahoma Press, 1959), 35–36; Paul C. Nagel, "The Man and His Times," in Shapiro, *Bingham* (1993), 15–53, 24.

9. Shapiro, "River," 146; Elizabeth Johns, "The 'Missouri Artist' as Artist," in Shapiro, ed., *Bingham* (1990), 93–141, 133; Shapiro, *Bingham* (1993), 55; McDermott, *Bingham,* 59.

10. Nancy Rash, *The Paintings and Politics of George Caleb Bingham* (New Haven: Yale University Press, 1991), 75, 69.

11. Johns, "Artist," 118; David Lubin, "Bingham's *Boone,*" in *Picturing a Nation: Art and Social Change in Nineteenth-Century America* (New Haven: Yale University Press, 1994), 55–107, 58–59.

12. Shapiro, *Bingham* (1993), 52.

13. Groseclose, "Historian," 62–63; Rash, *Bingham,* 69; *De Bow's Southern and Western Review* 12, no. 1 (January 1852): 1–13; Rash, *Bingham,* 87.

14. McDermott, *Bingham,* 62; Shapiro, *Bingham* (1993), 65.

15. Frances Trollope, *Domestic Manners of the Americans,* 2 vols. (London: Richard Bentley, 1832), 2:291.

16. Walter Benjamin, "Paris—The Capital of the Nineteenth Century" (1955), in *Charles Baudelaire,* trans. Harry Zohn (London: Verso, 1997), 161.

17. Richard D. Altick, *The Shows of London* (Cambridge, Mass.: Belknap, 1978), 199; Ralph Hyde, *Panoramania!* (London: Trefoil, 1988), 131.

18. See Ann Uhry Abrams, *The Valiant Hero: Benjamin West and Grand-Style History Painting* (Washington, D.C.: Smithsonian Institution Press, 1985).

19. Hon. Charles Augustus Murray, *Travels in North America during the Years 1834, 1835 & 1836,* 2 vols. (London: Richard Bentley, 1839), 1:233. Murray also met Martineau on his travels.

20. Altick, *London,* 276; Timothy Barringer, "The Course of Empires: Landscape and Identity in America and Britain, 1820–1880," in Timothy Barringer and Andrew Wilton, eds., *American Sublime: Landscape Painting in the United States, 1820–1880* (London: Tate, 2002), 38–66, 49; Altick, *London,* 278.

21. Alan Wallach, "Making a Picture of the View from Mount Holyoke," in David C. Miller,

ed., *American Iconology* (New Haven: Yale University Press, 1993), 80–91, 84; William Gilpin, *Observations on the River Wye and several parts of South Wales* (1782; London: T. Cadell, 1800), 128.

22. Miller, *Eye,* 45; Wallach, "Holyoke," 85.

23. Thomas Cole, "Essay on American Scenery," in Graham Clarke, ed., *The American Landscape: Literary Sources and Documents,* 3 vols. (Mountfield, East Sussex: Helm Information, 1993), 2:337–47.

24. Miller, *Eye,* 33; Barringer, "Empires," 52; Miller, *Eye,* 37.

25. Barringer, "Empires," 53; Stephen F. Mills, *The American Landscape* (Edinburgh: Keele University Press, 1997), 58.

26. James Duban, *Melville's Major Fiction: Politics, Theology and Imagination* (Dekalb: North Illinois University Press, 1983), 192; Anders Stephanson, *Manifest Destiny* (New York: Hill and Wang, 1995), 32; Kevin J. Avery, "Movies for Manifest Destiny: The Moving Panorama Phenomenon in America," in *The Grand Moving Panorama of Pilgrim's Progress* (Montclair, N.J.: Montclair Art Museum, 1999), 1.

27. Mark Twain, *Life on the Mississippi* (Boston: James R. Osgood and Co., 1883), 577; John Bell, "The Sioux War Panorama and American Mythic History," *Theatre Journal* 48, no. 3 (1996): 279–99, 282; [John Banvard], *Description of Banvard's Panorama of the Mississippi & Missouri Rivers* (London: W. J. Golbourn, 1848), 10; Risley and Smith, *Professor Risley and Mr J. R. Smith's Original Gigantic Moving Panorama of the Mississippi River* (London: John· K. Chapman and Co., 1849), vii. Smith, the artist, had previously worked in the theater, designing backdrops for Noah Ludlow ("The Hunters of Kentucky") in St. Louis.

28. Reps, *Cities,* 4.

29. *Commercial Review of the South and West* 1, no. 2 (February 1846): 145.

30. John Francis McDermott, *The Lost Panoramas of the Mississippi* (Chicago: University of Chicago Press: 1958), 161.

31. Paul Collins, *Banvard's Folly: Thirteen Tales of Renowned Obscurity, Famous Anonymity, and Rotten Luck* (London: Picador, 2001), 2; [Banvard], *Description,* 3–16.

32. [Banvard], *Description,* 3–16.

33. John Francis McDermott catalogued the variations in Banvard's pamphlets: "Banvard's Mississippi Panorama Pamphlets," *Bibliographical Society of America Papers* 43 (1949): 48–62.

34. Hyde, *Panoramania!* 133; Collins, *Folly,* 11; McDermott, *Panoramas,* 43; Robinson quoted in Slater, *Dickens',* 2:135; "Banvard's Panorama," *Scientific American* 4, no. 13 (December 1848): 100.

35. Dickens, "Panorama," 135–37.

36. Charles Dickens, "Some Account of an Extraordinary Traveller," in Michael Slater, ed., *Dickens' Journalism,* 4 vols. (London, 1997), 2:201–12, 211; Scott Wilcox, "Unlimiting the Bounds of Painting" in Hyde, *Panoramania!* 13–44, 40, 24; C. R. Leslie, *A Handbook for Young Painters* (London: John Murray, 1855), 4.

37. Michel Foucault, "Panopticism," in *Discipline and Punish,* trans. Alan Sheridan (1977; London: Penguin, 1991), 317; Wallach, "Holyoke," 83; Dolf Sternberger, *Panorama of the Nineteenth Century: How Nineteenth Century Man Saw Himself & His World & How He Experienced History,* trans. Joachim Neugroschel (Oxford: Blackwell, 1977), 8.

38. Altick, *London,* 174; Oettermann, *Panorama,* 7; Altick, *London,* 470, 231.

39. John F. Sears, *Sacred Places: American Tourist Attractions in the Nineteenth Century* (1989; Amherst: University of Massachusetts Press, 1998), 4.

40. Wolfgang Schivelbusch, *The Railway Journey*, trans. Anselm Hollo (Oxford: Blackwell, 1980), 57–60.

41. Schivelbusch, *Railway*, 60; Sternberger, *Panorama*, 39, 46; Christopher Mulvey, *Anglo-American Landscapes: A Study of Nineteenth-Century Anglo-American Travel Literature* (Cambridge: Cambridge University Press, 1983), 216; Trollope, *Manners*, 1:4.

42. Risley and Smith, *Panorama*, v; Ida Pfeiffer, *A Lady's Second Journey Round the World*, 2 vols. (London: Longman, Brown, Green, and Longman, 1855), 2:301; Risley and Smith, *Panorama*, vii; Oettermann, *Panorama*, 335.

43. Dickens, "Panorama," 137; Longfellow's journal quoted in Henry Wadsworth Longfellow, *Evangeline, The Song of Hiawatha, The Courtship of Miles Standish* (London: George Routledge, 1886), 10; Henry David Thoreau, "Walking," in *Civil Disobedience and Other Essays* (1862; New York: Dover, 1993), 60; Dickens, "Traveller," 212.

44. Umberto Eco, "Travels in Hyperreality" (1974), in *Travels in Hyperreality*, trans. William Weaver (London: Harcourt Brace, 1986), 1–58, 19, 44–45; McDermott, *Panoramas*, 77.

45. Rathbone, *Panorama*, 16–17; McDermott, *Panoramas*, 171; Rathbone, *Panorama*, 16.

46. The front cover of Banvard's "Description" showed above the proclamation "THREE MILE PAINTING" with the much smaller adjustment: "extensively known as. . . ." [Banvard], *Description*, 1; McDermott, *Panoramas*, 167.

47. Rathbone, *Panorama*, 16. See also Bernard Comment, *The Panorama*, trans. Anne Marie-Glasheen (London: Reaktion, 1999), 172–77.

48. Oettermann, *Panorama*, 338; McDermott, *Panoramas*, 34; Dickens, "Panorama," 137; Dickens, "Traveller," 205.

49. Reps, *Cities*, 25.

50. William Petersen, *Mississippi River Panorama: Henry Lewis' Great National Work* (Iowa City: Clio Press, 1979), 11; Reps, *Cities*, 27.

51. Charles Lanman, *A Summer in the Wilderness, Embracing a Canoe Voyage up the Mississippi and around Lake Superior* (New York: D. Appleton and Co., 1847), 59; John Francis McDermott, *Seth Eastman's Mississippi: A Lost Portfolio Recovered* (Urbana: University of Illinois Press, 1973), 7.

52. McDermott, *Eastman's*, 12.

53. Ibid., 16; Trollope, *Manners*, 1:29. Lady Emmeline Stuart Wortley, *Travels in the United States, etc. during 1849 and 1850*, 3 vols. (London: Richard Bentley, 1851), 1:209.

54. Trollope, *Manners*, 1:45.

55. See Frank Luther Mott, *A History of American Magazines*, 5 vols. (Cambridge: Harvard University Press, 1938–68), 1:43–45; Reps, *Cities*, 36; "Arrowsmith's Panorama of Western Travel," in *Harper's New Monthly Magazine* 18, no. 103 (December 1858): 141–42.

56. John Grafton, *The American West in the Nineteenth Century: Illustrations from "Harper's Weekly" and Other Contemporary Sources* (New York: Dover, 1992), vii. See also Frederic E. Ray, *Alfred R. Waud: Civil War Artist* (New York: Viking, 1974).

57. Alfred Waud's unpublished plans and drafts for *The Father of Waters*, ca. 1885 (Historic New Orleans Collection, Williams Resarch Center, MSS 106: Alfred R. Waud Papers, 1860–87, Folders 5–10).

58. Bryan F. Le Beau, *Currier and Ives, America Imagined* (Washington, D.C.: Smithsonian Institution Press, 2001), 296–98.

59. Collins, *Folly,* 1, 15, 17; Phineas T. Barnum, *The Life of P. T. Barnum, Written by Himself*, ed. Terence Whalen (1855; Urbana: University of Illinois Press, 2000), xv.

60. Collins, *Folly,* 17–18.

5. CRIME AND PUNISHMENT: "EXTRAORDINARY METAPHYSICAL SCAMPS"
IN THE MISSISSIPPI UNDERWORLD

Title. Herman Melville, *The Confidence-Man: His Masquerade* (London: Longman, Brown, Green, Longman, and Roberts, 1857), 190. All citations to Melville's *The Confidence-Man* are to this edition unless otherwise stated.

Epigraph 1. Melville, *Confidence,* 276.

Epigraph 2. J.F.B. Lillard, *Poker Stories* (London: Gibbings and Co., 1896), 42–43.

1. Melville, *Confidence,* 352; George Byron Merrick, *Old Times on the Upper Mississippi: Recollections of a Steamboat Pilot from 1854 to 1863* (Minneapolis: University of Minnesota Press, 2001), 138–39.

2. Alexis de Tocqueville, *Democracy in America* (1835–40; London: Folio Society, 2002), 21. Melville, *Confidence,* 9–10. Anacharsis Cloots led a cosmopolitan, multicultural deputation into the French National Assembly in 1790 to symbolize the support of the French Revolution by all mankind. He was later executed by the French.

3. Charles Mackay, *Memoirs of Extraordinary Popular Delusions,* 3 vols. (London: Richard Bentley, 1841), 1:2–3.

4. Mackay, *Delusions,* 1:11; Thomas M. Kavanagh, *Enlightenment and the Shadows of Chance: The Novel and the Culture of Gambling in Eighteenth-Century France* (Baltimore: Johns Hopkins University Press, 1993), 258; Hodding Carter, *Lower Mississippi* (New York: Farrar and Rinehart, 1942), 36. In truth, there "never was any Mississippi Company": it was called "*La Compagnie d"Occident* and later [. . .] *La Compagnie des Indes,*" but popularly it was known as the Mississippi Company.

5. Mackay, *Delusions,* 1:15; Kavanagh, *Enlightenment,* 86; Mackay, *Delusions,* 1:38; Alexandre Dumas, *The Count of Monte-Cristo,* 2 vols. (London: Chapman and Hall, 1846), 2:319; Buford Rowland, "William Wordsworth and Mississippi Bonds," *Journal of Southern History* 1, no. 4 (1935): 501–7.

6. Albert Phelps, *Louisiana: A Record of Expansion* (New York: Houghton, Mifflin), 60; Mackay, *Delusions,* 1:31.

7. William Grattan Tyrone Power, *Impressions of America, during the Years 1833, 1834, and 1835,* 2 vols. (London: Richard Bentley, 1836), 2:197–98.

8. *Niles Weekly Register* (Baltimore), August 8, 1835, 401; Michael Gillespie, *Come Hell or High Water* (Wisconsin: Heritage, 2001), 165.

9. Stahl [George Wharton], *The New Orleans Sketch Book* (Philadelphia: A. Hart, 1853), 34–35. Monte, played with three cards, is now better known as "find-the-lady." It was favored by steamboat gamblers.

10. Gerda Reith, *The Age of Chance: Gambling in Western Culture* (Routledge: London, 1999), 128–33.

11. Otto A. Rothert, *The Outlaws of Cave-in-Rock* (1924; Carbondale: Southern Illinois University Press, 1996), 175, 37.

12. Michael Allen, *Western Rivermen, 1763–1861* (Baton Rouge: Louisiana State University Press, 1990), 112; Jackson Lears, *Something for Nothing: Luck in America* (New York: Viking, 2003), 117; Allen, *Rivermen*, 112–13; Christian Schultz, *Travels on an Inland Voyage*, 2 vols. (New York: Isaac Riley, 1810), 1:203; Ned Buntline [Edward Zane Carroll Judson], *The Mysteries and Miseries of New Orleans* (New York: Akarman and Ormsby, ca. 1851), 25. The approximated date of 1851 in the British Library Catalogue is supported by internal evidence. Buntline's novel features an account of Narciso López's third and final filibustering attempt on Cuba, which resulted in his execution by the Spanish in 1851. The swift turnaround of action in this novel suggests a change of tack to satisfy a popular demand for the contemporary story.

13. From *The Crockett Almanac for 1840*, 11. Reprinted in Michael A. Lofaro, ed., *The Tall Tales of Davy Crockett: The Second Nashville Series of Davy Crockett Almanacs, 1839–41* (Knoxville: University of Tennessee Press, 1987).

14. From *Col. Crockett's Exploits and Adventures in Texas,* written by Richard Penn Smith, in *Davy Crockett's Own Story, As Written by Himself* (New York: Citadel, 1955), 275–78.

15. Raymond W. Thorp, *Bowie Knife* (Albuquerque: University of New Mexico Press, 1948), 126; Herbert Asbury, *Sucker's Progress: An Informal History of Gambling in America from the Colonies to Canfield* (New York: Dodd, Mead, 1938), 206; Thorp, *Bowie*, 128–29. For one of the popular versions of Bowie versus the riverboat gambler (with two variant endings), see Asbury, *Progress*, 206–9.

16. B. A. Botkin, ed., *A Treasury of Mississippi Folklore* (New York: American Legacy Press, 1955), 218–22. (Originally published in 1847 in *The Earthquake of 1811 at New Madrid and along the Mississippi Valley,* by Capt. Chas. Ross. Emil Klauprecht appropriated Girty's monologue for the character of the "Alligator" in *Cincinnati, or The Mysteries of the West.*) Asbury, *Progress*, 212.

17. Jack Brace [Justin Jones], *Marie; or the Gambler of the Mississippi* (New York: E. D. Long, n.d.), 16, 107. The story is set in 1847 in the third municipality of New Orleans. The author is given as "Jack Brace." The British Library Catalogue notes that Jack Brace was one of the pseudonyms for Justin Jones (better known as Harry Hazel), a prolific writer of popular fiction in the antebellum years. Of the forty-four works attributed to Jones in Lyle Wright's bibliography *American Fiction, 1851–1875,* thirty-three were published before 1855, five have no date, and only two were published after the Civil War, both stories of the war. As such, it would also seem safe to include this important novel as an antebellum text.

18. Percy Gardner, "Greek River-Worship," *Transactions of the Royal Society of Literature of the United Kingdom,* vol. 11 (London: John Murray, 1878), 173–218, 187; Gary Lindberg, *The Confidence Man in American Literature* (New York: Oxford University Press, 1982), 147.

19. Melville, *Confidence*, 183; William Lenz, *Fast Talk and Flush Times: The Confidence Man as a Literary Convention* (Columbia: University of Missouri Press, 1985), 129; Melville, *Confidence*, 161, 192, 113; Lenz, *Fast*, 129.

20. Melville, *Confidence*, 2; Mackay, *Delusions*, 1:641. See also Gerald Howson, *Thief-Taker General: The Rise and Fall of Jonathan Wild* (London: Hutchinson, 1970).

21. *Niles' Weekly Register* (Baltimore), August 8, 1835, 404; Mark Twain, *Life on the Mississippi* (Boston: James R. Osgood, 1883), 312; Herbert Asbury, *The French Quarter: An Informal History of the New Orleans Underworld* (1936; New York: Thunder's Mouth Press, 2003), 89. James Lal Penick Jr., *The Great Western Land Pirate: John A. Murrell in Legend and History* (Columbia: University of Missouri Press, 1981), 7–8.

22. Augustus Q. Walton [pseud.], *A History of the Detection, Conviction, Life and Designs of John A. Murel* (1835; Cincinnati: n.p., n.d.), 50.

23. Ibid., 36, 42, 47, 40, 54, 62, 41.

24. Ibid., 57, 24, 48; *Niles' Weekly Register* (Baltimore), August 8, 1835, 404; Christopher Morris, *Becoming Southern: The Evolution of a Way of Life, Warren County and Vicksburg, Mississippi, 1770–1860* (New York: Oxford University Press, 1995), 123. See also Mark Carnes, *Secret Ritual and Manhood in Victorian America* (New Haven: Yale University Press, 1989).

25. *Niles' Weekly Register* (Baltimore), August 8, 1835, 404; Christopher Morris, "An Event in Community Organization: The Mississippi Slave Insurrection Scare of 1835," *Journal of Social History* 22, no. 1 (1988): 93–111, 95.

26. Henry S. Foote, *Bench and Bar of the South and Southwest* (St. Louis: Soule, Thomas, and Wentworth, 1876), 66; Morris, "Organization," 95; *Niles' Weekly Register* (Baltimore), October 17, 1835, 119.

27. Jonathan Green, *Secret Band of Brothers: A Full and True Exposition of All the Various Crimes, Villanies, and Misdeeds of This Powerful Organization* (1847; Philadelphia: T. B. Peterson and Brothers, ca. .1858), 9–10, 16, title page; Penick, *Murrell,* 155; *Niles' Weekly Register* (Baltimore), August 8, 1835, 403.

28. Botkin, *Treasury,* 196. George Devol told a version; see George Devol, *Forty Years a Gambler on the Mississippi* (Cincinnati: Devol and Haines, 1887, repr. 1998), 53–55.

29. Henry Watson, *Narrative of Henry Watson, A Fugitive Slave* (Boston: Bela Marsh, 1848), 26; Devol, *Gambler,* 295; Penick, *Murrell,* 47; James Haskins, *The First Black Governor: Pinkney Benton Stewart Pinchback* (Trenton: Africa World Press, 1996), 7, 12.

30. Haskins, *Pinchback,* 18; Devol, *Gambler,* 216–17.

31. Henry Bibb, *Narrative of the Life and Adventures of Henry Bibb, An American Slave* (New York: self-published, 1849), 143–51.

32. Thomas Buchanan, *Black Life on the Mississippi* (Chapel Hill: University of North Carolina Press, 2004), 76; Thomas C. Buchanan, "Rascals on the Antebellum Mississippi: African American Steamboat Workers and the St. Louis Hanging of 1841," *Journal of Social History* 34, no. 4 (2001): 797–816.

33. Penick, *Murrell,* 28–31.

34. Power, *Impressions,* 2:199–200; *Niles' Weekly Register* (Baltimore), August 8, 1835, 401; ibid., October 17, 1835, 120.

35. *Niles' Weekly Register* (Baltimore), October 17, 1835, 120; ibid., November 28, 1835, 220.

36. Tony Horwitz, *Confederates in the Attic* (New York: Vintage, 1999), 201–2; H. R. Howard, ed., *The History of Virgil A. Stewart and His Adventure in Capturing and Exposing the Great "Western Land Pirate" and His Gang, in Connection with the Evidence; Also of the Trials, Confessions, and Execution of a Number of Murrell's Associates in the State of Mississippi during the Summer of 1835,*

and the Execution of Five Professional Gamblers by the Citizens of Vicksburg, on the 6th July, 1835 (1836; New York: Harper and Brothers, 1839), 264–68.

37. Penick, *Murrell*, 155; *Niles' Weekly Register* (Baltimore), August 8, 1835, 401, 405; Penick, *Murrell*, 147.

38. Hon. Charles Augustus Murray, *Travels in North America during the Years 1834, 1835 & 1836*, 2 vols. (London: Richard Bentley, 1839), 2:177; *Niles' Weekly Register* (Baltimore), August 8, 1835, 401–2.

39. Watson, *Narrative*, 26–27; *Niles' Weekly Register* (Baltimore), August 8, 1835, 401–2.

40. *Niles' Weekly Register* (Baltimore), August 1, 1835, 373; ibid., November 28, 1835, 219–20.

41. Twain, *Mississippi*, 386; Jonathan Green, *Gambling Exposed* (1847; Montclair, N.J.: Patterson Smith, 1973), 150. Ann Fabian, *Card Sharps, Dream Books, & Bucket Shops: Gambling in Nineteenth-Century America* (New York: Cornell University Press, 1990), 35–37; Morris, *Southern*, 123.

42. Frederick Law Olmsted, *A Journey in the Seaboard Slave States*, 2 vols. (1856; New York: Putnam's, 1904), 2:209. Herman Melville, "The River," in Hershel Parker, ed., *The Confidence-Man* (New York: Norton, 1971), 222–23.

43. Kenneth S. Greenberg, *Honor & Slavery* (Princeton: Princeton University Press, 1996), 135; W. J. Cash, *The Mind of the South* (New York: Vintage, 1961), 39; Robert V. Remini, *Andrew Jackson and the Course of American Empire, 1767–1821* (New York: Harper and Row, 1977), 28–31; Joseph G. Baldwin, *The Flush Times of Alabama and Mississippi* (New York: D. Appleton and Co., 1853), 199–200.

44. Emil Klauprecht, *Cincinnati, or The Mysteries of the West*, ed. Don Heinrich Tolzman, trans. Steven Rowan (New York: Peter Lang, 1996), 185; J.F.B. Lillard, *Poker Stories* (London: Gibbings, 1896), 43; Henry Adams, *The Education of Henry Adams*, ed. Jean Gooder (1918; New York: Penguin, 1995), 100. Green, *Exposed*, 150; Karen Halttunen, *Confidence Men and Painted Women: A Study of Middle-Class Culture in America, 1830–1870* (New Haven: Yale University Press, 1982), 17; Greenberg, *Honor*, 143.

45. Halttunen, *Confidence*, xvi, 3, 27, 25.

46. Howard, *History*, 264; Henry Ward Beecher, *Lectures to Young Men* (1844; London: James Blackwood, n.d.), 147–48; Green, *Exposed*, 42.

47. Halttunen, *Confidence*, 20.

48. Crockett, *Texas*, 287; *The Female Land Pirate; or Awful, Mysterious, and Horrible Disclosures of Amanda Bannorris* (Cincinnati: E. E. Barclay, 1847), 15–16; J.R.S. Pitts, *Life and Confession of the Noted Outlaw James Copeland* (1858; Jackson: University Press of Mississippi, 1980), 37.

49. William Gilmore Simms, *Richard Hurdis: A Tale of Alabama* (1838; New York: W. J. Widdleton, 1864), 293, 402.

50. William Gilmore Simms, *Border Beagles: A Tale of Mississippi* (1840; New York: W. J. Widdleton, 1855), 494–95. Edgar Allan Poe, "William Gilmore Simms," in *The Works of the Late Edgar Allan Poe*, 3 vols. (New York: J. S. Redfield, 1850), 3:272; Simms, *Hurdis*, 11.

51. Jones, *Marie*, 29, 10–11, 31.

52. Frederick Gerstäcker, *Western Lands and Western Waters* (London: S. O. Beeton, 1864), ix. Originally published in *Mississippi-Bilder: Licht und Schattenseiten transatlantischen Lebens* (Dres-

den und Leipzig: Arnoldischen Buchhandlung, 1847). The preface notes that all the sketches had previously appeared in translation in the *Boy's Own Magazine* and the *Englishwoman's Domestic Magazine*. Friedrich Gerstäcker, "Up the Mississippi," in *Western Lands and Western Waters* (London: S. O. Beeton, 1864), 3–86, 26, 50, 77, 84; Botkin, *Treasury,* 242.

53. Frederick Gerstaecker [Gerstäcker], *The Pirates of the Mississippi* (London: G. Routledge, 1856), iii, 49, 235–36. Originally published as *Die Flußpiraten des Mississippi* (Leipzig: Otto Wigand, 1848).

54. Eugène Sue, *The Mysteries of Paris* (London: W. Dugdale, 1844), 2; Philip Penchant, *Mysteries of Fitchburg* (Fitchburg: Charles Sepley: 1844), 1.

55. Richard Maxwell, *The Mysteries of Paris and London* (Charlottesville: University Press of Virginia, 1992), 15–19; Baron Ludwig von Reizenstein, *The Mysteries of New Orleans,* trans. and ed. Steven Rowan (Baltimore: Johns Hopkins University Press, 2002), xxvii. In *Melville's Reading,* Merton Sealts recorded a copy of F. Thiele's *Mysteries of Berlin; from the Papers of a Berlin Criminal Officer* (1845). Merton M. Sealts Jr., *Melville's Reading: A Check-List of Books Owned and Borrowed* (Madison and Milwaukee: University of Wisconsin Press, 1966), 100; Melville, *Confidence,* 8, 77.

56. Buntline, *Mysteries,* 85.

57. Ibid., 28, 23, 28.

58. Klauprecht, *Cincinnati,* xxii.

59. Ibid., xi, 214–15.

60. Ibid., 48, 99, 299, 80.

61. Reizenstein, *Orleans,* 1, xxxiii.

62. Ibid., 463, 416, 462–63, 418, 538.

63. Timothy Flint, *Recollections of the Last Ten Years in the Valley of the Mississippi* (1826; Carbondale: Southern Illinois University Press, 1968), 69; John Milton, *Paradise Lost,* ed. John Leonard (1667; London: Penguin, 2003), 190.

64. Robert Burns, *The Works of Robert Burns,* 4 vols. (Liverpool: J. M. Creery, 1800), 3:10–11; William Andrew Chatto, *Facts and Speculations on the Origin and History of Playing Cards* (London: John Russell Smith, 1848), 303; Crockett, *Texas,* 276, 292; *Niles' Weekly Register* (Baltimore), August 8, 1835, 402; Fabian, *Sharps,* 29; Reizenstein, *Orleans,* xxiii, 262.

65. Phineas T. Barnum, *The Life of P. T. Barnum, Written by Himself* (1885; Urbana: University of Illinois Press, 2000), 333–35.

66. John S. Robb, "The Second Advent!" in John Francis McDermott, ed., *Before Mark Twain: A Sampler of Old, Old Times on the Mississippi* (Carbondale: Southern Illinois University Press, 1998), 264–69; McDermott, *Mississippi,* xiv; Jonathan A. Cook, *Satirical Apocalypse: An Anatomy of Melville's "The Confidence Man"* (Westport, Ct.: Greenwood, 1996), 50.

67. Flint, *Recollections,* 198; Robert Bruce Flanders, *Nauvoo: Kingdom on the Mississippi* (Urbana: University of Illinois Press, 1975), 23, 6, 278.

68. John W. Nichol, "Melville and the Midwest," *Publications of the Modern Language Association of America* 66 (1951): 613–25, 613; John D. Seelye, "Timothy Flint's 'Wicked River' and *The Confidence-Man,*" *Publications of the Modern Language Association of America* 78 (1963): 75–79; Johnson J. Hooper, *Some Adventures of Simon Suggs* (Philadelphia: Getz and Buck, 1851), 12;

Melville, *Confidence*, ed. Parker, ix. See also Hershel Parker, *Herman Melville: A Biography, 1819–1851* (Baltimore: Johns Hopkins University Press, 1996), 176–78; James Hall, *Legends of the West* (1832) and *Sketches of History, Life, and Manners, in the West* (1835); John W. Shroeder, "Sources and Symbols for Melville's *Confidence-Man*," *Publications of the Modern Language Association of America* 66 (1951): 363–80; Egbert S. Oliver, "Melville's Picture of Emerson and Thoreau in *The Confidence-Man*," *College English* 8 (November 1946), 61–72; Elizabeth Foster's introduction to her edition of Herman Melville's *The Confidence-Man* (New York: Hendricks House, 1954); Harrison Hayford, "Poe in *The Confidence-Man*," *Nineteenth-Century Literature* 14, no. 3 (December 1959): 207–18; Egbert S. Oliver, "Melville's Goneril and Fanny Kemble," *New England Quarterly* 18, no. 4 (December 1945): 489–500.

69. Seelye, "Flint," 79; Shroeder, "Sources," 365.

70. Melville, *Confidence*, ed. Parker, 276; Hugh W. Hetherington, *Melville's Reviewers, British and American, 1846–1891* (Chapel Hill: University of North Carolina Press, 1961), 260; Melville, *Confidence*, 270; Hetherington, *Reviewers*, 255; Melville, *Confidence*, ed. Parker, 275; Melville, *Confidence*, ed. Parker, 346.

71. Melville, *Confidence*, 273, 236, 261.

72. Ibid., 30, 53, 68, 144, 353; Howard C. Horsford, "Evidence of Melville's Plans for a Sequel to *The Confidence-Man*," *American Literature* 24, no. 1 (March 1952): 85–89, 85.

73. Melville, *Confidence*, 354; Cook, *Apocalypse*, 214; Melville, *Confidence*, 354.

74. Allan Pinkerton, *Mississippi Outlaws and the Detectives* (New York: Carleton, 1879), vii.

75. John Morris, *Wanderings of a Vagabond* (New York: self-published, 1873); Mason Long, *The Life of Mason Long, The Converted Gambler* (Chicago: Donnelley, Loyd., 1878); Henry Edward Hugunin, *Life and Adventures of Henry Edward Hugunin, or Thirty Years a* Gambler (New York: Oliphant, 1879); Devol, *Gambler*, 190, 285–87.

76. Fabian, *Sharps*, 6, 38.

77. Edward Willett, *Flush Fred's Double; or, The Squatters' League of Six* (New York: Beadle, 1884), 2; Edward Willett, *Flush Fred's Full Hand; or, Life and Strife in Louisiana* (New York: Beadle, 1884), 3; Willett, *Double*, 3. There were, in total, four *Flush Fred* adventures: *Flush Fred, the Mississippi Sport; or, Tough Times in Tennessee* (1884); *Flush Fred's Full Hand* (1884); *Flush Fred's Double* (1884); and *Flush Fred, the River Sharp; or, Hearts for Stakes. A Romance of Three Queens and Two Knaves* (1888). See Albert Johannsen, *The House of Beadle and Adams and Its Dime and Nickel Novels*, 2 vols. (Norman: University of Oklahoma Press, 1950), 1:215, 216, 217, 224.

78. Lillard, *Poker*, 42–43, 50–51.

THE CIVIL WAR AND MARK TWAIN

Epigraph 1. Frederick Jackson Turner, *The Frontier in American History* (1920; Tucson: University of Arizona Press, 1994), 198.

Epigraph 2. Mark Twain, *Life on the Mississippi* (Boston: James R. Osgood and Co., 1883), 96–97.

1. Cora Montgomery, *The King of Rivers* (New York: Wood, 1850), 3; Shelby Foote, *The Civil War: A Narrative*, 3 vols. (1958, 1963, 1974; London: Pimlico, 2000) 1:90; Jack D. Coombe, *Thunder along the Mississippi, The River Battles That Split the Confederacy* (New York: Sarpedon, 1996), 6.

2. Louis Hunter, *Steamboats on the Western Rivers: An Economic and Technological History* (1949; New York: Dover, 1993), 481. Foote, *War,* 1:9.

3. Clement Eaton, *Jefferson Davis* (New York: Macmillan, 1977), 25; Foote, *War,* 1:10.

4. Stephen B. Oates, *With Malice toward None: The Life of Abraham Lincoln* (London: Allen and Unwin, 1978), 13; Carl Sandburg, *Abraham Lincoln: The Prairie Years* (New York: Harcourt, Brace, 1926), 87, 108. Sandburg's biographical works have long been superseded, but, perhaps because of his Illinois connections, Sandburg paid particular, and valuable, attention to Lincoln's time on the rivers.

5. From Andrew Adderup's *Lincolniana* (1864). Quoted in B. A. Botkin, ed., *A Treasury of Mississippi Folklore* (New York: American Legacy Press, 1955), 136.

6. Emanuel Hertz, ed., *Lincoln Talks: A Biography in Anecdote* (New York: Viking, 1939), 15; Botkin, *Treasury,* 132–33; Oates, *Lincoln,* 17.

7. Botkin, *Treasury,* 135–36.

8. Eaton, *Davis,* 17; Sandburg, *Prairie,* 154–55.

9. Hunter, *Steamboats,* 504, 481, 495–96. The term "critical decade" is Hunter's.

10. Dee Brown, *Hear That Lonesome Whistle Blow* (London: Pan Books, 1979), 11; Francis Parkman, *The California and Oregon Trail* (New York: Putnam, 1849), 3; *De Bow's Southern and Western Review* 12, no. 1 (January 1852), 37; Albert D. Richardson, *Beyond the Mississippi: From the Great River to the Great Ocean* (Hartford, Ct.: American, 1867).

11. Brown, *Whistle,* 16–17.

12. John W. Starr, *Lincoln and the Railroads* (New York: Dodd, Mead), 108; Brown, *Whistle,* 20.

13. Hunter, *Steamboats,* 547; William Petersen, *Steamboating on the Upper Mississippi* (1937; New York: Dover, 1995), 510; George Devol, *Forty Years a Gambler on the Mississippi* (Cincinnati: Devol and Haines, 1887; repr. 1998), 116–17; Hunter, *Steamboats,* 547.

14. Petersen, *Steamboating,* 185; Hunter, *Steamboats,* 549.

15. Coombe, *Thunder,* 22; Anthony Trollope, *North America.* 2 vols. (London, 1862; repr. 1987), 1:29; Trollope, *America,* 2:151–59.

16. Foote, *War,* 1:183–84; Kirkpatrick Sale, *The Fire of His Genius: Robert Fulton and the American Dream* (New York: Free Press, 2001), 157. See also Florence Dorsey, *Road to the Sea: The Story of James B. Eads and the Mississippi River* (New York: Rinehart, 1947).

17. James M. McPherson, *Battle Cry of Freedom* (New York: Penguin, 2002), 157; Foote, *War,* 1:308.

18. Kate Stone quoted in Edmund Wilson, *Patriotic Gore* (1962; Norton: New York, 1994), 259; Clarence Clough Buel and Robert Underwood Johnson, eds., *Battles and Leaders of the Civil War,* 4 vols. (New York: Century Co., 1887), 2:20; Mary Boykin Chesnut, *Mary Chesnut's Civil War,* ed. C. Vann Woodward (New Haven: Yale University Press, 1981), 330; Charles Dufour, *The Night the War Was Lost* (Lincoln: University of Nebraska Press, 1994), 331; Devol, *Gambler,* 121.

19. Foote, *War,* 2:346; David Dixon Porter, *Incidents and Anecdotes of the Civil War* (New York: D. Appleton and Co., 1885), 95–96.

20. James M. Perry, *A Bohemian Brigade: The Civil War Correspondents* (New York: Wiley, 2000), 138; Foote, *War,* 2:63, 193, 147, 192–94. For the 1876 Vicksburg cut-off, see Stephen E. Ambrose and Douglas G. Brinkley, *The Mississippi and the Making of a Nation, From the Louisiana Purchase to Today* (Washington: National Geographic Society, 2002), 108. Foote's account of

the Vicksburg campaign (available as a single volume, *The Beleaguered City: The Vicksburg Campaign* [New York: Modern Library, 1995]) remains the most readable. Alternatively, see James R. Arnold, *Grant Wins the War: Decision at Vicksburg* (New York: Wiley, 1997). For an exhaustive treatment, see Edwin Cole Bearss, *The Campaign for Vicksburg*, 3 vols. (Dayton, Ohio: Morningside Books, 1985). For a revisionist assessment of Vicksburg's importance (or lack of it), see Albert Castel, "Vicksburg: Myths and Realities," *North & South* 6, no. 7 (November 2003): 62–69.

21. Richard B. Harwell, ed., *The Confederate Reader: How the South Saw the War* (1957; New York: Dover, 1989), 209–12. Foote, *War,* 2:415; Ambrose and Brinkley, *Mississippi,* 108.

22. Foote, *War,* 2:640, 965; Walter Havighurst, *Voices on the River* (New York: Macmillan, 1964), 167; David Dixon Porter, *The Naval History of the Civil War* (New York: [Sherman Publishing Co.], 1886), 352; Nathaniel Hawthorne to Elizabeth Peabody, July 20, 1863, in Nathaniel Hawthorne, *The Letters, 1857–1864,* ed. Thomas Woodson et al. (Columbus: Ohio State University Press, 1987), 591; Tony Horwitz, *Confederates in the Attic* (New York: Vintage, 1999), 233; Foote, *War,* 2:319.

23. James M. Gregory, *Frederick Douglass, The Orator* (Springfield, Mass.: Willey and Co., 1893), 128; Gilbert Haven, *National Sermons: Sermons, Speeches and Letters on Slavery and Its War* (Boston: Lee and Shepard, 1869), 529–30, 546; [Aharles G. Halpine], *The Life and Adventures, Songs, Services, and Speeches of Private Miles O'Reilly* (New York: Carleton, 1864), 106.

24. Absalom Grimes, *Absalom Grimes, Confederate Mail Runner,* ed. M. M. Quaife (New Haven: Yale University Press, 1926), 46–63. D. H. Rule is currently preparing a book on the Confederate spies of the Mississippi. For the moment, the ample fruits of her research can be found at www.civilwarstlouis.com. Rule claims that "over sixty Union steamboats were destroyed by Confederate sabotage on the Mississippi River and in the surrounding area," with the loss of thousands of lives.

25. H. C. Castleman [Charles Austin Fosdick], *Frank on the Lower Mississippi* (Cincinnati: R. W. Carroll and Co., 1865), 35. (See also H. C. Castleman [Charles Austin Fosdick], *Frank on a Gunboat* [Cincinnati: R. W. Carroll and Co., 1865]; H. C. Castleman [Charles Austin Fosdick], *Frank before Vicksburg* [Cincinnati: R. W. Carroll and Co., 1869].) Wesley Bradshaw [Charles Wesley Alexander], *Maud of the Mississippi* (Philadelphia: C. W. Alexander and Co., 1864), 23. Wesley Bradshaw [Charles Wesley Alexander], *Pauline of the Potomac* (Philadelphia: Barclay and Co., 1862).

26. Jerry O. Potter, *The Sultana Tragedy: America's Greatest Maritime Disaster* (Gretna, La.: Pelican, 1992; repr. 2000), 70–73, x.

27. Epigraph from Mark Twain, *Mark Twain's Letters, 1853–1866,* ed. Edgar Marquess Branch, Michael B. Frank, and Kenneth M. Sanderson (Berkeley and Los Angeles: University of California Press, 1988), 327–29; Twain, *Mississippi,* 254–56; John W. Reps, *Cities of the Mississippi, Nineteenth-Century Images of Urban Development* (Columbia: University of Missouri Press, 1994), 204; Ron Powers, *Dangerous Water: A Biography of the Boy Who Became Mark Twain* (Cambridge, Mass.: Da Capo, 2001), 62–65.

28. Twain, *Mississippi,* 62; Mark Twain, *The Adventures of Tom Sawyer* (London: Chatto and Windus, 1876), 17, 252; Twain, *Mississippi,* 45, 530, 536; Powers, *Water,* 54.

29. Mark Twain, *Mark Twain's Own Autobiography: The Chapters from the North American Review*, ed. Michael Kiskis. (Madison: University of Wisconsin Press, 1990), 113–15, 121–22; Mark Twain, *Pudd'nhead Wilson* (Leipzig: Bernhard Tauchnitz, 1895), 203–4; Mark Twain, "Villagers of 1840–3," in *Huck Finn and Tom Sawyer among the Indians and Other Unfinished Stories*, ed. Dahlia Armon and Walter Blair (Berkeley and Los Angeles: University of California Press, 1989), 104; Albert Bigelow Paine, *Mark Twain: A Biography*, 3 vols. (New York: Harper, 1912), 1:64.

30. Harwell, *Confederate*, 27–28; Twain, *Mississippi*, 62; Stephen Foster, *Nelly Was a Lady* (London: J. Allen, [1856]), 2; Dana Epstein, *Sinful Tunes and Spirituals, Black Folk Music to the Civil War* (Urbana: University of Illinois Press, 1977), 229; Powers, *Water*, 48; Eileen Southern, ed., *Readings in Black American Music* (New York: Norton, 1983), 188. Higginson's memoirs were originally published in 1870.

31. Mark Twain, "The Dandy Frightening the Squatter," in *Early Tales and Sketches, 1851–1864*, ed. Edgar Marquess Branch and Robert H. Hirst (Berkeley and Los Angeles: University of California Press, 1979), 63–65; Andrew Hoffman, *Inventing Mark Twain: The Lives of Samuel Langhorne Clemens* (London: Phoenix, 1998), 48–49.

32. Twain, *Mississippi*, 87–88, 103–4, 119.

33. Ibid., 118–19; R. Kent Rasmussen ed., *Mark Twain A to Z: The Essential Reference to His Life and Writings* (New York: Facts on File, 1995), 318; Twain, *Mississippi*, 217, 166.

34. Twain, *Letters, 1853–1866*, 77; Twain, *Mississippi*, 217–18, 228, 245.

35. Mark Twain, "A Private History of a Campaign That Failed," in *Merry Tales* (New York: Webster, 1892), 9; Twain, *Mississippi*, 153.

36. Twain, *Letters, 1853–1866*, 327–29; Mark Twain, *Mark Twain's Letters, 1870–1871*, ed. Victor Fischer and Michael B. Frank (Berkeley and Los Angeles: University of California Press, 1995), 499.

37. Mark Twain, *Mark Twain's Notebooks and Journals*, ed. Robert Pack Browning, Michael B. Frank, and Lin Salamo, 3 vols. (Berkeley and Los Angeles: University of California Press, 1979), 3:606.

38. Mark Twain, *Adventures of Huckleberry Finn* (London: Chatto and Windus, 1884), 177–79.

Index